# Law and society

# International Library of Sociology

Founded by Karl Mannheim
Editor: John Rex, University of Warwick

Arbor Scientiae
Arbor Vitae

A catalogue of the books available in the **International Library of Sociology** and other series of Social Science books published by Routledge & Kegan Paul will be found at the end of this volume.

# Law and society

Adam Podgórecki

**Routledge & Kegan Paul**
London and Boston

*First published in 1974*
*by Routledge & Kegan Paul Ltd*
*Broadway House, 68–74 Carter Lane,*
*London EC4V 5EL and*
*9 Park Street,*
*Boston, Mass. 02108, USA*
*Set in 10/11 Times New Roman, Series 327*
*and printed in Great Britain by*
*Butler & Tanner Ltd*
*Frome and London*
*© Adam Podgórecki 1974*

*ISBN 0 7100 7983 4*
*Library of Congress Catalog Card No. 74–82785*

# Contents

# Preface

This book, *Law and society*, is based on my previous works. I have tried, in this book, to present a synthesis of my research and studies which were earlier published in Polish in the following books: *Sociology of Law* (1962), *Legal Phenomena in Public Opinion* (1964), *Prestige of Law* (1966), *Attitudes of Polish Population toward Law and Morals* (1971, co-author) and *Outlines of Sociology of Law* (1971). Dr J. Kurczewski is the author of Chapter 4, 'The ethnographic approach.'

I am indebted to my colleagues of the Committee on Sociology of Law of the International Sociological Association who, since the establishment of this Committee in 1962, were kind enough to discuss with me various problems and issues which needed broader, international perspectives.

I am also grateful to the Center for Advanced Study in the Behavioral Sciences at Stanford for giving me (during the academic year 1972–3 as a Fellow of this Center) the opportunity to try to pull diverse elements into a synthesis. Many and warm thanks are due to Miriam Gallaher who translated the main part of my English manuscript into English. Thanks also to Mary Tye who was kind enough to type the book.

# part one

# Contemporary sociology of law

# 1 Background

**Methodological problems**

My book, *The Sociology of Law*, published (in Polish) in 1962, had as its essential aim to show the possibilites of establishing a new branch of empirical legal science. Its main point was to bring into focus the merits and uses of a new look at the field of law. More than a decade has elapsed since then and sociological inquiries into law have become a fact both in Poland and elsewhere.

Underlying the present book is a different intention. By now a fairly large number of reflections on law have accumulated which call for a unification of the consistent generalizations. Obviously, the value of empirical research does not consist in multiplying the quantity of random contributions. Therefore it seems that now is the time to attempt to bring some theoretical order into the confusion of sundry inquiries.

Investigations on law can be either speculative or empirical. The speculative approach consists mainly in pondering over the essence of law and its main qualities and in conjecturing how it functions or could function. There is no systematic means of verifying the validity of general concepts and theories. Matters are even more complicated because of the ambiguities of law itself and because of the traditions of the profession. Lawyers tend to constrict their views on law to conform to the normative pressure of regulations, while at the same time acquiring a working knowledge resulting from professional experience which gives them some insight into the functioning of law. The speculative approach to legal science also presents a number of methodological problems. Various viewpoints which are admissible within it are often wholly or partially incomparable because of the total lack of concern for verification of the stated propositions. In principle, no verification is even attempted. And finally, the speculative approach leads to the reification of certain ideas which thus tend to assume an independent, hypostatized subsistence.

The empirical approach in investigations on law, though it has many advantages, reveals some drawbacks as well. Until recently, it has scarcely permitted of taking an overall view of the researches thus far carried out. Moreover, empirical studies on law have been made by means of many methods and techniques which are often resistant to reasonable comparisons. However, in spite of these limitations, a general image of law appears to emerge, though by no means smoothly, from various narrow-range researches and their interpretations. It is remarkable that this image is developed by the relatively young discipline of the sociology of law, rather than by the traditional judicial study of jurisprudence (philosophy of law or state and law theory).

By 1946, the tasks of the philosophy of law were conceived as follows:[1]

> [The philosophy of law] differs from the detailed judicial disciplines by its subject matter, as it deals with law in general, law 'as such,' rather than with any particular kind of legal relationships [civil, criminal, commercial, etc.]. In other words, the philosophy of law 'looks for the proper essence of law,' or 'it looks for the very idea of law which ought to underlie the valid principles of the state.'

We must add that philosophy of law meant at that time a discipline covering what is now labeled as introduction to the judicial sciences and the theory of law and state.

The most up-to-date exposition of jurisprudence in socialist countries, without claiming to cover the whole field of the theory of law, lists the following problems as essential:[2]

> (1) The problem of the place of law among other social norms. It is a general problem of the theory of norms, linking the legal considerations with other social disciplines and with ethics. (2) The problem of legal and judicial language. This concerns the ways of formulating the legal texts and the doctrinal as well as practical assertions. (3) Structural problems of the system of law. A general analysis of the system of law and its characteristics is a precondition of the requisite systematization of socialist law. (4) The problem of the binding force (validity) of law as the key theoretical dilemma. (5) Selected problems concerning the social functioning of law. These are to be focused on law as a means of social control. (6) Problems of law making, conceived as a theoretical model of legislation, with reference to legal policy and theory of the sources of law. (7) Problems of the

interpretation and application of law. These are to be presented as theoretical models based on empirical materials concerning the practice of law courts in socialist countries. (8) Methodological and systematical problems of the science of law.

Another writer sets forth the theoretical tasks of legal science in the following manner:[3]

The theory of the legal sciences is by no means homogeneous. There are even tendencies to include in it everything that cannot be covered by doctrinal jurisprudence, with the sole exception of the history of law which is no longer considered a science. Such a standpoint can hardly be accepted. In any case, the theoretical field includes at least two, clearly distinct groups of problems:

1. Considerations aiming to arrive at general propositions about legal systems (particularly contemporary systems), concerning their concepts of the sources of law, their structure, the social origin of their laws, the actual efficiency of certain kinds of legal norms and their social functions, motives for respecting legal norms, etc. An exemplary statement of this kind is the basic assumption of the Marxist theory of law that legal norms usually protect the interests of the ruling class and support the social relationships which are convenient for that class, with obedience to these norms being forced through coercion exerted by state agencies. Propositions of this kind can be historical generalizations with narrower or wider fields of reference.

2. Methodological problems of the science or meta-science of law, having to do with formulating propositions not about law itself but about the legal disciplines: e.g., about their terminological apparatus, about the ways of reasoning employed in theoretical and dogmatic legal considerations, etc. The fact that problems as diverse as these are considered as a single whole is an expression of the low level of methodological awareness of the lawyers and, on the other hand, a result of the situation in which the theory of law still remains only an appendix to the doctrinal legal disciplines with their much longer traditions and greater practicality. Another important factor is that the relationship between what is considered to be the science of law and what actually shapes the norms which are valid in a given country is usually complex and often difficult to be clearly determined.

The most 'traditional' approach to the tasks of the theory of state and law is formulated in the following terms.[4]

5

It is an independent study, with its own scope of inquiries. That scope consists of: (a) the basic notions of the science of law, such as the state, law, the legal relationship, the legal norm, justice, the legal order, etc.; (b) the regularities of development of state and law, particularly those which are embodied in all the spheres of administrative and legal activities; (c) mutual relationships between state and law and between either of these and the other phenomena of social life; (d) the ways of studying and appreciating the phenomena of administrative and legal activities, i.e. the methods which would be used in the investigations on state and law.

The source of the shortcomings of jurisprudence has been succinctly summarized by one who is at the same time a theorist of law and an empirical student of criminal law.[5]

Sociological problems of jurisprudence have recently been attracting more and more the attention of both the theorists and the practitioners of law. Soviet legal science has been 'sociological' since its earliest days. It has always seen law, the state and its institutions in a close relationship with the life of society and with the laws of social development. But precisely for that reason this relationship has been dealt with only on the most general level of sociological theory—within the limits of considering the basic conditions and social functions of state and law as a whole. But the particular legal institutions, not to mention the detailed regulations, have been understood by lawyers in their social significance only in lip service, rather than being systematically and deeply studied. The causes of such a situation are generally familiar. Even though the science of law has its own shortcomings, these causes have been largely related to the lack of sufficiently developed sociological theories and sociological research methods.

The scope of interests of jurisprudence allows for the following critical analysis of the tasks of this science. Jurisprudence as we know it has been studying, above all, abstract problems, such as the concept of norm, types of legal and other norms, their sanctions, validity, the legal system, subjective and objective law, judicial language, etc. All these and similar considerations, though they have their merits (mainly as a definitional introduction to basic researches), deal with normative concepts connected with the actual shape and content of the binding law. But any changes of the binding law lead, more or less directly, to related changes in the interpretation of normative concepts. Consequently, the research interests of the state and law theory depend on the actual shape of the binding law and its modifications. Thus, though science claims to pursue universal regularities, each change of regulations at any level of legislation may lead to changes in what claim to be universally valid scientific propositions.

As already noted, the traditional definitions of the scope of jurisprudence have been essentially modified during recent decades. However, what is the essence of this change?

Though some sociological procedures have actually been introduced into the study of law, they apply, according to law theorists, only to particular isolated problems, rather than being a means for generalizing so as to learn something significant about the functioning of law as a whole. In this perspective, the empirical investigations are mainly instrumental as tools to study the functioning of particular legal institutions, chiefly new ones.

In such a situation, sociological methods are employed for auxiliary researches, focused on how particular legal institutions function in specified economic, social and political contexts, instead of being applied to the task of discovering more general regularities of the functioning of laws, which would constitute the essential theoretical underpinning of the legal sciences. Studies which could be defined as basic, i.e. those which concern the working of law, its efficiency, its determinations, etc. are still left to formal and normative reflections, while the coexistence of sociological efforts with the established habits of speculative thinking in law is reduced to the acknowledgment of an auxiliary role for sociology.

This is a deplorable situation, if only for the simple reason that, except for historical knowledge about the social or class determinants of law, any attempts to discover the regularities of the emergence, functioning and impact of law can only be successful if they are cumulative theoretical interpretations of various detailed empirical researches. Any such attempts will not succeed so long as they remain abstract or phenomenological reflections.

It would appear that the style predominating in the sociology of law differs from the traditional way of thinking in terms of jurisprudence by four characteristic hallmarks:

The sociology of law aims at grasping law in its working, thus to determine the range of efficiency of short- or long-range impacts of law; it tries to find out what kinds of legal instrument are most suited for remolding political attitudes, economic relationships, or human interaction; it seeks to discover whatever negative by-products ensue from law; it exposes the myths about how law functions and points out whatever elements of truth may reside in them, and inquires into their origin. In several countries the philosophy of law, although not limited to mere apologetics, quite often pays lip service to the

7

implications of political legal theory instead of engaging in concrete analyses.

The main objective of sociological investigations into the functioning of law is to provide expert advice for social engineering, allowing for rational and effective remolding of the human condition. The state and law theory rejects this task, passing it on to the positivist legal disciplines. Thus, the sociology of law provides a theoretical basis for development of a scientific legal policy, whereas the state and law theory fails to do this.

The sociology of law makes an effort to shape its studies so as to make them useful for practical applications. For example, studies on delinquency should be performed in such a manner as to make it possible for actual policy-makers to translate the theoretical findings into the language of their professional activity. State and law theory has no such concern.

The sociology of law struggles with reality, trying to describe it in empirical terms and to give a fuller and clearer image of it than we now possess.

To be critical of jurisprudence is not to denounce it as completely useless. What is implied is rather the need to see clearly that the essential problem in the science of law is inquiry into legal and social reality, whereas the analytical-linguistic studies which are the main concern of jurisprudence are useful only as auxiliary and instrumental with respect to the basic concern. This is a reasonable diagnosis in terms of an adequate methodology for the social sciences; however, in terms of organization of science, it is state and law theory which is the discipline covering the actual basic theorizing and researches on law. This situation urgently calls for a radical change.

The traditional classifications of legal disciplines can lead to methodologically ambiguous situations. For example, it is not clear whether the doctrinal disciplines (normative and dogmatic) are legitimate fields of scientific inquiry. But according to the prevailing view, the doctrinal disciplines are the core of jurisprudence. They constitute the bulk of university curricula and they can be most strongly felt in legal education, legal thinking, and in the formal doctrinal approach of lawyers to the phenomena of social life. Let us remember that by doctrinal we mean such disciplines as the civil law, civil procedure, penal law, penal procedure, financial law, religious law, tax law, etc. The main task of these studies consists in elucidating or explaining the meaning of the precepts which are valid in the given field of law, in making them consistent and arranging them in orderly patterns, and finally in suggesting new solutions concerning matters on which the law is ambiguous or says nothing at all.

However, the doctrinal disciplines, as a rule being professional and service-oriented, do not pursue the primary aim of all science, which is the description and explanation of phenomena by discovering and formulating general regularities. The representatives of the doctrinal fields of law not only do not pursue general knowledge expressed in causal relationships, but since they remain under constant pressure of professional expectations exerted by judges, lawyers, executives, etc. they overlook what they otherwise would know quite well, that the main task of their studies ought to be the formulation of general relationships, and of causal ones in particular.

The traditions of the profession have led to a splendid flourishing of the doctrinal disciplines as ways of interpreting, elucidating and bringing to consistency the meaning of terms used in the precepts of law. For the primary task of lawyers has always been the reading and understanding of legal texts. This practical consideration, together with its developed theoretical rationalization, accounts for the neglect of the study of the empirical consequences of law, the need for which might otherwise seem obvious.

Reflection on the methodological status of the doctrinal disciplines brings out their mixed-up theoretical and practical character. On one hand the doctrine of law considers the problems of logical relationships between names and norms and between the propositions constituting the set of concepts and regulations of the existing law. Its general task is the logical arrangement of concepts employed by a given system of existing law so as to elucidate and interpret it clearly, consistently and without any gaps. On the other hand, the doctrine of law is in part a political concern, since doctrinaire scholars often have to decide which of the available concepts of relationships between legal formulas is right or just, and what the advantages or disadvantages of each decision might be. However, thinking along such lines is teleological in character, since the doctrinaire does not consider and evaluate his own judgments but employs them as an element of reasoning which is taken for granted within the given system of law. Thus in such cases the doctrinal considerations become teleological and at the same time belong to the sphere of a practical art, viz. legal policy.

If the doctrines of the several sections of law are devoted to the understanding and interpreting of legal texts, jurisprudence (the state and law theory) has the obligation to explain, in a general perspective, law as it is understood by the several doctrinal studies. However, state and law theory is not interested in law as an element of social reality, but as a phenomenon to be analyzed by the doctrinal disciplines. This accounts for a persistent misunderstanding involved in the label 'state and law *theory*'. If, according to the definition by K. Ajdukiewicz, we understand by theory the hypotheses or small sets of hypotheses which are sufficient to provide explanations of all the empirical regularities describing the manner in which the processes belonging to some more extensive field occur, we can hardly accept as theory the fruits of a discipline which offers no hypotheses at all concerning the functioning of law, but rather is concerned with law as a normative phenomenon and not as a part of social reality. The auxiliary character of the state and law theory is also thereby disclosed, as its main concern is the semantical ordering of notions which constitute doctrinaire generalizations.

In this situation an adequate classification of the legal disciplines is urgently required. Such a classification, like any other, ought to be based on clear and non-overlapping criteria. Theoretical disciplines describe their proper sections of reality; they generalize the descriptive data into regularities formulated as hypotheses. The practical disciplines are concerned with how certain objectives can be achieved by specific means, provided that certain judgments are granted.

The general disciplines formulate regularities in which the variables are not objectified norms, institutions, types of behavior, endeavors, etc., but rather the general types of judgment, attitude or behavior related to the legal norms. The particularist disciplines, on the other hand, are concerned with objectively determined behaviors which occur now or have occurred in the past. These can be supportive of the existing law, or they can be inconsistent with it and related to the breaking, trespassing against or evading of the law or to situations in which unlawful behaviors are apt to occur. The legal disciplines studying the two types of phenomena can be distinguished accordingly.

The sociology of law is a theoretical and a general discipline studying regularities in the functioning of law. It formulates hypotheses on how law influences and is influenced by the wider reality. From this standpoint, the state and law theory appears as an auxiliary discipline for the sociology of law, dealing with the semantics of judicial language so as to make it more capable of realistic and appropriate distinction among the legal phenomena.

The particularist disciplines would be the historical ones, such as the history of Polish or of church law. Though historical data can be used in formulating some general regularities, the formulations themselves belong to the theoretical discipline, which is the sociology of law.

Legal policy, as a practical science, would constitute a counterpart to the sociology of law. It would incorporate the more or less general sociological regularities and the values embodied in the system of law, and would offer practical directives aiming at rational social change, to be instrumentally brought about by law. The general legal policy would be partitioned into various detailed political studies connected with the relevant sections of the system of existing law, such as civil, penal and financial policy, etc. Policy would then take a position both toward existing law (*lege lata*) and toward its proposed changes (*lege ferenda*).

It is by no means the intention of the present discussion to mount an assault against the paramount and central position of the state and law theory. Should it be disposed to undertake the problems which are the 'natural' concern of the sociology of law—i.e. the study of the social functioning of law—then we would concede that the sociological problems of law be investigated under the label of state and law theory. We only propose that the central legal discipline, whether it is called sociology of law or state and law theory, or whatever, be concerned with problems which are essential to their importance for the other legal sciences.

But which are the problems that do have such an essential importance? Which are strategic for the whole field of legal science?

One of these is the problem of familiarity with the law. The traditional conception of legal awareness, ambiguous and normatively biased, does not appear to provide a convenient starting point for empirical investigations. Studies on familiarity with the law ought to yield information on such issues as the knowledge of law among various social strata; knowledge of law that is recorded in codes, and of law expressed in the actual working of various state agencies; the distribution of the social and legal needs among different social groups; the causes of deprivation of some groups as to their knowledge of law; the ways in which some may take advantage of the lack of knowledge of law by others; and knowledge of the legal precepts and the legal principles used in social life. A similar problem concerns the relationship between legal and moral norms. The available semantic considerations concerning the consistent or incompatible intuitions of the meanings of the two terms can be useful for the arbitrary terminological stipulations necessary to empirical researches tackling such issues as legal conformism; obedience to law as a function of the quality of its sanctions; supporting of legal attitudes by moral ones; the weakening of legal integrity by conflicting moral norms; and moral norms as guideposts determining the directions in which legal norms might expand.

Another basic issue for the legal sciences is the distinction between the functioning of the official and the intuitive law. The prevailing normative and formal conception which limits the meaning of law to what is deemed valid by the authorized agencies has excluded intuitive law from the field of observation and analysis. Actually, however, there are various legal sub-cultures which are not entirely reconciled with official law. Some are obviously at odds with it. Therefore, a research program claiming to cover the entire field would involve analyses of various social groups or strata as legal sub-cultures. A realistic diagnosis of the scope and forms of acceptance of law by these groups would provide the basis for an informed and thus a more rational social and legal policy.

Also the problem of social and legal rigorism *v.* tolerance is vital for a general jurisprudence. Within the theoretical approach that has prevailed up to now, this issue has been considered, if at all, a minor question relating to criminal law. However, the criterion of social rigorism *v.* tolerance is quite essential for evaluating the efficiency of penal sanctions as instruments of social policy. For example, what in socialist countries is called 'economic delinquency' (theft of state property by employees of state-owned enterprises being the most important subdivision of this class of offenses) can be fought by imposing more severe sanctions, but only if public opinion supports the range and degree of the more rigoristic measures. If such support is lacking, other preventive means and managerial regulations will be advisable instead, since any increase of rigorism that does not find support among the people would lead to many negative side effects and the sum total of the costs would most probably be greater than the advantages of the repressions.

The problem of the prestige of law is paramount for all the legal sciences. We should emphasize three kinds: the prestige of law in general, the prestige of the various sections of law, and the respect enjoyed by law in abstract declarations and in actual practice. If there is a considerable general respect for law, various social changes can be effected without resorting to sanctions and coercive means of control, whereas the prevalence of little respect requires more efficient apparatus of control and discipline, thereby making the functioning of the whole apparatus more expensive.

These and related problems ought to be brought to the fore of theoretical legal inquiries, if we do not want to see the society only through the peephole of legal norms as shaped by presently existing law. Legal norms should be viewed as products of the functioning of the social system, in which their origin and their effects should be looked for.

Legal science cannot proceed by purely speculative steps. It can make a start toward a theoretically fruitful phase of development only when it is supported by empirical investigations. This being done, speculation can sometimes be helpful, too. Many of the ideas which appear in the philosophers' disquisitions can explain more than the toilsome and systematic researches. We might well consider the way the essence of law is elucidated in a Chinese fable.

When the town of Lu was possessed by panic, fire, pillage, violence and death, the children, women and men ran in all directions, treading down and trampling each other. Si-tien stood by one of the town gates, giving one and the same answer to all the incessant, clamoring shouts asking for direction: 'Towards the Su Hill.' His pupil Meng, torn intermittently by curiosity and fear, turned to him and asked: 'My lord! Why do you give such advice? How do you know that is a safe escape?' Si-tien answered: 'If all the principles suddenly appear to be incompatible and to bring destruction, it is best to select one at random and strictly abide by it.'

The meaning of law is order.

## Beginnings of empirical sociology of law

Many ancient thinkers who spoke about law expressed ideas which seem only speculative. In fact, however, they sometimes uttered thoughts with some empirical load in them. For example, reaching back to Aristotle we could say that his concepts of legitimacy and justice referred to the *basic values* of a social system and were empirically meaningful in that they expressed the need of a social system and were empirically meaningful in that they expressed the need of a social group for some inner order. Aristotle's distinction between law and morality can also be considered as presaging the later empirical investigations. Thus, even in the early history of philosophical and legal thought we can single out a number of predecessors of the future empirical trend in law. Without reaching so far back into history, we can enumerate thinkers who, even though they were not yet exactly modern lawyers and made no empirical investigations themselves (and could not make use of any) still managed to voice thoughts which can be translated into empirical language.

Among the significant forerunners of the sociology of law was F. Savigny. According to him, law had usually originated as a custom and a sentiment, was then elaborated by legal science and inculcated into human beliefs, and, only in the final phase, was determined by a binding act of legislation. Savigny also recognized the relationship between law and social change.

The utilitarian ideas of J. Bentham and R. Jhering went even further in emphasizing the role of law as an instrument of social change. The early views of Bentham concerning the strategic role of pain and pleasure can be clearly read in the recent conceptions of Homans, especially in his idea of explaining human behavior in terms of reactions to reward and punishment. According to Bentham, nature submitted the human race to the regime of two sovereigns, pain and pleasure. It is the office of pain and pleasure to instruct us in what we should be doing; the standards of good and evil

13

on the one side, and the chain of cause and effect on the other, are fastened to their throne. According to Jhering, law is a means to a definite end; this view was even expressed in the title of his book, *Zweck in Recht*.

The Austrian lawyer E. Ehrlich, a contemporary of Leon Petrażycki, maintained (to what extent under Petrażycki's influence is not known) that legal behavior and its development do not depend essentially on legislation, legal science, or judges' decisions, but on society itself. Thus he considered law as a dependent variable. One of the prominent exponents of sociological jurisprudence, R. Pound, suggested that law ought to be studied in its actual working and not as it stands 'in the books'; law should be handled as an instrument of social control; it should be attentively checked what negative social effects, if any, are brought about by legislation: consequently, the social effects of legislative changes ought to be carefully analyzed; and the working of law must also be related to the economic factors geared to it. According to Pound, actual human behavior is determined less by abstract regulations than by decisions of judges in courtrooms. The Scandinavian school, to which A. Hägerström, V. Lundstedt, K. Olivercrona, T. Geiger and T. Segerstedt belong, perhaps also under some influence of the ideas of L. Petrażycki, emphasizes the social origin of law and encourages studying law as a social fact. Such thinkers as W. Holmes, K. Llewellyn and J. Frank were founders of what is called legal realism; they argued that law could be reduced to social and psychological phenomena and that it was a secondary elaboration of the set of available norms. They emphasized the importance of the decisions of judges as the main factor influencing prevailing legal sentiments and saw lawmaking as being determined by those decisions.

Ideas on the borderline of law and the political sciences are another source of inspiration for later empirical investigations. This trend of thought is marked by a tendency to connect studies on the social determinants of law with such related disciplines as history, economics, and social and political systems analysis. This encyclopedic or interdisciplinary trend has shed much light upon the relationships between legal and other phenomena, upsetting the traditional jurisprudential approach toward law as a monistic and unique field. In the early phases of general reflections leading more directly toward the sociology of law, other thinkers besides those mentioned above have contributed to the shaping of our discipline. Among them should be mentioned É. Durkheim, L. Duguit, G. Gurvitch, N. Timasheff, L. Fuller, and T. Parsons. A detailed discussion of their works would require separate analysis.

Finally, it is generally acknowledged that works by Marx, Engels and Lenin have contributed to the elucidation of the social and

14

particularly class origin of law and its instrumental character as it is more or less consciously applied by the classes in power.

Of course, we can only arbitrarily determine the moment (establishing the Research Committee of Sociology of Law (1962)) at which the sociology of law should be considered to have become institutionalized as a modern empirical science. Many sporadic empirical researches had appeared before the systematic trend of investigations began to develop. Analysis of the published investigations, their interpretations, and theories related to them makes it apparent, in the few years that have elapsed, that there are several geographically based groups of sociologists of law. We can discern the Scandinavian, Italian, American, Soviet and Polish schools.

The Scandinavian school sees as its founders A. Hägerström, V. Lundstedt, K. Olivercrona, T. Geiger, T. Segerstedt and A. Ross. The basic problem of the social meaning of justice, which has been the common theme in the thought of these authors, reappears in the subsequent empirical studies of law. Thus, T. Eckhoff and S. Naess recently investigated the sentiments of justice in school children; the study was based on an empirical classification of various types of justice and on the analysis of conditions in which decisions concerning the distribution of justice take place. A study of rural laborers in Scandinavia (by F. Schmidt) attempted to find out to what extent the judicial regulations concerning employment were actually respected. It turned out that in some farms the conditions of labor were fairly consistent with the law, while in others extensive discrepancies were found. Thus, for instance, though the right of laborers to a fully paid leave was acknowledged by all, it was frequently carried out in a manner inconsistent with the law. About one-third of the farmers allowed their employees shorter leaves, giving them extra pay in return. However, in general it was found that (perhaps because of the penal sanctions incorporated into the law) the precepts of the labor bill were respected.

In a study by V. Aubert, concerning the new Norwegian law on domestic servants, essential discrepancies were observed between what the law demanded and the actual practice. For example, in only 30 per cent of cases were the servants paid for work after normal hours, while in not a single case could the extra payment be precisely reckoned. Both the employers and the servants had heard about the new law regulating their relationship, but only a few could give any details of the law. It was also found that the regulations were broken with the same frequency by those who knew them and those who did not. The discrepancy between the demands of the law and the actual state of affairs was explained in two ways: the law on domestic servants was relatively new and nothing similar had ever been heard of by housewives;[6] and the servants in Norway were not organized

15

and thus had no means of executing their rights. One of the main conclusions of the study was the following generalization: 'The awareness of legal norms influences human behavior more strongly when its source is one's own reference group than when it comes from the mass media.'[7]

Another study by Aubert (who, by the way, is one of the foremost personalities in Scandinavian sociology of law, along with Eckhoff) concerned the control of prices and the attitudes of businessmen towards it. It was found that the businessmen play two conflicting roles. On the one hand, they are marked by a loyalty toward the state and the law and a general disapproval of unlawful behavior as such, while on the other they are loyal to the business ethics which lead them to seek rationalizations and justifications for their own attempts to outwit or break the law.

An investigation by H. Klette on drivers intoxicated by alcohol shed interesting light upon the efficiency of the legal sanctions employed in such cases. Thus it seems that the sanctions against drunken drivers, even when they involve imprisonment, are not felt as threatening. The punishments inflicted do not affect the job security of those convicted, neither do they cause economic deprivation or impair their social relations with others. Problems of evidence make such cases difficult for the prosecution. The investigations also revealed that only a small proportion of drunken drivers are apprehended—of the order of one out of every ten or twenty. The study was based on court files analysis, on observations of the behavior of policemen and law officers, and on interviews with those who had received sentences and with citizens who expressed respect for the law.

An interesting Danish study by V. Goldschmidt concerned the behavior of officials in respect to the criminal code prepared for Greenland. In 1948–9 Goldschmidt was sent with a group of other experts by the Danish government to Greenland to study the local legal customs and to investigate the influence of the Danish legal codes and Danish culture in general upon the local population. Goldschmidt presented a report of the researches to the Danish parliament. Subsequently he was assigned the task of preparing a penal code for Greenland. His project, with minor modifications, was accepted by the Danish parliament as a bill on March 5, 1954. Article 121, paragraph 2 of the bill demanded explicitly that the social effects of the introduction of the code be studied and that changes be made if necessary. A special team was subsequently dispatched to Greenland in order to study the consequences of the law, and the following was found: the stronger the pressure of public opinion, the less the need for sanctions incorporated into positive law. The reverse is likewise true: if the pressure is weak, sanctions are the more necessary. Public opinion exerts particularly strong pressure on human behavior when social groups—as in most cases in the small villages of Greenland—are small. It turned out that in such cases the infliction of the sanctions of positive law (implanted from continental Danish law) frequently disrupted the integrity of the existing groups, but rarely had the expected frightening effect.

A good example of a translation of the idea predominating in Scandinavian studies—the idea of the social meaning of justice—into the language of empirical researches can be found in the analyses by K. Mäkelä.[8] He investigated an average Finnish population (2,023 adults) and 143 judges from district and regional courts. A systematic and sophisticated analysis yielded, among others, the following results: various social groups differ only slightly with respect to the severity of punishments demanded by them; women usually demand more severe punishments for offenses against morality, but are more tolerant than men with regard to offenses against property; in cities, social groups with higher incomes ask for more lenient punishments than those with lower incomes, while in rural areas this relationship is reversed; there are significant differences among the judges with regard to the severity of the punishments they impose; the severity of punishments imposed varied as much as from 10 per cent to 80 per cent, depending on the type of offense; these punishments varied widely as applied to offenses related to alcohol; age and professional standing of the judges were not related to the degree of severity of their sentences; judges of lower level courts were apt to pass more severe sentences in cases related to alcohol than were judges of higher level courts, although with respect to all other types of offenses there was no difference between these two groups of judges. In principle, the average population and the judges agreed to their demands for punishments, though there was some tendency on the part of the public to demand more severe sanctions than those imposed by courts.

In a study[9] concerning a similar problem, B. Kutchinsky arrived at the following conclusions, based on two Danish researches (one carried out in 1953-4 was based on interviews with 79 men and 58 women; the other, in 1962, on interviews with 242 men and 107 women).

1 Women express more rigoristic attitudes than men toward delinquency as an abstract notion, but are more tolerant than men in their evaluations of concrete cases of delinquent behavior.

2 Education and social position are closely related to rigorism. Educated persons tend to be the more rigoristic, but the relationship is less marked than between rigorism and social position, those higher up on the social ladder being more rigoristic in their attitudes.

3 In principle, the population as a whole does not approve of

unlawful behavior. However, the repulsion against such behavior is more marked among older than among younger people.

4 A comparison of the views of imprisoned persons and the average population reveals only a few significant differences. The most remarkable is the difference as to knowledge of law in the two groups: in some fields the knowledge of law disclosed by prisoners was amazingly poor.

5 It is interesting theoretically that the variable of social position clearly determines the attitude toward law among the average population, while it plays hardly any role at all among the prisoners.

In Italy the remarkable development of the sociology of law is strongly influenced by the fact that the headquarters of the Sociology of Law Research Committee of the International Sociological Association is in Milan (industrial center, several research facilities, strong university) and that the president of the Committee, Professor R. Treves, endeavors to connect as tightly as possible the empirical investigations of law with the actual needs of the judicial apparatus in his country.

Investigations by A. Pagani and G. Martinotti reveal that the majority of Italian judges are persons with peasant backgrounds. It is southern Italy in particular which provides the judicial apparatus with a sizable number of judges, and also with members of the Supreme Court. This remarkable recruitment of people from peasant families to the legal profession is explained by the fact that in southern Italy clerical work, and the profession of a judge in particular, is one of the few opportunities of social advancement, and one which is very highly respected. E. Moriondo has also analyzed the system of values of Italian judges. It turned out that the Italian judges are grouped into two professional organizations which struggled against each other. They published separate periodicals, cherished opposing professional ideologies, and in their struggle, as well as in their fight for the improvement of the professional situation of the judges—in particular in their claim to be clearly separated from the rank and file of administrative clerical workers—they were on the verge of organizing a nation-wide strike of the judges. Moriondo showed in his study how the Italian system of justice tried to eradicate the socially and morally noxious burden of Fascist experiences, still prevalent in some spheres of social life.

The Milan project of investigations on judicial administration is a large-scale design carried out with great vigor. Within this complex venture, the following fields of study have been singled out as essential: (1) organization of the institutions (the general pattern of the organization of justice, reconstruction of the process of judicial decision making, financing of the justice apparatus, organizational problems of its functioning); (2) monographic studies, focused on a

single selected court of law; (3) the profession of a judge (social background of judges, their satisfaction with their work, their ideology,
attitudes of the other judicial professions toward the judges); (4)
public attitudes toward the judicial administration; and (5) social and
economic effects of the functioning of justice (the courts as a factor in
economic change, the quantity and types of lawsuits in Italy, and informal ways of arbitration and mediation).

A number of factors determined that the program should be so
extensive. Among them were the following: widespread disfavor of
public opinion toward the functioning of the judicial apparatus; the
striving of a considerable number of judges to advance their own
careers at the expense of the public weal; the example set by other
judges to change and improve the situation, i.e. both to make their
work better in its quality and to promote a more socially oriented
ethic and professional attitude; and a disposition on the part of legal
science to gain an insight into those social situations which until then
had been blank spaces in the inquiries of both the lawyers and social
scientists.

Interesting results have been achieved both by the analyses of the
professional ideology of the judges and the studies on the attitudes of
public opinion toward the judicial institutions. The following findings were made: there is a negative attitude on the part of the population toward law; one of the essential features of society is the lack
of a tendency to make use of the judicial apparatus; in those social
environments in which the relationships between people are more
impersonal, the reluctance to resort to the judicial apparatus is
relatively less marked; and in a group where attitudes toward the
legal system tend to be negative, the opinion of the whole group tends
to be more homogeneous. In northern Italy the judges are technically
oriented and are apt to solve individual cases instrumentally; in
central Italy their attitudes can be defined as humanistic, as they are
interested above all in the individual before them; the judges from
southern Italy reveal a marked authoritarian attitude. The general
population takes a clearly negative attitude toward the legal profession; those social strata which can be considered as under-privileged
believe more than others in the possibilities and efficiency of legislative influence.[10]

In a work attempting a synthesis of sociology of law in the USA,
J. Skolnick[11] emphasizes three features which he considers significant
for American society. According to him, American society is marked
by an egalitarian system of values on the one hand, and by an obvious
social stratification on the other. Second, Americans have traditionally been attached to local autonomy, but centralistic tendencies are
gaining strength and control the society more and more efficiently,
increasing the general feeling of 'depersonalization.' Third, Skolnick

maintains that American society is, on the one hand, ideologically committed to the functioning of individual capitalists with their individualistic model of success in life, while on the other hand nationwide organizations such as the federal government, corporations, stock companies, trade unions, etc. are increasingly gaining power.

It is by no means easy to classify the multitude of empirical investigations on law carried out in the USA. E. Schur in his book *Law and Society*, New York, 1968, suggests the following arrangement of what has been done: (1) studies of courts, judges and lawyers; (2) studies on the administration of criminal justice; (3) studies on the styles of judicial activity; and (4) studies on the attitudes of public opinion toward law.

One of the most renowned American researches was an investigation of the jury system which resulted in a national uproar. In 1954 jury sessions were tape-recorded by means of microphones hidden in the jury room. After the facts had been discovered, this procedure was forbidden by Congress, though it was established that the taping had served strictly scientific ends only. Subsequent investigations thus could not be based on authentic jury discussions, but on fake sessions, designed to be as similar as possible to the actual ones. However, the results obtained in this way have the features of a laboratory experiment, which is something very difficult in a field such as law. Here are some of the findings: the foreman of the jury, selected by it, is usually a man, better educated than the other members; when a group of people without legal training, with different social backgrounds, constituted together into a jury, begins to work toward a verdict, its activity assumes a new form, never before experienced by the members: the law influences them in a uniform and schematic manner, inducing them to accept the general standards and to give up their individual propensities; and in general, juries are apt to resolve their cases more leniently than professional judges.[12]

Investigations were also undertaken on the problem of the mechanism of decision-making by judges. These were sometimes labeled wittily as 'gastronomical law research,' as they saw the outcome of judiciary decisions as being influenced by the actual psychical state of a judge, including his mood as determined by a good or a poor breakfast. Anyway, it turned out that certain social characteristics of judges significantly influenced their verdicts. For example, judges who are Democrats differ remarkably from those who are Republicans in their verdicts concerning various types of legal suits. Democrats are more likely than Republicans to decide in favor of a defendant in criminal cases. They tend to favor the unions in contests between labor and capital; they decide differently in cases concerning the paying of taxes; they also take differing decisions in cases involving indemnities for damages.

20

Studies on the style of police behavior revealed, against normative expectations, that policemen behave quite differently in different concrete situations. A policeman in practice handles a juvenile delinquent in very different ways, depending on how he sees him socially. His behavior is not the same towards a well-dressed person as towards an unkempt and slovenly dressed one; it is different toward an arrogant one and one assuming meekness; it is not the same toward a Negro as toward an obviously upper-class person. These findings are in accord with common sense, but they are in some way surprising to lawyers, because the universalistic principles of law demand from its officers the same attitude towards all categories of people.

Studies on the styles of work of various legal professions, relatively neglected until recently, have made progress on many fronts. Thus, the huge legal firms which play such a significant role in American society were analyzed. It was found that the partners in these enterprises are most often Protestants, children of persons active in big business, directors or professionals. Lawyers employed in the large and prestigious firms are Ivy League graduates and often have been editors of their university legal faculty journals. They represent, in terms of D. Riesman's comment, the self-fulfilling myth in legal education and they believe themselves to be 'something better' as citizens. A lawyer employed by a big legal firm is almost exclusively concerned with the problems and affairs of big business. He looks upon himself as one of the significant elements of the establishment. In New York City such a firm will occupy a four- or five-story office in the downtown section and will employ 50 to 150, or sometimes even up to 250, persons as its personnel.[13]

Quite different is the situation of a lawyer who serves the lower social strata. He does the 'dirty job'; he picks the cases that the big or even medium-sized houses would not touch, those which require special approaches or endeavors beyond the limits of the formal. These are usually matters of taxes, indemnities, divorces and criminal cases. J. Carlin, who analyzed the situation of an average attorney in the USA, described his position as it is seen in his neighborhood in the following terms:[14]

> People look at their neighborhood lawyer differently than at a lawyer who works downtown. They treat him like the other service people or salesmen who are not in the professions. Lawyers of this category are treated more like businessmen next door than like professionals. Physicians have no such problems at all; a physician from downtown is treated like a suburban doctor.

The different styles of handling legal matters described above certainly mark out significant differences in the legal sub-culture of

21

those who are devoted to carrying out the requirements of legal precepts. Depending on these sub-cultural differences, the precepts can be realized in various manners, either consistent or inconsistent with the general requirements of the legal system.

Sociology of law in the German Democratic Republic and in the German Federal Republic has not been very well developed until recently, and though in the last few years it has enjoyed a remarkable spurt I shall cite here only a few of its results, i.e. those concerning the legal professions and thus comparable with the American studies described above.

H. Steiner, a GDR scholar, pointed to the essential difference in the social backgrounds of judges in the GDR and in the GFR. In the GDR, the judges are mostly of working class or peasant origin and they have no Nazi taint; the judges in the Federal Republic are largely persons from clerical bourgeois families. W. Kaupen,[15] a scholar from the GFR, attempted to establish the number of lawyers who practice in West Germany. Estimations in the literature are from 45,000 to 60,000. According to Kaupen's findings, the actual number exceeds 90,000 (82,000 among them being professionally active). The German lawyers consider themselves as state officials. Even attorneys with private practice—most of them at least—see their professional roles as the devotion to justice, and justice is largely identified with the state administration and power. The author points out that German lawyers are subject to professional indoctrination which is by no means limited to their university education and vocational career, but reaches deep into their childhood and early socialization. Thus, the bulk of them come from provincial, Catholic families of state officials. Most are sons of prosecutors and judges, and less frequently sons of lawyers employed in big business. Their personalities have been molded under conditions not favorable to flexible attitudes. They reveal interest in various problems of the contemporary world, but stick persistently to traditional notions and stereotypes—norms and manners of behavior which can only with utmost difficulty be made to fit into contemporary society. This process of socialization of young lawyers in the GFR is enhanced by their professional training. It is remarkably narrow compared to the education of other students. As a result, the professional curriculum tends to make their minds uniform and conformist, at the same time withdrawing them from the current matters of their society. This kind of education bears far-reaching consequences for their professional activity. According to Kaupen, the process involves an increasing gap between the conflicts which emerge in the daily life of the country and the domains governed by the administration and controlled by lawyers. The frame of mind of West-German lawyers also has serious implications for the authoritarian style of German institutions and is reflected in lines of political thinking and in the ways in which social reforms are undertaken.

The young and dynamic sociology of law in the Soviet Union has long-standing traditions and very thorough methodological grounds. In an interesting monograph on the subject, the assumed definition of sociology of law is similar to that accepted by some Polish scholars. It says:[16]

> Sociology of law is tightly connected with the legal sciences.
> They have a similar subject of investigations: the state and law.
> However, the sociology of law differs from the legal sciences in that it studies the general regularities of the development of state and law. Besides, it studies much more extensively than they the following problems: by what social phenomena is the state and law determined? how do the state and legal institutions influence the development of society? to what degree do they contribute to such development? Sociology of law in the USSR attempts to achieve knowledge on how law contributes to the construction of communism.

Sociology of law in the Soviet Union is concerned, for example, with studies on the social position of deputies to the Supreme Soviet and to the 'Soviet of Nationalities' (i.e. the collective organ of different nationalities living in the Soviet Union); there are investigations concerning problems of labor law; reasons why legal factors influence the fluctuation of factory personnel are studied; problems of marriage and family are investigated; causes of delinquent behavior are sought; and, finally, the essential problem of public opinion towards law is tackled.

It should be noted, by way of illustration, that the research on deputies included such issues as: the number of speeches a deputy made during a session; the amount of time he devoted to the performance of his role as a deputy, etc.; these data were compared according to the age, sex, education and personality traits of the deputies. It turned out that older persons devoted more time to their parliamentary duties; in particular, persons between fifty and fifty-nine years of age devoted the most time to their roles as deputies while those below twenty-nine years devoted the least. This finding is consistent with the fact that people under thirty have relatively more of other social involvements. The deputies who have managerial functions (directors of enterprises, managers of organizations) devote more time to their parliamentary roles than those deputies who are in the professions (such as physicians, engineers and teachers); workers devote the least time to their roles as deputies.

In general, Soviet sociology of law is marked by a number of singular features: it tends to design its empirical programs on a large scale; very large populations are subject to investigations; numerous methods of cross-control of results are employed, improved and tested; many unconventional research methods are applied which, supplemented by traditional ones, often bring new and unschematic results; and finally, there is an obvious tendency to undertake studies in fields which not only are theoretically important but are above all significant for social and political reasons. The latter characteristic is particularly remarkable: in the Soviet sociology of law, the problem of undertaking studies that are economically, socially and politically important is very sensibly felt by scholars. In this way Soviet sociology of law tries to avoid collecting facts which would make up a kaleidoscopic image of incomprehensible data, or hypotheses which have no apparent usefulness in practice. The bulk of research efforts is thus focused upon those fields which can in some way or other be useful for socialist construction.

## Socio-legal investigations in the socialist system

Since the sociology of law attempts to translate discovered regularities into the language of concrete practical advice, it is worth while to reflect on which fields of legal and social life should be exposed to intensive scientific investigation and what practical benefits can be expected. Turning to the socialist system for concrete cases, the following fields can be listed as appropriate for intensive analyses: the functioning of the new legal-political institutions established since the advent of the People's Poland; the functioning of the prior institutions carried over from a different social and legal system and now working within a system which is generically alien to them; various socio-legal institutions that are not recognized by the existing formal system of law, which acknowledges only those elements which are inherent in its own structure; the social and economic effects of various institutions and norms of law from the point of view of their overall impact; the legal sub-cultures found within the public institutions, and the legal sub-cultures found within the groups shaped or molded in some way by the system of existing law; and the full social meaning of the functioning of informal structures within institutions, which modify the working of the institutions in ways that are often quite crucial.

Such a research program is not intended to supplement the legal sciences by a mere mechanical application of sociological methods and procedures to their traditional problems. Its objective is not the addition of new illustrations shedding redundant light upon the available encysted legal concepts and ideas. What is really at stake is the dissipation of the myth that existing law is efficient merely because it exists. The aim is to reveal as fully as possible the conditions

24

for the efficiency of the working of law; it must be disclosed how the existing law interacts with various social and economic factors, enhancing or impeding, or even sometimes losing, its own effectiveness in the process. But it must also be made clear that law often happens not to be the proper instrument of social policy, and that some types of social change simply cannot be accomplished by means of legislative action.

In the socialist system this kind of consideration acquires particular significance. Here, law has become a tool of far-reaching and universal change. Thus, careless experimenting with law (e.g. promoting legal regulations which are not thoroughly considered, or are not sufficiently rational, or are downright irrational) can bear social consequences of great import. Sometimes legal moves which are clearly well meant can become really valuable pieces of legislation only when they are supported by a suitable range of socio-legal findings.

To illustrate this, I shall describe some research on a very important legal and social problem. To avoid any misunderstanding, let me say at the outset that the analyzed body of legal regulations seems to be correct and socially valuable; the objections that are raised against its functioning have their roots in the aforementioned neglect of the relevant socio-legal knowledge.

The research concerned the procedures in the 'penal-administrative collegiums,'[17] non-professional institutions for handling minor offenses. Organizationally, they are extensions of the presiding bodies of national councils; they have been functioning since 1952. The most material legislative changes were introduced in 1966. The penal-administrative collegiums work as an independent and separate system, detached from the courts of law and the apparatus of prosecution. Their members are not professional lawyers and they hold their offices not as remunerative jobs but as social positions of honor. The research was carried out in thirty-two collegiums of the lower level, in five voivodships (i.e. larger administrative divisions of the country). The following methods were applied: examination of the files of 3,441 cases which ended with final sentences (no longer subject to appeal) during 1965; observation of 786 proceedings in these collegiums during 1966; interviews with presidents of collegiums, members of the official prosecutors' offices, and militia (police) officers; and the study of supplementary materials obtained by observation of the conditions and organization of work of the collegiums. The 3,441 cases selected for study were sampled randomly; it was found later that the samples were quite representative in their structure of the general distribution of cases handled by collegiums throughout the entire country during 1965. Following are some of the findings of the study.

B

In 12·5 per cent of cases the defendants never participated in the proceedings of the collegiums. In 1,005 cases the defendants were absent from at least one session; in 438 of these the reason was failure to inform them of the date of the session, while in the remaining cases there were a variety of other reasons. Though non-professional defense assistance was allowed in all cases and professional legal aid was allowed in about 34 per cent of cases, professional solicitors actually appeared in only three cases and a non-professional advocate was seen only once. Prosecutors appeared in 12·8 per cent of cases. In 26·1 per cent of cases there were no witnesses, and experts were called in only 0·4 per cent of cases. In spite of the widespread view that the collegiums do not have technical facilities to admit the public to their sessions, it turned out that in most cases there were fairly good conditions for accommodating reasonable-sized audiences. Surprisingly, it was found that the only factor determining whether a session was open to the public or not was the behavior of the minutes clerk: when he summoned the involved persons by name, nobody else entered the room; when he read out the description of the case, the audience went in. Other observations support the general opinion that in the penal-administrative collegiums there is a tendency to evaluate evidence depending on the rank and importance of the official who brings an action against the defendant.

In general, it can be said that the formal institution of defense is 'dead' in the collegiums. According to the author of the research, this is due to faulty organization of legal aid services. A proper form of defense could be provided by establishing legal aid offices, but up to now it has not been because a relevant legislative act is lacking. A further, very interesting finding points to 'a broad differentiation in the practical application of the several principles of penal procedure.'[18] According to the author, 'the differences can be accounted for by the wide limits left for independent opinion or interpretation' and by 'insufficient knowledge of the existing law resulting from the very nature of the administrative collegiums, as they are essentially non-professional bodies.' Another general finding of the research is that in the various administrative-penal collegiums differing styles or habits of work have evolved, sometimes consistent with the existing law and sometimes not. Some have even arisen by mere accident.

The foregoing piece of research is a convenient illustration for our thesis. Awareness of the fact that the prescriptions regulating administrative-penal procedure will be carried out by people who are often personally involved in what they do, and who have the time diligently to pursue their duties in the collegium, would likely lead to provision of a suitable expert compendium of the abstract and scattered (and thus hard to locate) precepts, a compendium adjusted to the actual state of education and training of those who are expected to apply these precepts.

Underlying the situation is the assumption that it is the legislation and the interpretation of legal acts which constitutes the final phase of judicial activity, the crowning of the complex process of law-making. Actually, the opposite is the truth. The legal precepts which are issued and posed for interpretation are not the final product of the working of law but its beginning. The traditional way of thinking is based on the *a priori* assumption that legal regulations, once they are issued in a proper manner, will take on a life of their own, fully realizing their intended objectives. This is an atrociously fallacious idea. On the contrary, it can rightly be said that legal enactments realize their intended objectives only when, in the first place, they have been properly implemented as pieces of legislation and are based on theoretical knowledge underpinning the expectation that the implemented law will function as an independent variable; and in the second place, when it is established *ex post* that the intended effects have actually been realized without any negative and un-intended side effects.

If such a legislative procedure is to be at all possible, there must be available, as noted above, theoretical knowledge enabling prediction of the effects of projected legal enactments. Such knowledge would encompass, above all, awareness of the actual motivations governing the behavior of the general population, as well as motivations typical of various narrower groups. For if legal precepts are meant to be incentives to certain kinds of behavior, they will be effective only if they animate motives conducive to that behavior.

Let us consider the two possible approaches to law in terms of the following fictitious model. We will imagine two societies in both of which there is a very high degree of mass-scale conformity to law. An observer from outside seeking to describe the behavior of the people in respect to existing regulations would find the two societies very similar. However, in one there is a strong coercive control based on fear that discourages people from deviant behavior, while in the other there is an internalized obedience and a spontaneous acceptance of the legal norms. A traditional lawyer, like the outside observer, would be apt to view the two societies as similar to each other. However, there is an essential difference. In the coercive type of society, con-formity to law is inordinately expensive because of the necessity to support and maintain the apparatus of control, while in the other type law and order cost little or nothing as they are self-sustaining.

The psycho-social determinants on which a legislator or a politician may rely can be disclosed only by a study of motivations, their distribution and force. One of the reasons why the traditional approach to law is inadequate is its belief that legal stipulations are a kind of political sorcery. Normative spells, chants of what ought to be, and solemn formulas, are a kind of secular witchcraft which hardly ever has transforming power. To influence people efficiently, we must know, and know how to activate, the motivations controlling their actual behavior.

An interesting classification was set forth by J. Kwaśniewski in his study on the legal and moral views of Polish society. He distinguished empirically two orientations: an outer and an inner.[19]

An outer-oriented individual obeys the law as a result of consideration of what might happen if he deviated from a legal norm. On the other hand, we say that a law-abiding individual is inner-oriented if he accepts a given norm as his own, as well as knowing that he will meet disapproval if he behaves unlawfully; deviant behavior is for him not only grounds to expect some consequence or other but a sufficient reason or justification for such consequences.

Kwaśniewski's research based on this assumption sought to analyze various types of motivations for lawful behavior. It turned out that attitude toward obedience to law was highly correlated with the following factors: a tendency to condemn the breaking of minor regulations; high ratings on scales of rigorism (i.e. a strong tendency to condemn various behaviors offending the generally accepted social norms); age above thirty; education higher than elementary; a steady source of income; white-collar occupation; and urban residence in towns of up to 100,000 inhabitants. The declared reasons of this all-Polish urban sample for crossing the street only in accord with the traffic regulations were supplemented by observations of actual behavior in a similar situation. Even though the two samples (the interviewed and the observed individuals) could not be the same for technical reasons, the declarations and the behaviors turned out to be surprisingly consistent. And while the results of this study cannot be generalized routinely, still it is a type of approach that provides more knowledge than does mere guesswork.

The above research is similar to another, earlier study. In an American town 2,103 persons who happened to cross an intersection were observed (aged and handicapped persons and children were not considered). With the traffic signals either red or green during the crossing, 99 per cent of the sample respected the red lights and 1 per cent did not. After this was established, an extra factor was introduced by way of experiment. A specially instructed person crossed the street when the red light was on and the number of other trespassers was then counted. Two situations were arranged. In the first case the person who broke the regulation was well-dressed—in a white shirt, properly pressed trousers, clean shoes—looking like an upper-class citizen; in the second case the person who crossed the street against the red signal was a slovenly and unkempt, ostensibly lower-class fellow. Offenses against the regulation were recorded as 14 per cent in the first situation and 4 per cent in the second.

The experiment confirmed two general regularities: (1) an example provided by an offender induces imitation, i.e. encourages others to break a norm; (2) an offender with visible or known higher social status influences others more strongly than one representing a lower level of prestige.

These findings are not exactly trivial. They amount to saying that respect for law is influenced by reference models and consequently if the persons with greater prestige reveal more respect for law, they provide more valuable social models. The above relationship summarizes our knowledge as to degree of respect for the law as it relates to the social sources of models for imitation.

What seems clear from all that we know so far is that law and order will not prevail by mere exhortation. Lawful behavior can only result from our knowledge of human motives and of the means of influencing human conduct. Sociologists of law believe that the book learning of law fails to provide such knowledge and that there is an urgent theoretical and practical need to concentrate efforts towards a deeper understanding of these problems.

For example, in Poland the general science of law suggests that more repression is required to curb frequent offenses against social (state) property. However, our knowledge of the results of penal sanctions points out that severe punishment is only effective if the person exposed to it feels respect either towards the punitive agent or towards the norm underlying the penalty.[20] And we know from empirical research that the persons who steal social property are those who in general do not feel responsible for or obliged to protect it. In 1960, A. Siciński made a nationwide investigation of the problem, covering a representative sample of the urban population employed in socialized enterprises, composed of 1,744 persons. He arrived at the following conclusions:[21] the feeling of responsibility toward the company is related to the degree of involvement in the work done and to the degree of social stabilization (low rate of mobility); in general, there is more respect for 'good work' or 'decent craftsmanship' than for the discipline of work; less respect for social than for private property is confirmed; an interrelation is marked out once again between the appreciation of the degree of one's influence upon the company and the 'feeling of responsibility' for it; and skilled workers have more committed attitudes toward their jobs than do unskilled workers. Considering these findings, offenses against social property ought to be combatted by new, more efficient and rational means.

A sweeping look at the field suggests that the studies most likely to supply knowledge of how influence can be exerted by legal means are those focused on the following: the attitudes of the society toward law and judicial institutions; the informal functioning of these institutions; their practical effectiveness in achieving stated goals; and finally, the social and political values that the legal system should seek to promote.

An analysis of social attitudes toward law and legal institutions can reveal the potential reserves of pro-legal motivations and disclose the extent to which spontaneous human behavior may be relied upon. It can also bring out the scope and intensity of the actual or potential anti-legal behaviors. A diagnosis can also be provided as to which social strata and categories have the tendency to support the law, and which are more prone to deviant conduct. Such a diagnosis would allow for the determination of which categories of the population can best be relied upon in efforts toward realizing the postulate of law and order in the socialist sense.

The problem of what goes on within those institutions which are the substrate of the legal order has been amazingly neglected by the traditional legal science. No attempts have been made to understand the inner mechanisms or informal networks working within the various institutions—what styles of work emerge in them and by what channels the models of behavior are communicated, such as to either help or hinder the performance of their tasks. Institutions administering law are the strategic elements of the legal system through which law affects society. If the system is transformed or peculiarly refracted by inner processes within institutions, the system's overall impact can be different from what is intended, the more so the greater the 'angle of refraction.' Very often—in particular when the state administration shows a tendency to be transformed into a bureaucracy—the legal system is able to perform only a small fraction of its tasks, since the institutions which ought to serve it begin to consider their own subsistence as an end in itself, or as an autotelic value. An analysis of those dysfunctional processes within the working institutions can provide an image of the conditions which are necessary for the given legal order to become fully realized.

I have remarked again and again that it is mere illusion to suppose that a correctly enacted legal precept will bring about such effects as are anticipated. A study of the effectiveness of the working of legal institutions and precepts can reveal, on the one hand, the extent to which the intended rational ends can be made real by means of law and, on the other, whether law is after all the proper instrument for such ends, rather than, for example, educational undertakings such as popularization by the mass media of law-abiding behavior.

Finally, a legal system is an educative endeavor with large-scale objectives. It teaches people how they ought to behave. It assumes that human behavior is to some extent based on other values than those underlying the legal system. Precision and clarity as to the aims involved in a legal system, the hierarchy of accepted values and the rank order of preferences can be very helpful in determining the sequence of endeavors in social engineering which can be carried out by means of law.

Thus the aim of sociology of law is to have the principles of law and order realized in a rational manner, based upon well-grounded diagnoses. The sociology of law is opposed to the belief that effective change can be achieved by declarations, rhetorical exhortations or, as Petrażycki used to say, by shooting off postulative ammunition.

# 2 Defining the sociology of law

It is possible to look at the sociology of law from many points of view. It may be regarded as: (a) one of the branches of general sociology (a problem immediately arises as to what specific features distinguish the sociology of law from other sociological approaches, and also what the sociology of law may contribute to general sociological knowledge that is new and specific); (b) a modern version to replace obsolete, semantically vague and methodologically suspicious jurisprudence without abandoning an important field of inquiry (the analysis of basic philosophical notions which are inherent in the legalistic way of thinking and problem-solving); or (c) a cryptic and misleading term supposed to cover a new (in contrast to the old, traditional) approach but only introducing sociological techniques of investigation secondary to the basic legal ones (in which case a legitimate objection could be raised that the sociology of law is only a convenient and rather empty slogan which reveals several additional and helpful but nevertheless second-rate means of enlarging the traditional legal outlook on the law).

Which point of view is methodologically the most proper? Which is the most adequate for dealing with current empirical discoveries? Which one reflects most closely the insights generated during the still lively discussions pertaining to the basic problems of the legal sciences?

In order to answer these questions we must look at some existing definitions of the sociology of law. P. Selznick says: 'The sociology of law may be regarded as an attempt to marshal what we know about the natural elements of social life and to bring that knowledge to bear on a consciously sustained enterprise, governed by special objectives and ideas.'[1] He distinguishes three stages of the development of the sociology of law: (1) the primitive or missionary stage, (2) the stage which belongs to the sociological craftsman, and (3) the stage of true maturity where 'the sociologist goes beyond (without repudiating) the role of technician or engineer and addresses himself to the larger objectives and guiding principles of the particular human enterprise he has elected to study.'[2] J. Skolnick has a slightly different approach to the question: 'The most important work for the sociologist of law is the development of theory growing out of empirical, especially institutional, studies,' and also: 'The most general contribution that the sociology of law may make to social theory is that of understanding the relation between law and social organization.'[3] V. Aubert tells us that the sociology of law is part of a general discipline, namely the sociology of science, which deals with the specific legal way of thinking.[4] I myself have put forward as a definition[5]

> The Sociology of law has as its task not only to register, formulate and verify the general interrelations existing between the law and other social factors (law could then be regarded as an independent or dependent variable), but also to try and build a general theory to explain social processes in which the law is involved and in this way link this discipline with the bulk of sociological knowledge.

These definitions, like all definitions in the social sciences, try to focus attention on specified problems and to emphasize certain aspects of complicated social reality. Therefore, these and other definitions may be regarded as an academic attempt to contain within a general description the different tasks performed by scholarly specialists who consider and deliberate over various relationships existing between the law and social structure.

Nevertheless, despite these attempts to 'grasp the essence' of the sociology of law, a new, in some ways completely different approach (but one still rooted in previous, traditional attitudes) to the sociology of law emerges as a possible new pattern of inquiry. This attempt is visible in various other inquiries but is especially clear in a comprehensive Italian study on the administration of justice.[6] In this particular case several features of the new type of approach become visible: (a) a social issue of great importance was selected as the object of comprehensive, interdisciplinary analysis; (b) a social diagnosis covering a vast range of problems, issues and open questions was offered in an attempt to describe, in general language, a variety of different processes proceeding at different rates in different directions, but complying on the whole with a general pattern; (c) partial and more general explanations were proposed as to reasons for the interactions registered and described; and (d) some proposals having the character of social engineering were formulated as part of this comprehensive study.

Perhaps this new attempt is simply complementary to the old one in that it tries to stress the need for solving problems of great social importance which were overlooked by classical scientists. If so, many methodological possibilities remain open through a new combination of traditional disciplines. Let us, instead of looking for a perfect definition prepared in a somewhat analytical manner, take into account the achievements and difficulties which the sociology of law (a relatively new science in its empirical version) has accumulated up to now. Some of these problems are of a mainly methodological character. Thus, to what extent has the lesson to be drawn from the sociology of law by the legal sciences enriched these sciences? Perhaps an elliptical answer would be proper at the beginning. The lesson imparted by the sociology of law revealed with amazing sharpness that traditional legal reasoning is limited when used as the main tool and instrument in solving legal problems. A further question immediately arises: on what grounds is so-called legal reasoning based? Again, the answer—if given at all—is quite astonishing: legal reasoning is based on the grounds of common sense and specifically legalistic professional abilities. And yet common sense, with all due respect, is limited and yields to systematic knowledge. Moreover, the professional abilities of lawyers, unique to those possessing them, are biased by the experiences accumulated by a given profession. These short-comings create the major limitations of the traditional use of legal reasoning. But if this is the situation, what new and more specific sociological methods could be offered such as to enlarge, deepen and sharpen our insight into the complicated operation of legal and social processes?

In order to give a more satisfactory answer to these questions, a survey of the various methods which are useful in supplementing the traditional knowledge of the law is needed.

### The historical-descriptive method

The historical method in the sociology of law assumes the diachronic approach in research, reaching back into the past. It makes use of various documents, such as private and official records, memoirs, publications, etc., recorded in any type of writing, cuneiform, hieroglyphics, or in symbols such as seals or coats of arms. The historical method requires expert critical source analysis, immediate and direct. In some cases this method may lack sufficient precision; in others it may bring many interesting results.

Traditionally used, the historical method when applied to law was supposed to describe this or that legal enactment, status or institution in its unique historical perspective. The more historical facts, the more details describing the idiosyncratic flavor and atmosphere of a given legal event, the more productive the application of this method. The modern version, which could fruitfully be used in the understanding of law, has a different methodological orientation. It tries to compare types of social systems and the legal systems corresponding to them. Without going into detail, one might say there are at least three basic relationships between social systems and the legal systems attached to them: (1) obsolete legal systems (when social needs outpace the rigidified tradition-bound requirements of the legal system), (2) adequate legal systems (when social needs are in some harmony with the set of legal constructs and norms which constitute the legal system as a whole), and (3) progressive legal systems (when the legal system is more developed, more enlightened than economic and political social conditions which resist its creative pressure). Of course, the real situation is always more complicated: legal systems are not stable; they are, in general (as I. Raz says in this connection) temporary, due to the fact that they are changing all the time; new laws are enacted continuously and some legal norms lose their binding force. Perhaps it would be better to speak of 'jumping' legal systems (they 'jump' all the time, systematically changing their scope and content).

This new point of view offers a far-reaching theoretical perspective. It could illuminate the up-to-now obscure general problem: under what conditions can a legal system be adopted or taken over by other social systems? There are not only technical innovations; legal ideas, and legal norms and constructs can also be regarded as social innovations. Parts of Roman law were adopted in medieval Germany, France and Poland. Parts of German law (especially the parts connected with urban settlement) were adopted in Poland. These elements of foreign legal systems were adopted because they were needed; they were functional and in accord with the new social and economic trends. After the Second World War Japan (in addition to the previously adopted civil law taken mainly from France and Germany) borrowed and adapted American constitutional law.

All these 'travels,' 'transplantations,' and voluntary and involuntary adaptations are better understood when the more elaborated scheme of socio-historical thinking is adopted. Then the directions of and reasons for the flow of legal innovations can be grasped in a deeper perspective; not as the influence of Prince X on Prince Z, or scholar A on scholar B, but as a complementary interchange of legal innovations and ideas. Also, unexpected and undesired negative by-products of these exchanges could be better understood. Some elements of a newly adopted legal system which were adjusted and 'natural' in the paternal social system could be regarded as strange, alien and unacceptable by some members of the receiving social system; they do not carry the stamp of traditionally accepted

35

institutions. This point of view also explains why some new legal systems or their elements, although rational and potentially fully functional, are violently rejected, against all rational arguments. They do not have the traditional charisma which stems from their own nationally, socially or historically accepted background. The presence or absence of this charisma is an additional, independent element that could be historically detected and which could modify the social behavior of members of a given social system in an essential way.

### The ethnographic-comparative method

What does a scholar who has adopted the point of view of jurisprudence gain from an anthropological perspective? At least two very important new dimensions may be obtained. One is recognition of the limited validity of generally accepted legal definitions; the second, and even more surprising, is recognition of the relatively narrow validity of the law itself.

Traditional lawyers are inclined (even if they disagree in the details) to define the law as official norms promulgated by legitimized authorities and provided with sanctions which safeguard conformity to these norms. There are many weak elements in a definition of this type. For instance, what does 'official norm' mean? Which authorities are 'legitimized'? What sort of sanctions are recognized as legal (formal, informal)? Let us omit here the eternal discussions concerned with these questions and point out, instead, that anthropological studies show that informal (living, intuitive) law functions even where so-called legitimized authorities do not exist. In the absence of these types of authorities, phenomena which could be defined by an observer as legal norms are treated by the people for whom these phenomena have validity as 'law'. They produce behavior which in all so-called civilized societies is termed 'legal,' and they are surrounded by institutions (serving as mediators) which, according to general standards, would also be called legal institutions. The vast evidence furnished by anthropological studies thus shows— contrary to existing theoretical beliefs—that the law as such could exist and function without the feature that would seem absolutely necessary: compulsory sanctions enforced by legitimized authorities. Briefly, it is possible to say that anthropological studies support (through evidence gathered from different types of societies) the thesis earlier formulated by L. Petrażycki[7] and E. Ehrlich[8] in connection with industrialized societies. According to L. Petrażycki (intuitive law) and E. Ehrlich (living law), a more adequate (not crippled, too narrow and therefore biased) understanding of the law could be obtained through a definition which grasps the law in its entire scope of actual functioning, not only in the scope officially described. This is the core of the first lesson which emerges when the traditional point of view is enlarged by the anthropological approach.

A second dimension is also quite essential. Several empirical anthropological studies conducted by P. Bohannan,[9] V. Goldschmidt,[10] and M. Gluckman[11] as well as findings from a study conducted by Pyong-Choon Hahm,[12] which is on the borderline between anthropological research and public opinion investigation, show that the law has a limited influence on human behavior. When the interplay of all possible kinds of motives determining human social activities is analyzed, it becomes apparent that motives which have a strictly legal character play a quite limited role. In all those social situations where members of a given group are engaged in many additional activities influenced by membership in other than the basic primary group, the relations existing inside the primary group are strongly affected by the feedback from the relations outside this group. The multiple relations in which members of the society engage change and limit this pattern of behaviour, which is prevalent in impersonal, industrialized, rationalized societies. In these societies, individuals suddenly, mainly by chance or voluntary decisions which can always be changed, engage in legal relations, behave according to patterns provided by them, and disengage themselves in a manner that is prescribed *a priori*. Then they disappear from the social scene. This type of behavior is not possible in societies characterized by multiple relations created by affiliation to interrelated social groups. In such societies the pattern of a decent (or a 'reasonable') man emerges as a model which is more functional —from the point of view of an efficient instrument supposed to resolve social conflicts and also to smooth over social relations—than the limited, detached, rational, disengaged, impersonal model of a law-abiding citizen. And, as Macaulay has shown, using the example of interrelations between businessmen in the most technologically advanced industrialized society, the pattern of strictly law-abiding citizens does not prevail in these professional circles, but the pattern of the decent man, who seemed so typical in the so-called primitive societies, does.[13]

The anthropological perspective offers an additional intellectual tool which could be useful for the legal sciences: it provides criteria which make possible the classification of societies from the point of view of their relationship to the law. Before a more elaborate classification is proposed, a tentative one could be offered: (a) societies which avoid the law (members of these societies turn to the law only in ultimate situations when all accessible means of informal social control have obviously failed); (b) pro-legal societies which stress the importance of the law as a needed instrument of social change on an individualistic and global scale (members of these societies would be encouraged to use the law and thus give the state the possibility of control over all interrelations among its subordinates; also, members of these societies would have an intrinsic need to use the law as an efficient instrument to measure, manipulate and shape social distance, and social costs and gains); and (c) societies which regard the law as a useful tool for establishing social relations, but one of secondary importance (members, being skeptical about the immediate and constant use of the law, would still be willing to use it as a subsidiary device when other instruments of social control, regarded as more reliable and corresponding more to the image of a 'decent man,' have been found to be ineffective). If such a classification were to be accepted, an example of a society with anti-legal inclinations might be Italy. As an example of a pro-legal society, traditional Germany could be cited, or socialistic societies which stress the role of the law in shaping new forms of social order. So-called primitive societies, or some sub-cultures in modern complex industrialized societies, could be regarded—from the point of view of the proposed classification—as societies in which the secondary, subsidiary role of the law prevails.

### Method for the analysis of legal material

The obvious advantage of method for the analysis of legal material is that the same researcher, or another one (in order to check on the first one, or to supplement his findings), can utilize the same material several times. The data remain intact and accessible, and any necessary double-checks or additional studies for the verification of new ideas which might have emerged during the research procedure are possible. Another advantage is that usually the data which are stored in legal materials are indicators of actions which were possible or which in fact took place. In this way the legal data refer to behavior rather than to values and attitudes connected with legal problems. This important link makes the material especially valuable, for in socio-legal studies what really counts is the legal behavior itself. Lawyers (oriented as they are) ought to see legal behavior through the normative glasses of status, precedent or administrative decision; when asked about legal behavior they would go to the law as it appears in the books and would extrapolate this law into action. Agreements which are supposed to be contracts, different types of informal wills, notes, letters, statistics, complaints, economic records, administrative memoranda—all these are data which usually escape the normatively trained lawyer as a possible source of coded legal knowledge.

As J. Górecki has clearly shown in his studies on divorce, this sort of material can be of the utmost value.[14] In his inquiry he went so far as to include in his records even such gestures as relaxed or clenched fists. Additionally, he was able to show in a clear way that the legal material collected in contested cases—since quarreling parties engaged in a conflict have a tendency to disclose all possible documents to support their position—gives a more adequate picture of the existing marital situation because of the variety of the evidence. On the other hand, material delivered by uncontesting parties very often gives a fabricated story prepared for the judge who, in such a situation, is neither willing nor able to check it. The recorded material remains in the archives and later on, after the flavor of each case has evaporated, the possibility of evaluating its credibility gradually disappears. Another serious shortcoming is that a substantial portion of legal events does not come to the attention of legal institutions and is thus not recorded. Quite often, those actions which violate the law are covered in the records of legal institutions. Even then, only part of these represent law-breaking behavior. And still an important question is open: what of this type of behavior remains outside of recorded data?

Generally speaking, socio-legal studies require a co-operative and comprehensive use of different types of research methods and techniques. But the analysis of legal materials, more than any other type of research method, requires complementary support.

### The experimental method

As this author learned in the People's Republic of China in 1963,[15] a tentative family law was passed in that country with the intention of observing the results of the new legal enactment, checking them, improving the law, and giving the final version of the law the power of a binding state force. In Poland, in 1960, a new institution for the administration of justice, the workers' courts, was set up (it started in a single voivodship (province) and later gradually began operating throughout the country).[16] These courts, the members of which are elected from among the workers by their colleagues, have no prescribed formal procedure, but make use solely of the pressure of public opinion within the given group. The idea behind this limited, quasi-natural experiment was to collect and gain professional experience about this new institution (which, according to the Soviet pattern, was supposed to enlarge the instruments of formal and, at the same time, informal control over the behavior of social groups particularly exposed to lawbreaking). In 1965, a new law was passed in Poland which gave the support of official law to the workers' courts. Interestingly enough, the professional experience of judges, lawyers, prosecutors, administrators, and legislators at a lower level was carefully taken into account. Nevertheless, the sociological study which was to be carried on in a parallel manner was omitted, apparently because the habit of consultation with social science experts is still not established as a completely legitimate procedure.

However, despite the limited possibilities, the experimental method could be used to study the law in force because of the binding value of equality before the law. In fact, this method has enormous potential in venturing into one of the most critical areas of the legal sciences: the investigation of the link between expressed or internalized legal values and legal behavior. Knowledge of the conditions which make the ties between legal values and legal behavior strong or weak are still almost unknown.

## The questionnaire and interview method

This method would appear to be very useful in studying the problem of the acceptance of the law, especially if we distinguish at least three levels of acceptance of the law and basic moral norms: (1) lip-service and declaration (purely external endorsement of certain values often made to meet clearly perceived social expectations); (2) internal acceptance (commitment to internalized values which sometimes are not externally expressed; for example, in cases where values could be regarded as deviant or where there is a commitment to values which is not strong enough to be a vehicle for corresponding behavior); and (3) behavior that is consistent with the expressed values.[17]

The questionnaire and interview method is, for the normatively oriented lawyer, quite paradoxical. For him the operative law (functioning in social reality) is valid and has a binding force; if it is not operative then it is supposed not to have the binding force. For him, the only relevant question is: Is the law in question an obligatory one or is it not?

Thus, the presently existing version of jurisprudence is hardly able to grasp the real socio-legal, let alone normative, problems. For a normatively oriented lawyer the official, binding law ought to be accepted, and being accepted should be obeyed. If the law is not accepted and is consequently violated, he who violates the law should be punished. This is not only too simple to be true, it is also too simple to be a functioning model. The depth of acceptance of the law, the relationship between legal norms and moral values, rationalizations offered for and against the law, several invisible factors such as principled or instrumental attitudes, individualistic or social orientation in ethics, and directions of affiliation, make the situation more complicated than described by existing jurisprudence. The poverty of traditional methods used in jurisprudence is partially responsible for this narrow-minded point of view.

Interview and questionnaire methods, when effieiently used, could bring about a broader recognition of the many ramifications of a given legal system. They could also elucidate the uniqueness of each legal system under study. To some extent, they could investigate the most crucial problem of socio-legal studies: the link between expressed values and actual behavior pertaining to legal norms. However, to study this particular problem, other methods should be used as the basic tools of inquiry.

## Basic problems of the sociology of law

With such a battery of methods now available for the study of the sociology of law, what sorts of problem should be regarded as the targets for potential investigations? There are at least three areas of reflection and investigation which should be treated as the main fields of socio-legal studies:

(1) Questions accumulated through a theoretical heritage; (2) problems relating to the effectiveness of the law; and (3) problems relating to legislative tasks. The second and third problems belong to the broader area of theoretical reasoning described as social engineering through law or legal policy. Problems connected with the theoretical heritage are the most complicated. They create an accumulated stock of eclectical composition—enormously important questions, serious problems, ideas which should be translated into an operational and empirical language; concepts which should be rejected as too abstract for investigation; notions which are value expressions; and, finally, statements which enjoy the legitimacy of a lengthy past, but are a semantic pot-pourri. A list of these problems would include: legal norms, moral norms, legitimacy, natural law, official law, the state, justice, rightness, legal sanctions, elements of social control, conformity, deviance, prestige of the law, ethical systems, legal systems, and legal logic.

All these problems ought to be, after careful semantic analysis, translated into operational and empirical language evaluated from the point of view of the existing knowledge and prepared, if necessary, for empirical interdisciplinary testing.

This progression from the abstract to the empirical stage of reasoning in jurisprudence and the sociology of law leads to additional meta-problems. If so-called official (or positive) law is too narrow a subject for the formulation of adequate theories (because this concept omits the instinctive, living law), and if criminology does not appear to be a reliable enough basis for adequate theories (because the scope of criminology is determined by the continuously changing content of the criminal law), then maybe the theoretical understanding of jurisprudence, the sociology of law and criminology should be reformulated. Then the sociology of conformity and deviance would appear to be the proper subject-matter for adequate theories, from the theoretical viewpoint, while the sociology of law or criminology might limit themselves to the changeable scope of the content of the law. Jurisprudence could then play the role of a repository of heterogeneous problems accumulated for many reasons, some of them quite important, which await theoretical clearance.

The questions pertaining to the effectiveness of the law are also not easy to solve. First of all, there is a strong need for a clear recognition of the limits of the use of the law as an instrument of possible social change. The two theories of the omnipotence and the importance of the law are false. Undoubtedly law is efficient, but only under certain conditions; what are these conditions? There are, contrary to the usual expectations, many kinds of effect of the law: expected, unexpected, positive, negative, partially positive or negative, and the combinations of these, sometimes called by-products. In order to detect these effects (and also to evaluate them), it is necessary to have at one's disposal the methods available for their recognition. These methods should be able to determine not only the real distribution of effects resulting from legal intervention, but should also provide lawyers with techniques to foresee its possible effects before a law is enacted. The question of deterrence emerges here as one of the most important. But not only can the types of relationship between moral, economic, political and legal values bar or stimulate the law. Effective and ineffective law has many motivational effects and educational consequences which, after they have been internalized, have additional motivational functions.

All problems connected with the effectiveness of the law have several important theoretical aspects as well as practical ones. They are directly connected with legislative questions. The prevailing method operating in different countries is to rely on the common sense and professional knowledge of lawyers in helping to prepare legislation. Quite often, surprisingly enough, this procedure is rather sound. But is this always the case?

Generally speaking, it is better to rely on systematic knowledge than on common sense or professional 'wisdom.' Paradoxically, in the language of law school curricula 'legislation' is understood as 'drafting.' But drafting deals with the semantic make-up of law while the whole area of the social setting of the law is left to the lawyer's intuition. The proper methodology—and it is necessary to stress this fact—of legislation is very complicated and consists of at least seven procedural steps: (1) comparative studies of legislation taken from different states with special regard to the possible spectrum of expected and unexpected results; (2) recognition of limitations of legislation and awareness of the applicability of a proposed law to a given area of social life; (3) adequate diagnosis of the situation which is supposed to be covered by the legislation. The techniques of the adversary system, as currently practiced, are of some use, but the relevant factor behind these techniques is the question of the extent to which the social sciences are engaged in the process of preparation of the required diagnoses; (4) studies of values, not only the values of average citizens and of the élite, but also of the strata of the population having innovative and conservative ideas; (5) access to the bank of regularities (hypotheses) governing the area of social life which is supposed to be regulated by law (this procedural step is perhaps the most important one: if it does exist, a stock of known and tested regularities is of great importance to the social sciences; if it does not exist, then common sense and professional knowledge enter the picture); (6) the ability to unify all previously mentioned elements in a synthesis which creates a legislative plan and strategy; and finally (7) legislative technique (drafting) which is the articulation of the plan into legalistic language.

It is quite apparent that all these methodological and procedural steps are closely connected with the main interests of the sociology of law. But, in reality, is socio-legal knowledge utilized in order to meet these practical (for example, legislative) needs and demands? Only to a very limited extent. There are many reasons for this limited use: one is the reluctance of legislators to consult experts from the social sciences. Another is the prevalent academic, not practical, orientation of the social sciences, including the sociology of law. These two orientations partially overlap, but at the same time partially bypass each other.

If the sociology of law has such potentialities as were described in connection with the possible applicability of different types of methods, and if the sociology of law also has some basic theoretical and practical problems to solve, what areas of study, then, have special importance for this discipline? There are several.

## Areas of research

The studies, reflections and discussions which are going on within the confines set by the interests of the sociology of law point to the following main areas of research: (a) value systems, (b) processes of socialization of the law, (c) social determinants of the law, (d) social modifiers of the law, and (e) the dynamics of legal institutions.

The break with the traditional concept that the only law is a binding, official law has opened a vast area for investigation—that of legal values and attitudes. Although values have long been an important subject of legal studies, inquiries of this kind in the past were directed toward ideal law—the goal of the law. Indeed, studies on the axiomatic aspects of the law are of great importance, but for a long time these studies overshadowed the other possibility—the empirical study of the real attitudes which the different strata of a given social system have towards the law. At the present time this latter type of study is very popular.

When the law lost its sacred character it became apparent that law itself also served as an object of socialization. The law is thus not only a socializing entity, it is also the set, the structure of values, which could be—within this or that other scope, to this or that degree—socialized. With this, many problems emerged, pertaining to: (1) the agents of socialization (it was discovered that not only the state and church but also the family, school and peers are possible agents of socialization as they support, contradict and compete with each other); (2) techniques of socialization (it was found that rewards, punishments, and patterns of behavior could be regarded as a means for channeling expected behavior into desired roles); (3) degrees of socialization (it became apparent that not all declared values are accepted, that not all accepted values are declared, and, finally, that declared and accepted values are not the only motives for actual behavior); and (4) targets of socialization (it became clear that there are different types of targets for socialization: youth, deviants, sub-groups such as immigrants, etc.).

Traditionally, the role of economic, political, and demographic factors as determinants of the law has been well recognized. Thus it is not necessary to stress and develop this particular point of view. Nevertheless, it might be proper to say that sometimes these (and other elements) have been taken into account as multiple factors, and sometimes certain ones among them were particularly stressed. Economic factors, for instance, have been emphasized as playing an enormous role in shaping the structure of the legal system.

The influence exerted by sub-cultures in modeling the law was discovered only recently. There is still a lack of clarity regarding the possible types of sub-cultures which should be taken into account. However, at least three should be distinguished: negative (for instance recidivists), positive (for instance law officers) and neutral.

The nature of the interactions taking place inside institutions and organizations has been considered by those concerned with the sociology of organization. Let us avoid the fruitless discussion of the borderlines between the disciplines in the social sciences. In this particular instance, it would be better to incorporate some of the findings which traditionally belong to the sociology of organization into the sociology of law. The way in which the law is perceived, transformed, strengthened, weakened, made into a symbol, instrument, pragmatic device or defense mechanism by the organization has tremendous importance for the functioning of the law. Institutions and organizations generate, accumulate and emulate several social processes, and this takes place not only within a given institution but also between several legal or non-legal institutions, and molds the law in many different ways. All of them add some meaning to, or subtract meaning from, the abstract legal norms.

It would be a mistake to treat the above-cited areas of research as final and complete. These areas are interrelated with research methods and, above all, with the basic problems in which the sociology of law is involved. None the less, it might be useful to list them so as to cover the whole array of problems belonging to the sociology of law (or which should, for methodological reasons, belong there).

## Conclusions

The sociology of law has been able to accumulate several cognitive experiences which have validity not only for the bulk of legal sciences but also for sociology itself. For theoretical sociology the sociology of law creates a virgin area. The time is ripe to enrich vegetating sociological theory with new stimuli from the outside. The legal sciences and legal policy (social engineering through the law) need a set of middle-range theories.

One attempt of this sort was made through the formulation of the hypothesis of the three-factor functioning of the law (see Chapter 12) The hypothesis of the three-factor functioning of the law holds that an abstract binding law influences social behavior by means of three basic variables. The first independent variable is the content and significance rendered the given legal enactment by the type of socio-economic relations within which it constitutes a binding element of the legal system. The second independent variable is the kind of sub-culture functioning in the framework of a given socio-economic system as a link between the legislator's directives and the social behavior of those bound by the law. The third independent variable which may variously modify the functioning of an abstract law (within the framework of a given socio-economic system and legal sub-culture) is the type of personality of the subjects affected by the law. Abstract laws begin to function and to be expressed in social behavior in connection with their human subjects. Into this mediation enters the law itself and three meta-standards: those springing from the nature of the socio-economic system, those deriving their content from given legal sub-cultures, and those flowing from the individual personality of decision-makers and addresses of legal norms.

A second attempt could be made by a deliberate division which should be directed towards the very heart of the law—its concept. It seems reasonable to distinguish two incompatible definitions of the law: the practical and theoretical. The practical one (fixed for clearly practical reasons, to give a judge or a lawyer a guiding line between law and non-law) would hold that the law is a norm generated by the proper authority and supplied with a compulsory sanction. The theoretical one would say that the law is the functional norm in a given social system based on two reciprocal elements— obligation and claim—and socially recognized as valid. The fact that the norm is functional for the given system does not have merely the traditional meaning; it means that the norm is designed not only in such a way that it would be consistent with the legal system and its requirements, but also as an instrument which is supposed to contribute to the integrity of this social system. Formalized, norms prescribed for different occasions among different social strata with respect to the distribution of duties and claims work in a balanced way—as tested and verified by social experience—toward unifying and integrating the given social system, and against the possible anomie-oriented disintegration of this system. This is the theoretical definition. But in order to use the *existing* law, to apply it, the practical definition must be employed. In order to understand, to introduce a *new* law to modify an existing one or to annul it, the theoretical definition should be employed. Let us now suspend a more detailed discussion on this subject, with one salient remark: the practical definition gives a relatively good orientation as to what belongs within the scope of the binding law, but is not able to cover all types of the functioning law. On the other hand, the theoretical definition gives a clear recognition of the law in action, but due to its not directly clear-cut feature (functional), it does not provide direct indication of which norms should be applied. This dual structure of the definition of the law reflects the dual character of the sciences involved: the practical one, which is oriented towards efficient application, and the theoretical, oriented towards understanding and explanation.

A third attempt could be made by introducing some new notions into jurisprudence and the sociology of law. Many of the existing notions are obsolete or inadequate: legal concepts tend to be abstract; sociological concepts are often alien to legal problems; psychological problems do not grasp the social reality of the law; and finally, the relevant concepts in the area of social psychology have not yet been generated. Therefore it would be advisable to work in the direction of elaborating such concepts as: principled and instrumental attitudes (attitudes which spontaneously support the law or are inclined to use it as an instrument); individualistic and social orientations in ethics (orientation toward conformity to norms characterizing behavior in small groups, or the orientation which takes into account the consequences of a person's social role or position); and types and degrees of affiliation to an institution, group or social system.

A reasonable answer to the question 'What is the sociology of law?' may, in the light of these considerations, be formulated as follows. The sociology of law consists not only of the bare application of sociological methods to the old problems of the philosophy of law. The sociology of law in its mature version would be an empirical replacement of jurisprudence. Attempts to deal with the traditional problems of jurisprudence from the viewpoint of the sociology of law would open a rich new area to research. The sociology of law brings something unique to general sociology: new notions which have potential explanatory power and a new sense of the integrity of the social system. And, finally, the sociology of law is now a field which is broader than it was traditionally perceived. The studies on the functioning of the law take into consideration not only sociological methods, but also such methods as the historical, statistical, comparative, experimental, anthropological, etc. The approach which is now needed is more comprehensive, more holistic. Therefore it is not ruled out that the sociology of law should now have the name of anthropology of law.

# part two

# Research methods in the sociology of law

Several methods can be applied in researching the sociology of law. Before discussing them and presenting examples of their application together with the results and interpretations, it seems useful to define the term 'method' as follows: 'a method is a systematically employed mode of performance.'* 'Method' is often used as a synonym for research 'technique.' However, this is not quite a correct usage. A method implies a more general approach to problem-solving in various situations; a technique usually indicates more narrowly defined procedures. Various techniques can be applied within a given method, while a technique rarely offers alternative ways of performance.

A method is a general directive on how a goal-directed process should be arranged; a technique provides a tool or a tested device or know-how most adequate to a given research task. For example, observation can be called a research method including such distinct techniques as studying the court files, overt or secret participation, etc.†

*The historical-descriptive method* The historical method in sociology assumes the diachronic standpoint in research, reaching back into

* T. Kotarbinski, *Elementarna teoria poznania, logiki formalnej i methodologii nauk*, Warsaw, 1961, p. 524.
† Analysis and description of all the methods in social researches is beyond the scope of the present work. These problems have been extensively developed in many publications.

the past. It makes use of various documents, such as private and official records, memoirs, publications, etc., recorded in any type of writing, cuneiform or hieroglyphics, or in symbols such as seals or coats of arms. The historical method requires expert critical source analysis, indirect or direct. In some cases this method can lack sufficient precision; in others it can yield many interesting results.

*The ethnographic-comparative method*   This method is similar to the historical. It consists in studying the functioning of various cultural phenomena in what are called the primitive societies. Contemporary civilized social relations are extremely complex. Primitive societies can sometimes offer opportunities to observe legal behaviors reduced to laboratory simplicity. Since the researches performed by means of the ethnographic-comparative method are usually carried out in cultures which are different from the student's own, the data obtained by it must be very carefully cross-controlled by as many means as possible. The technique of participant-observer can be very useful here, for after some time it allows the scholar to become more or less identified with the studied cultural environment.

*Questionnaire and interview methods*   The interview method consists in a structured or controlled conversation according to a prearranged schedule, and is designed to provide data on facts, opinions or judgments. Such a procedure allows for:

> face-to-face contact of an interviewer with a respondent;
> asking a number of follow-up questions about the same problem;
> asking control questions;
> controlling the situation in which the declarations are made.

Moreover, such a face-to-face conversation permits assessment of the degree to which a respondent is involved in the problems he is asked about. Finally, it allows the perception of new problems which otherwise could have passed unnoticed and the supplementing of the schedule during the research.

A questionnaire is a much less versatile method. It is based essentially on what are called closed questions, offering a list of ready alternative answers. These answers can be quickly and systematically compared.

Methods of opinion polling are sometimes considered as a distinct method because of the importance of the problem, though from a strictly methodological standpoint they can be reduced to either the interview or the questionnaire, or to a combination of the two. These methods can be applied in particular to the study of attitudes toward law and the legal awareness of society. We know that the statutory law is not always known by everyone in detail and that it is by no means accepted by the whole society. We also know that the officially enacted law can sometimes be in actual conflict with the sentiment of the society or of some of its groups. These phenomena have been relatively little investigated and there is now urgent need to fill this gap in our knowledge.

*The monographic method*   This method aims at gaining a thorough knowledge of the functioning of a specified legal institution, and its inherent interactions and tensions, by means of detailed description supplemented by interviewing techniques. The main thrust is a confrontation between actual behavior, and opinions and attitudes about and toward it. Sometimes a participant-observer of the studied unit may be involved, as when a sociologist takes a job in a factory as a worker so as to gain insight into some particular phenomena.

*The experimental method*   In spite of the prevailing belief, the experimental method can be applied to investigations on the functioning of law. Even though intentional experimenting in law-making by passing normative acts so as to obtain some cognitive results is quite exceptional, still unintended experiments do occur quite frequently, especially when law is used as an instrument in administration.

*The statistical method*   Statistical techniques can be very useful in investigations of the functioning of law. Though they are actually applied by lawyers, it must be noted that the use made of them is quite narrow: they serve mainly the purposes of description and reporting. They provide quantitative illustrations of the dynamics of certain social processes or serve to arrange the sets of available data in numerical terms. However, they ought always to be called upon for verification of hypotheses concerning the influence of definite factors upon law, or vice versa.

*Analysis of legal materials*   Studies of court and administration files, of statistical data contained in or related to them, of minutes, reports, legislative justifications, motions *de lege ferenda*, are among the materials used in analysis of legal problems. These assist in gaining insights into the functioning of legal precepts—e.g. a deficient functioning of a precept will cause an increase in the number of appeals in cases regulated by it. They also yield data on whether certain precepts are or are not being violated—if they are, the number of relevant cases, appellants, suits, etc., will be magnified. By means of these materials we can also collect data for verification of hypotheses underlying legal precepts or normative enactments.

The above list of the essential sociological methods applied to the sociology of law is by no means mutually exclusive: e.g. the mono-graphic method can involve interviews; the questionnaire and interview methods require the use of statistical processing. However, a presentation of various possible and useful approaches allowing study of the functioning of law seems to be more important than the requirements of any formal classification.

Thus, abandoning the subtler points of the logic of classification, we shall consider as a sociological method any set of procedures applicable in any science, as for example in economics, which can also contribute to sociological investigations. The statistical method and techniques applied in chemistry, biology, etc., should be acknow-ledged as sociological procedures to the extent that they can be applied in solving social problems.

# 3 The historical method

It must be noted that whoever does not improve his conduct or abide by law calls for calamity for all. . . . Thus it would be to the advantage of the commonwealth that nobody have bestowed on him the honors becoming men of learning who has failed to set forth some evidence of his scholarship, thereby to win the respect of the learned for himself and for his merits. Therefore, such men should be selected who could stand as critics and as public censors of the scholars. Thus neither would we be easily misled by asininity, nor would those who are truly devoted to wisdom be deprived of their due honors.

Andrzej Frycz Modrzewski

## The problem

The historical method brings home to us the experiences of past generations. We have already looked briefly at various means by which we can learn from them. Now let us examine the intellectual portrait of a Polish politician and thinker of the sixteenth century whose teachings, though remote in time, are still vital for us in some essential parts. It often happens that when the experiences and lessons of an epoch are cumulated and blended together, the wisdom born of them extends beyond the limits of their time. But when various roles are superimposed and interwoven in a single person who observes, participates in and gives advice regarding the important events in the life of his society and nation, the scale of his perspectives and experience can be amazing. The collective wisdom of nations is coded in many texts by many authors throughout history. But some societies focus their learning and experience in individual members— and if we can read out their thoughts we win access to what the social system, embodied in them, succeeded in arriving at. Moreover, their actions and writings, besides helping us to diagnose the situations contemporary to them, can also provide us with data for deciphering their plans and intentions, as well as the germs of forthcoming events. Therefore an attempt at phenomenological insight into the condensed experience of historical personalities representing the sense of their epochs can also be an essential element in our understanding of our own epoch and its dilemmas.

## The person

Andrzej Frycz Modrzewski was born about 1503 near the town of Piotrków, at Wolborz, the seat of the bishops of the province of Kujawy. His family were noblemen from the village of Modrzew or Modrzewie in Great Poland. He signed his name as Frycz or, in the Latin manner, Fricius. His father held the office of 'wójt' (a village executive official). Modrzewski studied in Cracow; after he had graduated from the trivium and quadrivium he entered the theological faculty of the Jagiellonian University.

After his studies he went to the court of a magnate, 'for the career,' as he put it himself. Thus about the year 1523, with his minor orders and unfinished theological studies, he assumed a job in the office of the primate Jan Łaski. His collaboration with Łaski and with his nephew Hieronim Łaski continued for several years; it seems that Hieronim Łaski intended to make use of Modrzewski's capabilities for his own ambitious plans, as he acted as an agent of Turkey and later of the Habsburgs. With Łaski's assignments Modrzewski went to southern Germany; he studied at the University of Wittenberg and became a friend of Melanchton, one of Martin Luther's associates. During his ten-year stay abroad Modrzewski was able to master Latin, in which he wrote all his works, as well as to learn German, but more importantly he gained knowledge of the ideology of the German and Swiss bourgeois world. During his absence from the country, significant social changes had occurred in Poland. A comparison of what he remembered from before his departure with what on his return he saw with more mature eyes exerted a deep influence upon him.

In 1547 he was awarded the office of King's Secretary, but neither income nor steady duties were attached to the post. His only obligation was to accept diplomatic assignments from time to time. Thus when, in the first year of his office, he was sent by King Sigismund the Old as a deputy to Emperor Charles V, Modrzewski performed his first duty as ambassador. Subsequently, he served as an envoy to Prince Albert's Königsberg, to King Ferdinand's court in Prague in 1549, and again to Emperor Charles in Antwerp and Brussels. When in 1552 a delegation was selected to attend the Trident Council,

Modrzewski was assigned as its secretary. The Council was deferred for two years; for Modrzewski the occasion became a motive for publishing his previously confiscated book *De Ecclesia* as preparatory material for the prospective envoys to the Council. After publishing in Poland his basic work, *Commentatorium de Republica emendanda* . . . , he sent the manuscript to Basel, where it appeared in 1554 and again in 1559 and brought him European fame. A Paduan humanist John Giustiniano translated one part of this book into Spanish as *De Bello*, and offered it to the King of Bohemia, Maximilian, as well as to the King of England. In 1557 *De Republica* was translated into German, and a little later into French. In his own country, the author of these works became not only famous, but also a target of assaults, envy and intrigues. Towards, the end of his life Modrzewski gave up the King's service and returned to his native Wolborz to become the 'wójt' of this township of craftsmen, an office that was hereditary in his family. He died in 1572.

**His work**

Three basic themes can be distinguished in Andrzej Frycz Modrzewski's extensive output. The first is a systematic, unprejudiced and courageous social, economic and political diagnosis. The second is related to the systematical development of a positive, ideal model of Polish society. The third refers to certain ideas of government which form the link between the diagnosis and the normative recommendations based on it.

The situation in Poland in the sixteenth century as it was seen by Modrzewski can be epitomized as follows: the peasants and burghers were oppressed; the noblemen fought arrogantly against everybody in spite of their tactical alliance with the great lords; the king's power was weak; and there was no sound conception for Poland's foreign policy.

The normative model as a proposed result of the reforms suggested by Modrzewski was summarized by W. Voisé in the following terms:[1]

> The peasants protected by a humanitarian penal law; with the title to use of their land; settled on it on tenancy principles. The trades and crafts given over to the burghers whose interests Frycz advocated in his opinions, as he favored the development of the germs of a primitive accumulation of capital. Strong power of the king, permitting him to control the relationships among the estates. The power of the grand lords broken down or at least counterbalanced. Sound foreign policy. The church reformed and the treasury founded on a regular

income tax. These are the most essential features of the 'improvement' extending over the whole of the social and political establishment.

From the retrospective point of view, in attempting to select from Modrzewski's output whatever is of significance for present-day legal science, it is not so much his diagnostic conceptions concerning the situation in Poland in the sixteenth century or his image of the ideal model, but rather his means and methods of reconstruction, that are the most interesting.

It must be emphasized that Modrzewski embodied the collective wisdom of his period of history. He was well aware of this himself:[2]

What has been told here about the customs can be related to all the people, and most of all to those who hold offices. More could be said about it (for this is a very broad matter indeed, extensively discoursed upon by the greatest of philosophers); but I decided to speak only about what is most conspicuous to the eyes of all.

Modrzewski was aware that his conceptions aimed at a synthesis of the experience of his epoch; he was thinking in terms of the whole of a social system, comparing it to a living body in which its several members do not serve their own ends but contribute to the welfare of the whole and do well or badly as the whole does.[3]

And as some member torn away from the body no longer deserves its name, since it can neither survive nor perform its duty if it is disconnected from the body, so none of the citizens can live properly or fulfill his duties outside the commonwealth.

Modrzewski understood very clearly the function of law and saw its role in social engineering. He was also aware that the efficiency of legal means, as well as the relative importance of law as an instrument of social influence, is related to and dependent on an adequate diagnosis of the actual state of affairs. He believed that the more critical the actual situation is, the more the prestige of law should be engaged in its improvement:[4]

Many traps and betrayals threaten innocent people every day; there are crowds of rascals everywhere; the poor, the kind and the weak are oppressed by the rich, the arrogant and the powerful; they must listen to their insults and threats, look at their countenances swollen with pride, beware of their naked swords, suffer the floggings, injuries and murders. Such atrocities, such cruelly harsh offenses and crimes thou canst not stop looming over the heads and property of your subjects, my King, if the customs, laws and courts are not improved and if there is no just and adequate punishment for the crimes.

Modrzewski also formulated the paramount directive for legal policy. It declared that the use of law as an implement of social engineering should not only aim at immediate and partial advantages, but should be directed towards the good conceived in terms of the whole. For it often happens that laws are enacted which produce good results in particular fields, but bring about losses and harm in other sectors of the same social system. Thus, he suggests:[5]

A lawmaker must then see to it first of all that he always keeps in mind the principle of reason and that in respect to all laws (as reason itself advises) he has either decency or common advantage in view. For as that medicine is good which heals the whole body, or in healing some part of it does so without detriment to the others, so that law should be praised which assigns similar rewards for the same virtues, while for the same degenerate or offensive acts it applies the same medicines or punishments. By the good God, whoever would readily take a medicine that repelled fever from the liver, but introduced cold to the stomach? None, I believe.

Modrzewski knew that a reasonable legal policy must involve at least two elements: a diagnosis based on a proper knowledge of social life and a sound methodology of purposive changes: 'I could not deny that the experiences of life had helped these lawmakers in enacting their laws; but what is certain is that they drew the juice and the core of the laws from the sources of philosophy.'[6]

In our own century there is widespread belief that laws can be issued on the basis of reflection only, or, scarcely better, on professional knowledge supplementing such thought. There is still lacking a sufficient recognition of the merits of a systematic, tested knowledge based on research and capable of correcting the arbitrary ideas or the biases of the profession. But Modrzewski pointed out, as early as the sixteenth century, that subjective conviction, however deeply anchored, must give way to data supplied by rational methods. He wrote:[7]

The laws stand in need of a great improvement; their dignity and splendor can certainly be returned to them only by those who are versed in them; for only they are able to transform into science the enactments which are unscientific in character. If someone believes that faith can be defended without knowledge gleaned from a number of sciences, he must come to realize that he is certainly most dangerously wrong; and how all too easy it is to leap from such an error into the pitfall of misdeeds, just as a ship can be wrecked on rocks. This has been taught to many by experience, which is the best teacher.

Neither did Modrzewski miss the point that not only must reasonable legislation be based on diagnostic experience, as well as on a rational method allowing proper use of the diagnosis, but lawmaking must also take into account certain controlling and supreme values. For a reasonable legal policy aims not only at enacting efficient bills, but also at making them right and just. He said:[8]

In general nothing can be law which is not related to justice, for it is as a source from which all bills flow. So if there should be but a single measure of justice by which the just shall be told from the unjust, it follows that those laws which are just should also be constant and unwavering; unless the things governed by them be so sundry that the laws must perforce differ at various points as well.

The reflections cited so far from the writings of Andrzej Frycz Modrzewski concern the field now defined as the policy of law. These comprise only a few of his statements on policy issues, mainly those which are more general in their intent. In various discussions concerning the problems of power, courts of law, schools or the church, Modrzewski derived more detailed suggestions from his general assumptions. Naturally, those detailed recommendations were related to the actual conditions of his time and nation. However, the general principles underlying them reach beyond those limits and are still significant for us.

The above ideas, expressed mainly in *De Republica emendanda...*, allow us to see in him as well a predecessor of the more general science of social engineering. He says: 'To govern the people really means to give order to their thoughts, to calm their hearts, to silence the tempests of their passions. But this can be done by a wise remark, a non-injurious censure, or a solemn admonition.'[9]

An essential principle of social engineering is the appropriate and effective distribution of rewards and punishments, so as to guarantee the proper selection toward the upper parts of the social ladder within the spontaneous processes of social mobility. Such selection, systematically and intensively promoted by expert social engineering, aims at advancing to higher positions those who are the better trained and skilled and at placing lower in the hierarchy those who are less capable. Such a method of selection not only brings important

c

advantages to the social system that applies it—in the form of economic, cultural, social and other bonuses—but motivates a great many people to strive to achieve the relatively higher social positions, or to avoid the threat of being demoted because of inadequate qualifications.

Modrzewski's reflections on the system of promoting army officers applies to other contexts as well:[10]

In what, then, should this dignity consist? Certainly not so much in family and wealth as in industry, knowledge of warfare and integrity which could be seen and acknowledged in battles. Nobody challenged to fight for his life would prefer a horse from his own stable that is skittish and easily frightened to one born in Turkey or elsewhere that is strong and bold. What stupidity then, by deuce, when the salvation and life of the motherland is said to be at stake, to push forward for friendship's sake those without any merits, merely because they happen to be someone's kith or kin, and to prefer them to industrious and brave folk who happen to be strangers! It is all too easy to bear the title and be addressed as hetman, a commander, a captain, a decurion, or a standard-bearer, but it is much more difficult to be any of these and to do what such an office requires. Those dignities are bestowed on people merely because of their families and property, though they lack any training in these matters, with scarcely a soldier's exercise being recorded on the army file; how they fulfilled their duty can easily be seen even by a blind man, as the saying is.

Modrzewski also refers to 'the honours and fame which are frequently the share of the least deserving and which often result from a lord's whim or from the recklessness of the government, rather than from a reasonably considered cause.'[11] It must be noted, incidentally, that clear and intelligible criteria of social selection, once they have become established and recognized, function automatically. If people are aware that certain types of behavior and activity are apt to give them the chance to advance socially, their behavior will be controlled by this awareness, i.e. by the underlying principles of selection.

Another essential principle of social engineering is that the crucial, strategic or decisive social factors be given their proper priority. Of course, these must be identified to begin with. Once they have been located on the map of possible factors influencing the social processes, they must be set in motion in such a manner as to make the most of them. Four hundred years ago Andrzej Modrzewski pointed out—and his remarks are still significant—that teachers are a strategic element in the network of social interaction and that their role is neglected.[12]

In the old days, exercises in rhetoric were cultivated in schools mainly in order that those who mastered them could, according to necessity, praise those matters of human life which came from virtue, and censure those that sprang from vice. The scholars were given full freedom to do so, for so great was the respect that learning enjoyed. I wonder why the present customs have gone astray from the roads and tracks of the past; why the schools are little respected and the people who are devoted to the sciences believe that what I have said here does not concern them. The old attitude toward the school and the old customs should be restored and brought back to us, so that we might also gather the flowers of the good sciences which serve their worshipers. Not only are those scholars who take care of public affairs useful to their states, but those, too, who work in schools. For they educate numbers of people and inculcate in them the sciences which are indispensable in controlling public affairs.

In some important cases Modrzewski himself applied in practice the postulates of social engineering. One of the problems which involved him most was the punishment for homicide. At that time, according to the bills of the Diet of Piotrków of 1496, a nobleman who killed another nobleman was sentenced to one year and six weeks of severe imprisonment and had to pay 120 'fines' (such was the name of the monetary unit) of 'head-penalty,' while for killing a burgher or a peasant a nobleman paid only 10 fines, without any prison sentence. A peasant or a burgher was unconditionally sentenced to death for killing a nobleman. Though the 1538 diet consented to make the punishment a little more severe for those noblemen who committed a murder, the subsequent later diets refused to confirm the amendment. Modrzewski argued very strongly against such injustice and demanded equal punishment for homicide. He wrote several orations concerning this issue, but to no apparent effect. The first in the series, 'An Oration concerning the Punishment for Homicide', was addressed to the king, the senators, the bishops and the noblemen. However, the fourth and last of the 'Orations' was addressed to 'the Polish nation and people.' Considering that his earlier appeals had been addressed to those who seemed not to wish to change effectively the discriminatory judicial treatment of persons belonging to different social estates, Andrzej Frycz Modrzewski decided to seek another audience, believing that what the leaders of the nation had failed to do the nation itself might undertake. Not only was the shift of the direction of his appeal remarkable but so too, perhaps intentionally

59

was the crescendo of its dramatic tone. At the beginning of the 'Complaint on the Repudiation of the Divine Law against Manslaughter' he wrote:[13]

> My words were formerly directed to men of high position for them to judge my speeches and enact what they deemed good to the commonwealth; but they did not taste of this feast of my thoughts. . . . Thus it occurred to me that you should be invited to it, you who stay away from the court and government, who are not conspicuous in the commonwealth, but are busy in its streets, market places and barnyards. Nor should you expect to be joyously or generously received; indeed, for other days than the present are such feasts. To the house of mourning you are invited, to a feast where food must be mixed with tears.

The fact that after the Second World War the number of homicides in Poland suddenly decreased may seem difficult to account for to those who are occupied with criminal studies now. On the other hand, the violent increase in such crimes in the USA is a constant source of anxiety to those who would like to counter it effectively. Modrzewski offered a recipe for reducing the threat to the people from murders and other crimes:[14]

> Historians tell us about many laws of the very ancient and very famous city of Marseilles, among them one forbidding anybody to enter the city with arms: there was always a warden on watch who took the visitor's weapons and kept them for him until he left. The purpose was to see that the visit did not threaten the citizens, as well as to ensure security for guests. And the advantage that citizens of Marseilles gained from such an arrangement was related by Valerius Maximus as follows: 'The sword for beheading malfeasors is so rusted in their city that it can hardly be used.' The rust, in this case, is strong evidence that where nobody is allowed to bear the sword all opportunity for crime and thus all need for punishing it has been got rid of and the most thorough peace prevails. Who can fail to see the advantages of a similar law in our commonwealth?

In the language of social engineering we speak of facilitation. This means creating or allowing some real situation which is conducive to, or stimulates, certain types of behavior in a foreseeable direction. Its opposite can be called anti-facilitation. Modrzewski, in demanding that the bearing of arms be forbidden, made use of anti-facilitation, on the premise that if weapons cannot be used there will be fewer crimes or even none at all, whereas when arms are handy violence occurs all too easily.

One of the basic concepts of the sociology of law is the opposition between statutory law and living law. This idea was congenial to Modrzewski: 'The law depriving the burghers of their countryside properties is cruel, inhuman, downright contrary to all reason and incompatible with divine and human laws.'[15] By 'human laws' he meant nothing else but feelings of justice, incompatible with the statutes that deprived the burghers of their landed properties. Quoted earlier was another relevant fragment, conveying a more general formula of the relationship between statutory law and 'justice' (see the quotation following note 8, above).

In principle, statutory law is based on sentiments of justice. It is the latter which acts as the motivating force, setting in motion the statutory law which, in such a situation, need not depend extensively on coercive sanctions. Of course, the enacted statutes by no means always find such strong support in the prevailing sentiments. Nevertheless it is desirable from the standpoint of rational legal policy that there be as much consistency between the two as possible. Many theorists of law fail to understand this today, but Modrzewski saw it very clearly:[16]

> For he who forms such a habit will later fulfill the duties of virtue either with delight or at least, if they are painful and heavy, without reluctance. Such a man will not need the statutes of law; for neither the rewards nor the punishments which are the perquisites of law will be needed to sustain him in his obligations. He will find the law in himself; he will know which things are the most righteous; his will shall be trained and accustomed to good deeds. These shall be his guides in all his life and demeanor.

Another problem to which Modrzewski devoted much attention was the mode of preparing the laws and the related issue of the scope of expert advice or the means of using available knowledge. This problem remains with us today. It must still be decided in what ways and by what methods we can make use of our store of social knowledge, much more abundant than it was in Modrzewski's epoch. Sufficiently developed 'relay' roles or mechanisms are still lacking for the transmission of findings of the social sciences so that they might be used by practical legislators, or for formulating the problems which are important to the lawmakers so that their empirical meaning would be readily obvious. If we set aside the minor differences, the problem was the same four centuries ago as it is today:[17]

> When I deliberated much on these things, it seemed to me that it would be best for the commonwealth if educated people were

61

selected from all the estates, and not only those who knew
various kinds of courts and the principles of their working, but
also those who knew other types of law, such as the canonical
law, the Roman law and the statutes of other nations; those
who knew the history of all ages and the dissertations of
philosophers on the customs and laws, and the sacred enactments of the Holy Scripture; those who have looked with their
own eyes at the customs of other nations and at their cities;
those, in the end, who were the most versed in all the liberal
sciences. That such were the ancient legislators and lawyers who
gave the laws to the Greeks and Romans is witnessed by their
writings. And so they arranged and wrote down the laws properly and neatly, passed them on to posterity for a long life. It
is certain that only such people, if anybody at all, are apt to
create something enduring.

The guiding values which should be the principles of lawmaking
were, according to Modrzewski, the egalitarian values, above all. We
read in his book: 'Thus, I believe, I can conclude by saying that all
those who live in this commonwealth, as well as all others, should
suffer the same punishment for the same offenses.'[18] At another
place he developed this idea more extensively.[19]

The first argument is that the laws and enactments of perhaps
all nations except ours punish homicides by their throats; next,
reason itself which is like the light and illumination in life
brings the judgment that it is shameful to make money out of
the killing of a man, a killing which cannot be compensated for
but by putting the slayer to death. For if the punishment is to
equal the crime, how else can it be made equal except by
punishing the homicides by death? Nothing should be held so
precious as human life. But if according to our laws those who
have taken something by theft are deprived of life, then why not
those, too, who have taken life? Indeed, what is given as an
apparent argument in favor of penalty in cash—namely, that if
the homicides were punished by their throats the commonwealth
would always have to get rid of a citizen after it had lost one
already—is by no means valid. For who does not know the
numbers of people who are killed by the law for theft? If, then,
we are not moved by the loss of people when thieves are involved, why should we be so moved when the life of a
homicide is at stake? It seems, indeed, as if the objects in our
possession had been more precious than life itself, or as if the
commonwealth suffered greater loss by the death of a slayer
than of a thief. And what is said about the merits of the noble

estate, because of which there are these differences in justice, is a great stupidity; and I wonder if those who have prized the plebeian heads as worthy of 10 fines wanted perhaps to play dice with them, while they punished by decapitation a plebeian who had slain a nobleman. So many absurdities are involved in this inequality in punishment that it must be wondered how it could ever have occurred to anyone; it is an insult to human reason, a scorn for the views of other nations, a darkness shed upon the light of justice which is the most beautiful of all virtues, and an abrogation of the divine orders.

It might be thought that Modrzewski, in thus sharply criticizing the inequity of punishment for homicide as applied to persons belonging to various estates, had not understood that the law was influenced by the vested interests of the ruling class. However, such an inference would be wrong: 'The laws are prevalently so arranged as to bring advantage to the powerful, and to oppress the miserable, so that the latter are caught by and entangled in the nets which are torn like cobwebs by the former.'[20]

While emphasizing that the egalitarian idea should be the principle underlying legislation, Modrzewski also pointed to other positive or negative values which were affecting for better or worse the functioning of law. He presented a list of faults which often prevented even well-meant laws from bringing about the intended effects. These failings were related either to the basic constitution of the state and its main agencies, or to some customary modes of conduct.

The following is an abridged catalogue of such faults and foibles: 'It is a particularly mean and corrupt habit that the common people cannot utter a sentence without an obscenity almost every third word.' 'It is absurd that the imputation of lying so shocks the ears of those whose mouths and tongues do not hesitate to speak untruth.' 'It is out of stupid pride or ambition that the greed for flattery and titles is born, when people favored by a few splendors would not suffer to be addressed without the use of very solemn words; and the greater their supremacy over others in splendors and riches, the more they love the prolixity of such words and foot-and-a-half long titles.' 'Since those who are devoured by the desire for dignities usually want great luxuries that would give them more splendor, it must be understood what a corruption of manners is spread thereby.' 'Let us talk about the duels which are sought for trifling reasons and which should be forbidden in a law-abiding commonwealth . . .'. 'Thus the habit of quarreling, struggling and hatred ought to be avoided, while peace and reconciliation should be pursued by all means.'[21]

On many specific issues Modrzewski expressed ideas which went far beyond his epoch. For example, he suggested the establishment of various institutions which would regulate social welfare:[22]

> Just as it should not be permitted that those who are able to work be beggars, so should care be taken that there be hospitals with everything that is necessary for life for those who are really miserable, i.e. for those who have no means of life whatever.

He also suggested establishment of an agency which would contribute to the reduction of idleness. This idea was in accord with his generally high appraisal of work as the means of acquiring basic satisfaction in life (in this he was close to bourgeois ideology, while remaining in sharp opposition to the general *Weltanschauung* of the noble estate):[23]

> It would be by no means pointless that every citizen disclose each year to an official agency what work he was engaged in, how he acquired the means for his expenditures, both those necessary for survival and those required by the dignity of his rank. Indeed, such a practice would curtail the luxury of many, and all would be discouraged from idle leisure and induced to decent labor. Many of the noblemen, and other citizens as well, have acquired the habit of spending beyond their means; and they feed herds of servants, not hesitating to use them in their cunning attempts against the property and life of others.

As can be seen, Modrzewski's ideas reached far into the future. Some are being realized only now (e.g. he demanded that church services be conducted in Polish); others are still waiting until the obstinate resistance against them gives up. The abolition of celibacy for priests may be an example.

Modrzewski's discourses on various minor legal institutions contain a remarkable amount of sociological–legal knowledge. Thus, for example, some of his arguments relating to the functioning of the courts were realized only after the Second World War. As we know, before the war the adversary principle was in force in the Polish civil procedure, i.e. the litigation in the court was determined by the opposing arguments of the parties involved. The role of the judge was reduced to settling the matter solely on the ground of what was brought forth by the contending parties. Modrzewski asked: 'Is it not worth considering whether the judge be allowed to seek for the truth beyond what the parties offer and relate?' And he answered: 'I believe it is the duty of a wise judge to discover all that can serve justice, or would stand in its way.'[24] The principle thus formulated is today one of the bases of both the civil and the criminal procedure in the socialist system.

It is not essential to present here all the ideas of Modrzewski that relate to sociological–legal considerations. Such a task would require a great deal more space; in the second place, there are many interesting publications along these lines; and third, such a detailed discussion would be apt to blur the main theme. What I wish to emphasize is that his ideas remain remarkable to this day because they are a successful crystallization of the collective experience.

The selection made by history brings to the fore the output of such great predecessors as Andrzej Frycz Modrzewski, and clearly reveals which of the problems they tackled are significant and can still bear fruit, and which are no longer relevant. If we wish to avoid multiplying spurious problems, we should not spurn reaching for the experiences of the past to see whether what we are trying to solve has or has not sustained the test of time. A Chinese tale tells us the following:

Su-teng asked Si-tien: 'Your honor! Why should Lu-wang, the most idle, careless and ignorant man, harvest more fruit from his orchard than all his neighbors who labor from dawn until sunset?' Si-tien answered: 'Think what fruit Lu-wang would gather if he cared for the noble stocks of his forefathers.'

# 4 The ethnographic approach
Jacek Kurczewski

There are many definitions of ethnography. The most reasonable of these seems to be that which describes it as a discipline studying socio-cultural entities, i.e. those human aggregates which have their own unique culture understood as 'the totality of objectified elements of social acquisitions common to several groups and, due to their objectivity, stable and apt to be spread in the area.'[1] Possession of a definite and specific culture is a characteristic of the types of social group studied by ethnography or cultural anthropology. However, when one looks into the practices of scholars in the field it will be found that they have been predominantly concerned with the object which cuts across the object previously defined. Aiming at a description, we should say perhaps that ethnography is a discipline studying traditional societies and communities, i.e. those which are exclusively or mainly based upon interpersonal audiovisual techniques of communication of the patterns and norms of conduct, beliefs and evaluations. According to this definition, ethnographical investigations are concerned with two different types of social collectivities. One type comprises independent cultural wholes, labeled as traditional or primitive societies. The other refers to the segments of developed societies (or those based on depersonalized communication) within which the transmission of culture is still effected on a face-to-face basis. This criterion of the technology of communication does not help much, however, in delineating the ethnographical research tools from those of sociology. The student interested in the description of a given traditional culture will never refuse to use written data, even from such possibly unreliable sources as the records of travelers, soldiers, missionaries and tradesmen of past centuries. On the other hand, the student of modern society will rarely omit making face-to-face interviews with the people whenever there is the opportunity to do this.

The history of the ethnography of law can be roughly divided into three periods. During the first, which ended at about the beginning of the First World War, the works consisted mainly of more or less coherent collections of the rules of marriage, property, etc. Their starting point was modern European law, its categories being used as the ground for singling out the legal phenomena characteristic of traditional societies. Colonial powers such as France or Germany evolved a model for the systematization of the common laws, collecting and compiling them in the manner reminiscent of ancient *coutumiers*, for the purpose of determining how one or another problem in civil law was to be solved in the colonized society. As to the criminal law, it was reorganised in accordance with principles already accepted in the metropolis. This period produced a number of works devoted to the description of various legal institutions whose 'legal' character in the conquered territories was determined by whether the given type of social action was regulated by law in the metropolis.

Bronislaw Malinowski, who spent the First World War on the islands of Melanesia, brought about the first important change in the field of primitive law. He studied, along with what was imposed on the aboriginal communities by European rule, all the norms of behavior obeyed in a traditional society. According to him,[2]

> The rules of law are distinguished from the rest of the rules in that they are felt and acknowledged as the obligations of one person and the legitimate claims of another. These rules find their sanctions not only in psychological motivation but also in a definite social mechanism of binding force, based . . . upon a reciprocal dependence and expressed in a balanced sequence of mutual services, as well as in the interweaving of such claims into a manifold relationship.

The sources of this definition can be traced to the views of another eminent Polish scholar, Leon Petrażycki. According to this approach, the law is to be studied not through the abstract rules of behavior objectified in writing or orally (as is the tradition of European jurisprudence) but through the observation and psychological interpretation of social actions performed in all fields of human activity. Norms are not given at the beginning of empirical study but must be inferred from other data. It is more difficult when one considers the necessity of distinction of rights and duties within the routine flow of everyday actions. Only in exceptional situations is nonconformist behavior likely to occur; and as Petrażycki averred, the study of law from pathological cases—i.e. when it is broken and the offenders are dealt with by courts—is incomplete and one-sided.

Malinowski's greatest originality was not in the formulation of a specific ethnographical definition of law, but above all in the development of the holistic analysis of the traditional society along functional lines. According to this mode of analysis the various local institutions together with their legal aspects are not investigated in isolation but as fragments of the whole of social life with mutual relationships interpreted in terms of rational although not necessarily self-conscious adaptive actions of individuals and groups. As to the *do ut des* principle involved in this conception, many charges have been brought against it, especially because of alleged oversimplification of traditional society, neglect of the phenomenon of power, authority and authoritative sanction, and excessive broadness of the concept of law on which it is based. On the other hand, scholars like R. Thurnwald, M. Mauss and C. Lévi-Strauss have further developed Malinowski's reciprocity principle in their works on traditional societies thus proving its theoretical usefulness.

The third phase of ethnographic inquiry into law can be dated with the appearance of a fundamental work by the ethnographer, E. Adamson Hoebel, and the lawyer, K. Llewellyn, on the law of American Indians, published in 1953.[3] Their investigations were focused on the reconstruction of the past legal and political system as it had existed before the colonial administration was introduced, or during the initial phase of its functioning. This factor together with the concern of Anglo-Saxon law for actual court cases rather than for abstract regulations or enactments has been especially favorable for the study of traditional systems. The study has led to the rejection of the traditional approach to primitive law in favor of asking what are the prevailing ways of solving specified types of legal problems, as well as what obligations and rights are involved in them. According to E. A. Hoebel's views, 'a social norm is a legal norm if its breaking involves the use of, or threat of using, physical force by an individual or a group enjoying a socially recognized privilege to do so.'[4] Application of this concept, with so different and so much narrower a range of denotata from that of Malinowski, has one thing in common with the latter, namely, the necessity of deducing the legal rules, norms from the results of empirical investigation. Llewellyn and Hoebel's study was based mainly on the analysis of concrete cases of internal conflict within a community and the ways of resolving it. These cases are observed where it is possible, or are recorded thanks to interviews made with reliable informants. The functional (in the sense: how it functions) approach of Malinowski has been enriched by putting emphasis on the question of who is entitled to settle the dispute or punish the law-breaker, what procedures are applied and, above all, what directives are practically employed (in contrast to abstract norms) in conflict resolution. This approach was strongly developed in the following years providing legal ethnography with extremely instructive works containing the case material on law in traditional society's practice.

While during the first period of the ethnography of law it was commonly assumed that 'law' in traditional societies comprised all the rules corresponding in their contents to what was considered as law, substantial and procedural, matters became more complicated in the European legal tradition during the subsequent phases of development. For if European law could be considered as a certain stage in the history of social institutions or the moral beliefs corresponding to them, or as a network adapted to a definite type of economic and social organization, then why should this particular stage or type provide a general yardstick for measuring the development of civilizations? This problem led to several controversies among scholars which largely assumed the form of definitional disputes.

As ethnography progressed from the hobbyist or administrative gathering of exotic customs to the status of science, a by no means minor role was played by scholars intrigued by the rules and sanctions of the so-called primitive peoples. On one hand, the advocates of the *etatist* conception of social order pointed to alleged anarchism as being typical of traditional societies; on the other hand, the adherents of the theory of the transient character of the state pointed to egalitarianism and collectivism as typical of their systems. The dispute between these ideologically different positions shaped the directions of ethnographical studies on 'primitive law' for the next generations. It must be remarked that empirical investigations have confirmed the theoretical possibility that a social organization without the state is able to subsist. There have been, and still are, several communities, formally or actually independent, in which not only is any class differentiation lacking, but there is also no overall institutionalized government, though there are feelings of belonging to a common culture, or of sharing the same rituals or common economic undertakings. Thus, for example, making their survey of traditional African political organizations in 1940, M. Fortes and E. E. Evans-Pritchard were able to observe that there were two types of system:[5]

(a) societies with central authorities, administrative and judicial in short, with a government—in which there existed discrepancies as to wealth, privileges and social position corresponding to the distribution of power in them; (b) societies in which there were no central authorities, administrative agencies or formally constituted judicial institutions, in short, no government—and in which there were no clear differences with respect to social position, wealth or political rank.

In a situation where there is no state or even any central authority, the classical definitions of law deriving from the Austinian model—

viz. as norms originating from the will of an authority and supported by the state's coercion—are obviously useless. Some scholars are disposed to say that in such cases there is no law at all. Others, however, noting the ways of introducing and enforcing norms and the ways of settling disputes in stateless societies, feel the need of a broader concept enabling comparisons with the law of societies that do have a state organization. The previously quoted definitions of Malinowski and Hoebel are good examples of two opposite ways of resolving this problem—first, through elimination of the notion of power, second, through broadening its meaning.

If we take a look at the subject matter of investigations of the ethnography of law during the three phases of development, we can distinguish the following types of phenomena: (1) specific duties and rights approved and/or practiced in traditional societies; (2) the ways of establishing and enforcing norms comprising these rights and duties; (3) the ways of dealing with controversies between individuals and groups within identifiable social units, such as family, village or tribe; and (4) social agencies and roles responsible for the establishment and enforcement of norms and for the settlement of conflicts. Some ethnographers working on these subjects, while bored by the disputes over the definition of primitive law, have been inclined to label their interests as 'social control', 'conflict resolution', etc.

From the purely methodological point of view, all disputes over formally correct definitions seem to be spurious. These conceptual conventions usually reflect some more important ideological and theoretical standpoints. Their practical implication is also that there are differences of approach in the technology of data collection. A normativist of the old school would be satisfied with collecting norms, postulated objects with so frequently ascribed strange ontological status. Assuming that each culture has a built in mechanism for assessing the validity of norms, it should suffice then to search for norms already assessed as valid, or to do the work the culture is supposed to do for itself by applying the criterion of validity to different norms. The necessary data are collected from the people best informed about the normative system which is accepted by a given collectivity as its own.

The second tradition combines the study of norms with the study of the actual behavior and inferred states of mind of the people. Norms accepted in a given culture are frequently not the norms accepted in social transactions. Some well-patterned expectations as to what should be done in a given situation mixed with equally well-patterned sanctioning reaction could not find its way yet to the official normative stuff of culture; old norms may still be accepted as valid albeit they undergo the processes of *desuetudo*, and normative

70

dissonance may be sustained for some reasons, e.g. for preserving the structure of whole culture intact, and resolved by others, e.g. the simple negation of its existence. Thus systematic and detailed study of everyday behavior is needed to discover the elements of the 'living law,' a concept of which the foundations may be found in the socio-legal theories of L. Petrażycki and E. Ehrlich.

The third approach consists in analyzing the decisions and social processes underlying the two other approaches mentioned above (p. 70). These decisions are allocations of particular rights and duties among the actors in the social system and this approach may be traced back to the fourth one mentioned above, if the fact of its very narrowness (conflicts only) is kept in mind.

This approach is emphasized by those writers who consider that an intervention by third parties who do not immediately suffer from the breaking of a given norm is the decisive feature for distinguishing the legal norm from other cultural norms. Evans-Pritchard, describing the mechanism of 'blood revenge' among the Nuer shepherds in Africa, wrote:[6]

> The Nuers have no law in the strict sense. There is no person performing legislative or judicial functions. . . . There is no impartial and constitutional power deciding who is right and who is to blame in a controversy, and there is no outer force to carry out such decisions if they had ever been taken.

The criterion of the presence of institutions established to judge and settle controversial and non-controversial issues leads to the classification of many traditional societies as not possessing any law at all. Among them, however, we can discern those in which only the parties directly involved in a controversy ever take part in it, and those in which third parties can step in by invitation of the contestants, though they have no executive power, or even any power to make authoritative decisions. At this point, some writers are disposed to acknowledge as legal the institution of a mediator or an arbiter, as well as the norms established or suggested by them.

The problem of defining traditional law is related to the objective of the research. The selection of one or another concept can be inconsequential, if only one society is being analyzed. However, the situation changes if we want to compare traditional communities with each other or with developed societies. One of the notions allowing for such comparisons is the concept of the 'rights and duties' of individuals or of subgroups of the studied human aggregate. By 'duties' is meant required obedience to the specific patterns of behavior imposed by the culture. Since 'rights' refer to actions which are permissible, the rights can be deduced from what the culture imposes and forbids. In principle, anything that is neither imposed

71

nor forbidden is left to the free decisions of individuals. In practice, however, the scope of such freedom is additionally limited by the cultural patterns, i.e. by certain habits of performing specific activities in specified ways. To this are added biological limitations and individual patterns of action. Moreover, it can turn out that a new type of behavior, even though it has not been forbidden by the general norms, can meet with a negative reaction from others and lead to the formation of a new interdiction.

In a traditional culture in which written records are lacking, direct questions must be asked and firsthand observations must be gathered in order to learn the rights and duties. In a society which has a state organization, a professional lawyer can contribute the most useful information about official law; in a traditional community an ethnographer will ask the most respected, aged and experienced persons, since they are the acknowledged sources of authority, transmitting and often creating the traditions.

Applying the notion of the system of rights and duties we can compare traditional law with the public and private law of state societies. From the formal point of view, for example, two types of controversies can be discerned. In the first type, an individual A feels injured because an action of another individual B has disturbed some of A's rights, e.g. his right to use some implement. At the same time B's action is, from the point of view of the culture, a disturbance of some duty, e.g. the prohibition against stealing. In the second type, the controversy is between two individuals A and B who claim their rights without trespassing against their duties, because the substance of the controversy is not normatively regulated. In the first case, the injured party is at least tacitly supported by the rest of the community of which B is also a member. In the second case, an eventual action by the community would only lead to the posterior establishment of a rule. The latter type of controversy is frequent in stateless communities, where obligations are most often defined with reference to the clan or family members and there are no rules defining who is right if there is a collision of interests. This is related to the fact that in these communities groups of relatives are units of economic collaboration, while the neighborhood or tribe community is seen as a secondary reference.

Until a central authority arises and a state organization begins to develop, the settlement of controversies is mainly the domain of independent action of the involved individuals or groups. But this does not mean that family vengeance is the only or even the most important form of settling conflicts between individuals in all the stateless communities. Various types of procedures can be distinguished, depending on the extent and character of the intervention of third parties.

The South American 'head-hunters,' the Jibaro Indians,[7] can serve as an example of a cultural community in which all the conflicts are left to those who are directly involved. Their basic unit of social organization is the family, living in a common homestead, governed by the father whose power is theoretically unlimited. During a war the families unite into a tribe under the leadership of the most experienced warrior. Once in their remembered history all of the tribes even united together to wage a defensive war against the Spanish conquistadors and were victorious. However, any political organization above the family level is only transient among the Jibaro. In relationships between persons belonging to different families the principle of retaliation is normal. A blood revenge for the murder of a family member is something more than a moral obligation, for it is supernaturally sanctioned by fear of the wandering and vindictive ghost of the victim. The relations between tribesmen are strictly regulated by the principle of a life for a life, though the vengeance need not reach the actual murderer but instead a member of his family. Once such a balance has been achieved, if the party exposed to revenge thus accepts responsibility for the death of the initial victim, the controversy is considered at an end. If he does not, the chain of vengeance can continue and many persons may in turn fall victims.

A similar procedure for conflict-solving is found to be true historically for many, though by no means all, traditional communities. It is remarkable that its relics have been maintained for the longest periods in two types of social environment in which family and clan have played the basic role: among the politically independent feudal noblemen and among the mountain dwellers, ecologically scattered in their family farms.

However, even the Jibaro are aware of the need for some limitations of the struggle imposed by the principle of 'one for one.' Such a limitation is afforded by the duel. Regulated combat of this type has been observed even among peoples at the lowest, gathering and hunting level of technology. For example, in Australia during the ritual ceremonies uniting the small groups of nomads, isolated during the rest of the year, duels were fought under the control of the elders. The parties fought very fiercely, but only until the 'first blood,' and then the conflict was put to an end. The Greenland Eskimos evolved the famous institution of singing duels; the contestants, applauded by the audience, sing out songs ridiculing the adversary, as well as boxing and ramming each other's heads. In this case the community as a whole controls the course of the struggle, without (apparently, at least) entering the contests. It should be noted that it is customarily the right of the party that feels injured to choose whether it is to be a bloody or bloodless vengeance or duel.

73

A further step toward the community's interference is represented, for example, by the mountaineers of Assam, of the Dafla tribe.[8] Among them, as among the Jibaro Indians, there has been no organization above the level of the so-called long house, consisting of a few kindred families under the leadership of the patriarch who is considered the owner of the house and the plots of ground surrounding it. Controversy is basically a matter of private revenge, but at some moment either of the parties can refer to a mediator called the *gingdung*. The requirement is that he be a neighbor maintaining good relations with both contesting parties.[9]

A mediator must be a talented diplomat, he must know well the customs of the tribe and stand beyond any suspicion that he might use the conflict to his own advantage. If he is successful, he is generously paid by the contending parties and his royalty is provided for in most agreements. Some of the gingdungs rise to a high prestige and their 'services' are sought for very much. Though they have no power to solve the conflicts or to impose their decisions, they can do much towards a solution satisfactory for both sides. [In some cases] their main task is to arrange for a contact between the parties and to make them meet and discuss their different positions.

The mediator enjoyed immunity. Any assault against him would call forth a general condemnation. This was the only sanction, as broader political organization was lacking, but there was no report of its ever having been breached.

Whereas an Assamite mediator acted only if he was invited by one of the parties, among the Papuans described by Pospisil, when a quarrel begins:[10]

Important men from the village, as well as from allied communities, appear on the scene. First they squat among the onlookers and listen to the arguments. As soon as the exchange of opinions reaches a point too close to an outbreak of violence, the authority steps in and starts his argumentation. He admonishes both of the parties to have patience and starts questioning the defendant and the witnesses himself, as well as investigating other evidence which would lead to the identification of the criminal, such as remnants of bones, feathers, etc. found on the place of the crime or in the defendant's house (cases 62, 74). This activity of the authority is called *boko petai*, which loosely can be translated as 'finding the evidence.' After he secures all the evidence and makes up his mind as to the factual background of the dispute, the authority starts the activity called by the natives *boko duwai*, which means the process of making a decision and inducing the parties to the dispute to follow it. This process could hardly be compared in its form to the adjudicating activity of our judges. The native authority makes a long speech in which he sums up the evidence, appeals to a rule, and then tells the parties what should be done in order to terminate the dispute. If the disputants are not willing to comply, the authority becomes emotional and starts to shout reproaches, and makes long speeches in which evidence, rules, decisions, and threats form inducements. Indeed, the authority may go as far as to start '*waini*, the mad dance,' or change his tactics suddenly and weep bitterly about the misconduct of the defendant and the fact that the latter refuses to obey him. Some native authorities are so skilled in the art of persuasion as to produce genuine tears which almost always break the resistance of the unwilling party.

Though this might seem at the least a strange procedure to an outside observer, it is as efficient as many of the decisions of European judges. The authority's action results from his own initiative only, and he has no means of forcing the parties to obey his 'sentence.' This is a frequent phenomenon in communities without a state organization. However, in every traditional society there are some basic social groups, such as the family or clan, within which the decisions of a recognized leader are respected and the conflicts do not assume the form of disputes between two equal and independent parties. Even though the principle of revenge may be valid between strangers or even between neighbors, some offenses within the family may carry no negative sanction at all. Among the Jibaros the killing of an inhabitant of the same homestead does not lead to the execution of the murderer. The Indians explain that there is no point in increasing the losses to the family. Such conduct can be accounted for by the principle of maintaining the basic economic unit at any price. Usually it is only when a family member repeatedly breaks the norms of behavior, or if he becomes dangerous and incorrigible, that his relatives will react by killing him, or—more frequently—by banishing him.

In some stateless communities the family and personal network are the only levels at which a group reaction toward a breaking of the obligations by an individual can take place at all. In other communities, more or less formalized reactions of this kind occur at a localized group level, the group often consisting of families related to each other by birth or marriage. Among the Eskimos there is no formally established authority, though there is a local leader, usually an eminent hunter, who enjoys some personal authority. A single homicide is subject to revenge by the victim's relatives. If, however, someone has killed a number of people, he becomes dangerous to the whole community. The leader can then ask all his neighbors for their opinion and, if they all approve, he will kill the murderer. In many traditional societies an overly aggressive person, an incorrigible thief, a multiple killer, a blasphemer, etc., may be subject to attack by the apparently neutral local community, acting as a whole or through its representatives. We can thus speak of a threshold of tolerance to treat, beyond which a purely private matter becomes subject to public interference.

It may be recalled at this point that many of the duties imposed upon the individual by a traditional culture have only supernatural sanctions as their warrants. Involved are such threats as actions by the ghosts of dead ancestors, or by anthropomorphic gods, or spirits, or amorphic magical powers. The failures of an individual or a group are thought to be due to more or less malicious activities on the part of the supernatural forces, and the vivid feeling of their presence never abandons a man brought up within the traditional culture.

Control of an individual's behavior by the ghosts of his ancestors or by the gods can assume the form of a relationship between the individual and the supernatural forces without any interference on the part of his social environment. There are always a number of taboos which, if broken, can bring harm only to the individual or his family. It is up to him or to them to redeem the offense by a proper offering. Interference by others occurs in two circumstances: if the interdictions which are the most important for the community are broken, or if taboos of any kind are broken repeatedly. In both cases, underlying the community's action is perhaps a conviction that certain misdeeds by individuals can call down the wrath of the insulted supernatural forces upon the other members of the community. Two examples from Africa may illustrate these statements.

In the social system of the Ashanti in Ghana the central power—the tribal chief and his privy council of the heads of clans—concerns itself only with those breaches of obligations which could undermine the good relationships of the community with the gods and the ghosts of ancestors that were necessary for the group's success and welfare. The Ashanti believed there existed a world of ghosts, *asaman*, where their ancestors lived in a manner similar to that in this world. Upon burying their dead they provided them with food, potions, clothing, adornments, golden sand and other objects necessary in travel and in the afterlife, and in the funeral prayers they asked the dead for their benevolence and care. The ancestors were believed to be incessantly observing the life of their living descendants, punishing those who breached the obligations, sending misfortunes and illness or even death. Those who obeyed the laws and customs and scrupulously fulfilled their duties enjoyed the protection and blessing of the ancestors.[11]

Similarly, among the Kabre in Northern Togo the norms derived either from the will of the creator or from the will of the ancestors. An offender disturbed the sacred order by his misconduct, so that his deeds required that justice interfere in its double form, sacral and lay. If he were not put to death, it was necessary to reintroduce him into the community, thereby restoring the disturbed balance. A proper means was for the transgressor to offer an animal as a sign of repentance, under the control of a priest.[12]

Faith in the immortality of ancestors and their intervention in worldly matters has great force for maintaining the old customs and manners or rules of behavior. Since they have their origin in the ancestors' enactments, they are sacrosanct and unchangeable, and the act of breaking them is believed to bring about an impromptu reaction on the part of their initiators, who remain invisible but are supposedly the actual distributors of failures and successes among the living. Nevertheless, in spite of all this, the rights and duties in a traditional culture are hardly changeless and fixed once and for all. The conservatism of the traditional systems of law may be due to the fact that those communities have only faced repeatedly similar situations. Still, an unexpected or unusual occurrence may frequently have led to undertakings which can only be called legislation. For example, Hoebel reports a Cheyenne tale of a soldiers' society having to consider the case of a warrior who had 'borrowed' a horse from another and refused to return it for rather a long time; the chiefs ordered him to restore the horse and announced that hereafter all deeds of this kind would be classified as theft and duly punished.[13] Among the Papuans, the changing of the marital law by a local chief was observed by Pospisil. The chief fell in love with a girl who was a close enough relative for marriage between them to break the rules of incest. He fled with her to the forest, succeeded in evading the pursuit of the indignant father-in-law, and after the moral outrage of the tribesmen had calmed down came to an agreement with them, at the same time declaring more liberal rules of marriage with reference to the permissible degrees of kinship. His avowed justification was that other tribes followed similar lines, but he confessed to the ethnographer in secret that the beauty of the girl had been the actual reason.[14] Similar cases of creating and modifying norms could certainly be found in the histories of all traditional societies.

Indeed, the notion that the traditional ways of thinking are inherently conservative is disproved by many cases of adjustment of primitive legal institutions to the new conditions brought about by colonialism and by the progressing modernization of social life (e.g. in Africa and Oceania). The apparent conservatism turned out to be the wise application of those rules of conduct which had been tested in the past. No wonder, then, that any attempt at innovation must arouse suspicion and mistrust as to its future consequences. In this respect the mentality of people who live in traditional communities hardly differs at all from the way of thinking of an average citizen of the developed countries.

The examples of traditional legal mechanisms cited so far have referred mainly to societies with very loose organization above the family level, with leaders appearing in times of emergency only and without means to enforce their decisions. However, the time comes when a village or a number of settlements will unite into a tighter political organization. This may be related to the development of economic collaboration, or to the diminishing role of the bonds of kinship which are not coextensive with geographical proximity. The political structure that immediately precedes the appearance of the state can be along any one of the following dimensions of specialization of social functions: (1) ascribed seniority status by lineage; (2) leadership over a few neighboring family groups engaged in common task performances; (3) war leadership; and (4) sacral leadership and mediation between an individual or a group and the supernatural world. Any of these dimensions of specialization can lead to an emergence of positions of power with adequate means of compulsion toward the other members of the community.

In societies where the mechanism of power is more or less established, courts may be called forth which have the authority to pass sentence for offenses against obligations, or to settle controversies. Such a court often assumes the form of a meeting of the elders, with the leader of the group as its chief; daily hearings may be held in the center of the settlement under the big tree. Only on rare occasions are the judicial functions performed by a single individual; even when the power of leadership is centered in one person, such power must often rely on the support of the elders or of the adult population. Institutions of power are in a position to impose specific obligations, fines or indemnities, or to sentence to death, flogging or banishment. It appears that no rule can be formulated as to the severity of repression in traditional societies, since this depends on the general orientation of a culture. In warlike communities severe physical punishments are frequent, while in economically flourishing groups fines and indemnities may prevail. In a simple subsistence community there are few things which can be confiscated and consequently it is the principle of positive or negative equivalence which most often is the chief mechanism of economic and social balance: the losses are made good, but without any surplus.

In stateless societies the main objective of the judicial body, if this exists, is to maintain internal harmony in the community, good relationships between neighbors and their mutual benevolence, as well as to warrant the benevolence of the supernatural forces. Thus a judge or a court settling a controversy would not attempt to maximize the indemnity for damage or injury, or to mortify the offender, but would rather appease the injured so that he could resume good relationships with the transgressor. Various minor ceremonies to mark the end of the controversy can be helpful, such as a common feast, a collective offering for a deity, etc. The striving for internal harmony may even lead to the abandonment of a rule which in principle is acknowledged as valid. Indeed, in these societies the abstract rules are more like models for trial decisions than like strict principles. What is really intended is not the rendering of formal justice but rather the reconciliation of the contestants. This is possible only in those societies in which the political organization is coextensive in its scope with the actually felt need for economic or ritual collaboration, under conditions of more or less full equality of the basic sub-groups, i.e. the families. Since the supernatural forces are more powerful than men, it is more important to calm down their wrath than to guarantee the interests of individuals. This accounts for the fact that all taboos or interdictions deriving from gods or ancestors are much more rigorously exerted when they become subject to public control than when they are left up to individual members of traditional societies.

As an example of the change in methods of sanctioning the rights and obligations during the transition from local community to a quasi-state organism, let us take the evolution of the Ashanti legal system.[15] In the beginning, before regal power developed in the eighteenth century, all controversies between inhabitants of the same village were settled by mediation rather than by physical coercion. The procedure was informal and it aimed at reconciliation between the contesting parties. If the controversy involved two clans, it was settled by the leaders of both, in the presence of the most respected old man in the village. Blood vengeance was unknown.

At the beginning of the eighteenth century one of the tribal leaders, Osai Tutu, united all the Ashantis by force into a state with a rather predominantly military character. All offenses were then considered to be mortal sins and, as such, left to the king's jurisdiction. Among them were homicide, suicide, sexual offenses, some thefts and robberies by force, treason, cowardice in battle, witchcraft, the breaking of the king's orders or of the local taboos and abuse of the regal oath. They were all punishable by death and the exclusive control of the sword belonged to the king. Nevertheless, though the law rarely prescribed fines, the king's courts accepted redemption from the death sentence. If the criminal was poor, his entire property was confiscated and his heirs were disinherited, although they retained title to the next harvest. Moreover, making abuse of the regal oath a capital crime meant that civil law came almost completely under the penal code. For example, the only warrant for a loan was often an appropriate oath in the king's name. A refusal to pay the debt meant that the debtor 'hated the king' or that he wanted to kill him. And this meant invoking capital punishment. In any controversy either party could resort to the regal oath by pronouncing the text, restricted in principle to the members of the king's family. If a common citizen uttered the oath, his case must be subject to examination by the king. Thus the case was transferred to the king's jurisdiction, and the losing party was sentenced to death for 'abuse' of the oath. Any civil process could end in this manner.

In the state of Ashanti there had begun the process of emergence of the ruling class, basically consisting of the sovereign, the members of his family and his officials. Law was one of the means by which the bureaucracy and the king could win the property necessary to maintain their power. A number of subsidiary political and economic instrumentalities made use of law for the purposes of exploitation.

Three basic types of systems of traditional law can be discerned, all related to the character of the prevailing economic order and to the political and social structures associated with it. It must be remembered, however, that any attempt at a systematization of the diverse forms of traditional societies must involve a simplification.

To the first type belong the systems in which the rights and duties of individuals and subgroups are sorted out in actual confrontations or conflicts. The parties consider themselves as equal, and any loss B causes A must be counterbalanced by a corresponding loss to B. It can assume the form of a blood vengeance in the case of a homicide, or of an assault upon the thief's property in the case of stealing. The principle of vengeance appears to be a negative version of the more general principle of reciprocity, according to which every gift must be answered with an equal one, and with every service rendered comes an expectation of and a right to a service from the recipient. The community interferes in the relationships between individuals and reacts upon their behavior only in extreme cases, when the threshold of tolerance has been exceeded. Above this threshold are, in particular, obstinate disregard of cultural imperatives and interdictions, and abuse of one's rights to the detriment of the interests of all the other members of the community. Public opinion is usually only a minor factor in private controversies, though the parties must take it into account when they plan their subsequent actions. Sometimes mechanisms for mediation by third parties, upon the invitation of those directly involved, are developed.

To the second type belong the communities in which some institutions of unilateral power have been established, usually only at the local level. These institutions can be either collective, such as the council of elders, or individual, as when a member of a certain lineage has the right to assume leadership of the village or of the tribe. The local political structure begins to perform judicial functions. In many tribes, the capability for solving controversies is a necessary requirement for leadership. Where there is no stable diversification of social positions within a local community, while it is necessary that all its members co-operate at least temporarily—e.g. for their defense—justice is not a matter of determining who is right and who is wrong in a controversy, but of striving for internal reconciliation and harmony. The local courts also execute the duties imposed upon the people by supernatural forces. In such cases, the court acts in concert with these forces to guarantee the survival and welfare of the whole society, in accordance with the religious principles of the culture.

Finally, to the third type belong the quasi-state organisms. This kind of society, arising in consequence of conquests or through unions of subgroups of common ethnic origin, at one time flourished in Africa. The penal laws of the African kingdoms were often very severe. Death sentences and mutilations were common. Characteristic of these political organisms was the exploitation of law as a tool for enrichment of the king and his officials or of the aristocracy, justified by doctrinal arguments. Such devices were employed as court taxes in kind, fines as a substitute for or supplement of indemnities, the possibility of redemption from the death punishment and from flogging, or the sale of the sentenced as slaves to white or Arab merchants. The Ashanti law can stand as an exceptionally consistent example of this kind of approach, based on the public and penal character of the whole legal system. The king strove to limit local jurisdiction by incorporating agencies of self-government into the broader hierarchy of administration, by reserving some types of cases to the crown's exclusive competence, and/or by making it possible to present any conflict to the king or his representatives.

These three types of legal system operating within a given cultural entity, which need not be a political one, may also be used in describing particular aspects of one society. It is possible to point out in counter-reaction to the theory of amorphous social organization that power always exists at some level of society and usually at more than one so that a multiplicity of legal systems may be conceived. If one does not consider unilateral power a necessary attribute of law as some do, then not only the multiplicity of levels of law but also the multiplicity of its types may be observed within a given unit of ethnographic or sociological analysis. The ethnography and the anthropology of law have not yet provided us with the general theory of factors which underlie these or other characteristics of legal systems. The widening of our viewpoint for different possible types of law and legal institutions still remains the most fundamental merit of cultivating the approach briefly discussed in the preceding pages.[16]

# 5 Questionnaire and interview methods*

## Surveying public opinion

Lawyers and legal scholars educated in the spirit of positivist law whether it be civil, penal, administrative or whatever, usually maintain that law is defined by its validity, that is, by its having been enacted by the authorized state agencies. They seem not to be troubled by the vicious circle inherent in this definition. For if valid law is whatever is on the books, while what is not so is not law, the question arises: Upon what principle is validity based? On a legal one, is the retort. Thus the vicious circle reappears, though its circumference is enlarged.

The problem of the validity of law is a complex one and, as is usual in such cases, any of several positions can be assumed. Along lines similar to distinguishing positive or valid law from that which is not positive, statutory law is distinguished from the intuitive 'sense of justice' and from common law.[1] The latter gives us extra trouble, as sometimes it is incorporated into that which is enacted and sometimes not. Nevertheless, one thing should be made clear, without entering into semantic details and arguments (which are perhaps doomed to failure in advance because of the a priori assumptions underlying the respective position), the concept of law as limited to that which has been legitimately enacted is too narrow for analysis of the social efficiency of legal measures. Such a concept, apart from being theoretically fallacious, can lead to a number of undesirable practical consequences.

Let us consider the fact that if a legislature enacts a bill which is

* This chapter is based in part on the author's 'Attitudes toward the law', a paper prepared for a symposium on studies of public experience, knowledge and opinion of crime and justice, arranged by the Bureau of Social Science Research, Inc., Washington, DC, March 16–18, 1972.

not consonant with the prevailing attitudes of the society, it must expect resistance motivated by those feelings. The difficulty in enforcing the law will be in proportion to the scope of such resistance. Officers of the law may increase the pressure for compliance (by bureaucratic measures, by tighter control, etc.), but then the public costs will increase proportionately. A law which is, on the other hand, compatible with the sentiments of the society acts smoothly on its own; it hardly needs control or supervision at all. It can be said that this kind of legal measure is cheap. Sometimes, however, a lawmaking body or a court may be aware that a given bill or ruling is counter to some popular viewpoint, and yet will not hesitate to take such a drastic step anyway. But such decisions should be backed by particularly important political or social considerations. The school bussing for the racial 'integration' issue in the USA is a case in point.

A legislature that attempts to introduce new values into a society will encounter resistance which delineates the struggle between new statutory law and traditional public sentiments. In such situations, a calculation of eventual social profit and loss is essential. The lawmaker will consider as profit all the expected consequences of application of the new law (if it works efficiently), while as loss will be counted all the hindrances (such as court actions, faulty performance by the administering apparatus, attempts to outwit the law, and the stiffening of social resistance likely to result from persistent public attitudes).

Such calculation obviously assumes that the legislators would act rationally on the basis of projecting the actual distribution of gains and losses. Reality, however, does not often live up to this model. Thus it becomes the task of science, and of the sociology of law in particular, to inform the legislators to what extent a proposed law is apt to be obeyed, how much support it will find in the existing popular sentiment, or what possible discrepancies might emerge between the new statute and prevailing attitudes on the particular issue. It should then be up to the legislature to reckon the costs of its enactment, the extent of any undesirable effects, and the social importance of the projected or intended objectives and values. It is not the job of science to make the legislators' decisions for them; the task is to provide them with such data that they can act, not on intuition, guesswork or sudden revelation, but upon adequate evidence.

The concept of law tends strongly to be universal and this tendency is apparent in every society. It demands a unity of the legal system (though various classes or groups of cases can be handled differently) to the extent that there can be no insoluble cases, i.e. there are no problems which are not regulated by it. This tendency to unity or universality is by no means limited to enacted law; it is also typical, though to a lesser degree, of the 'sense of justice' of a society. The tendency is, however, peculiar to law. In other areas the picture is different. For example, it can be seen from surveys that in choice of careers, patterns of leisure, consumer decisions, etc., there are many factors involved which tend to differentiate opinions. Public opinion on these and other issues is broken up into many segments depending on such factors as education, occupation, income, sex, family status, etc. But there is no general acceptance that legal prescriptions can be chosen at will or that pluralistic legal systems should be introduced into a given society. Thus there is a general demand for uniformity of the system of law and for a similar uniformity of legal sentiment throughout the society.

In this connection a fundamental problem arises which can be reduced to the question: Is there any such thing as *the legal sentiment* of a society?

The matter is a difficult and complex one. Indeed, can a sum total of individual responses, even if they are all consistent, be understood as the fixed view of a whole society? Would the votes in an eventual poll on what a particular law should be like really reflect the views of the society? Or would they perhaps be different depending on whether or not we asked for an uncommitted opinion without any afterthoughts; or on whether or not those questioned could answer after a calm consideration of complicated arguments peculiar to the legal issue? Would the answers be different if they were made after a discussion compelling the taking of sides? Finally, would the answers remain the same when they involved no practical consequences for the respondents as when they would supposedly be binding on the respondents' actions? All these caveats have been set forth to point to the essential fact that when a man is asked his opinion on a certain issue (and this is particularly true with respect to legal issues) he usually responds as a person who has no actual interest in the answer and, moreover, as a person who can have no influence upon the issue at stake.

This is not a matter that can be neglected, inasmuch as we do talk about society's attitude toward a law, and it is not at all easy to explain what is meant by this notion. Is it the attitude of social and political leaders? Of intelligent, progressive-minded and well-meaning people? Of working people? Of the man in the street? Or does the term refer to the numerical majority of the population? All of these questions require consideration.

## Two basic research strategies

The way law is rooted in values, beliefs and attitudes presents an especially difficult problem for research, given the weakness of theoretical underpinnings. There are two major reasons why this question, so important and so loaded with consequences, has not yet had a satisfactory theoretical solution.

First, it is not an easy task to link research on attitudes toward the law with the type of behavior which is relevant to the norms that are under study. Usually we have either research that deals mainly with norms of research that deals predominantly with behavior. Studies of moral and legal norms continuously take into consideration such questions as: knowledge of the law, knowledge of moral norms or customs, links between legal and moral norms, and the level of moral condemnation, the risk (or lack of risk) in using legal sanctions, preferences among different kinds of sanctions, and so on. Studies on behavior consider such problems as: types of anti-legal behavior, their incidence and prevalence; the 'dark number of crimes'; semi-criminal behavior; and deviant behavior and its causes. There are very few studies that try to combine the study of attitudes with research on the relevant behavior. The lack of studies of this type is due not only to the complexity of the matters involved, but also to the fact that this type of study is technically very difficult.

The second reason is even more complicated. A given legal norm is usually an element of the whole legal system. In principle, however, it is not proper to study the acceptance, effectiveness or possible ramifications of a given, isolated legal precept. The reason is that this precept is connected with similar norms which constitute a status, a code, a set of norms. Consequently, the proper subject of the study is a legal system. But again, it is not methodologically easy to study the legal system as a whole. Too many complicated problems are involved here: it is necessary to investigate its acceptance, costs, gains, and undesired by-products, and the posture of the apparatus of control which sponsors the given legal system. Again, the complexity of the matter and technical difficulties play an important additional role.

Is it possible to overcome these methodological stumbling blocks? There are several promising approaches, with which it would be useful to link two basic research strategies: partial research and global research.

*Partial research* takes into consideration a given element of the legal system and sets out to investigate this element in its unique function. Laboratory experiments would, of course, be the best methodological solution for this type of study. But binding, official law is not convenient material for any type of experiment, especially in a laboratory setting. Moreover, the perplexity and multiplicity of the law makes the selection of suitable issues for investigation a complicated undertaking. Thus, it might be more auspicious to start our discussion with the second strategy.

86

*Global research* takes into consideration the legal system as a whole, focusing on several important elements of the system. This type of study investigates problems relating to the whole system: its prestige; its social, political and moral acceptance; and differences in acceptance and prestige in different areas (civil, criminal and behavioral sub-systems, and so on). By penetrating the strategic elements of the legal system, a study of this type makes clear which parts of the system are amenable to more detailed and thorough examination, i.e. 'partial research.'

So that they may be studied in a comprehensive manner, these complex problems require some, albeit tentative, theoretical framework as a starting point. Such a point of departure might be found in the concept of the three-step hypothesis on the functioning of legal norms.

The hypothesis of the three-factor functioning of the law means that an abstract binding law influences social behavior by means of three basic variables. The first independent variable is the content and significance rendered the given legal enactment by the *type of socio-economic relations* within which it is a binding element of the legal system. The second independent variable is the *kind of sub-culture* functioning in the framework of a given socio-economic system as a link between the legislative directives and the social behavior of those bound by the law. The third independent variable which may variously modify the functioning of an abstract law (within the frameworks of a given socio-economic system and a legal sub-culture) is *the type of personality of the individuals* in the social system. Abstract laws begin to function and to be expressed in social behavior in conjunction with their human subjects. Into such conjunction enter the law itself and the three meta-standards: those springing from the nature of the socio-economic system, those deriving their content from given legal sub-cultures, and those flowing from individual personality traits. This general hypothesis is pregnant with many theoretical implications.

The variable connected with the social system in which a given legal system operates is, in itself, enormously complicated. It is possible to distinguish underdeveloped—developed, stable—unstable, coercive—permissive, and law-oriented—law-avoiding social systems. It is also possible to distinguish total, partial, and ephemeral (momentary) legal systems as well as stable, functional, dysfunctional, fully petrified or partially petrified ones. Of course, there are many possible interrelations between the different kinds of social systems and the legal systems that exist, as a binding force, within them.

The second variable is not a simple one either. The concept of a legal culture or sub-culture is rarely used. The positivistic attitude of lawyers rejects this notion; indeed, the legal system should be a unity, normatively prescribed, free from regional or parochial traits. But social reality is more complicated than the expectations of those who study jurisprudence. There are negative legal sub-cultures—not only those connected with crime directly but those which cultivate various other types of deviance. There are positive legal sub-cultures (positive from the point of view of a given social system; in fact, these can be negative if the social system, like Nazism, is negative in itself) which set out to socialize the members of the social system in a way which is most favorable for the implementation of values embodied in the legal system. There are also—and this possibility is the most interesting theoretically—neutral sub-cultures: sub-cultures which do not aim to strengthen or weaken the legal system but which change their functioning by adding something to the purely legal and normative 'messages.' These provide local or regional habits, 'folklore,' and pragmatic devices which adjust the abstract legal system to the concrete situation in which this system is supposed to work.

The third variable was discovered only recently. Again, for a 'pure' jurisprudential mind, the idea that the law—the legal norm— could be changed or modified by individual preferences, traits or characteristics is shocking. But, as a Polish study shows in a dramatic example, the case of the death penalty, only three variables significantly modify attitudes toward the law, and these are not the classical sociological ones, but rather subjective-personality variables. Those subjects who manifest some elements of insecurity, maladjustment, or severe upbringing are inclined to accept capital punishment; such established and traditional variables as age, socioeconomic status and education do not have any significant influence.

Taking into account the fact of the normative unity of legal systems, the two possible research strategies take on a clearer shape. If research on a given legal norm or institution is in progress in various countries, then not only should the differing social systems be considered in order to understand fully the meaning and functioning of these norms and institutions, but so also should the uniqueness of the various legal systems. Therefore it seems methodologically proper first to study legal systems as independent entities, as elements which are able to change the functioning of their own norms or institutions, in addition to and separately from the many factors which are specific for social systems.

The accepted and usual research approach is to study, in different legal and social systems, what are regarded as similar legal institutions, making cross-comparisons. But this strategy overlooks the danger of mechanical transmission of findings from one socio-legal system into another, a danger that is even more obvious when the general hypothesis of three-step functioning of the law is taken into account. To counter this, the second type of strategy may be employed. Although it might appear more complicated at first glance, it could well be more rudimentary from a methodological point of view. This strategy aims to study the legal system and attitudes towards it without neglecting its normative uniqueness, traditional relics, historical background, specific values and motivations. Up to now the global research strategy has not been used with all the potentialities it affords. Therefore, studies on public attitudes towards a number of basic elements of the given legal system can be regarded as probably the closest approximation to this ideal research strategy.

## Research basis

There are several reasons why the Polish legal system seems especially interesting from the socio-legal point of view. Briefly, there is a general feeling that—for many peculiar reasons—it does not itself enjoy high prestige in the mind of the average person. If this is so, how are we to account for it?

The enumeration of the various factors is an exhausting task in itself. We will, then, take into consideration only some of them:

1   During the period of lack of independence (1795–1918) the law was a symbol of a foreign state. Disregard of the law and disobedience of the authorities were often considered as a national virtue.

2   In the absence of independence no effective school of government and administrative management developed.

3   The attempt to regain lost independence through national uprisings was regarded as the most important national issue, and questions of order remained subordinate.

4   Between 1918 and 1939 the Polish state was not strong in the area of law and order. A systematic discrepancy between goals to be achieved and the means at the disposal of the state, along with long-postponed, intense national expectations, did not make the task of civil order any easier.

5   Moral devastation was wrought during the Second World War by the invisible social poison that the Germans poured in Poland when they created two levels of order: (one official, unaccepted, enforced with sadistic cruelty, and the other unofficial but accepted).

6   A conflict of authority was generated by the change from a capitalistic to a socialistic system, and succeeding conflicts ensued between such powers as state, church, family, tradition on the one hand and, on the other, the new party loyalty which was spread gradually through the use of a variety of deliberate techniques.

7   The old 'face-to-face,' neighborhood-oriented, personal, informal forms rooted in rural needs for mutual aid (and based on the

D

experience which requires immediate help) have residues in the bureaucracy in Poland today that often do not work in harmony with the impersonal requirements of national and efficient law systems.

These and other factors have created in Poland the climate for an extensive cycle of studies on public attitudes toward the law. In 1962, a nationwide study of a new institution of divorce law (established in 1945) was conducted with 2,355 subjects. In 1963, a nationwide study on parental authority was made with 2,723 subjects (based on a similar American study with 800 subjects). In 1964, a basic study in the area of law and order—research on the prestige of the law—was conducted with 2,820 subjects. In 1966, an inquiry on legal and moral attitudes of the general Polish population took place with a sample of 3,167 subjects. Research on knowledge of the law was done in 1970 using 2,197 subjects.

Together, these studies,[2] when interrelated and mutually controlled, yielded a substantial amount of data aimed at approaching a single legal system from all possible angles. Control groups of judges, students, recidivists, and lay judges were introduced. All the investigations were preceded by pilot studies. Findings from other countries—mainly Scandinavian—were also taken into consideration.

## Major findings

Taken together the above studies gave quite a broad and in-depth diagnosis of public opinions and attitudes toward the law and basic moral issues. We shall discuss here three essential problems which constituted the key issues of the studies.

### Knowledge of the law

Various previous studies have thrown some light on the question of society's knowledge of the law. On the whole these sporadic, fragmentary investigations have suggested the general hypothesis that the extent of knowledge of the law is directly proportional to the subject's social position.

In the research referred to (1970) respondents were asked twenty-two fundamental questions relating to knowledge of the law. These were followed up by a series of additional problems which, in sum, constituted an examination on legal knowledge. The questions, which constituted an index of such knowledge, pertained to various departments of law: civil, penal and administrative. Every effort was made to obtain information on the respondents' knowledge (true or erroneous) of the questions asked, not to disclose their opinions on how things ought to be. The analysis of the results was based on this index. Respondents were divided into three categories, according to the number of correct answers: (a) those with a good knowledge of the law (23 per cent), (b) those with a median knowledge (65 per cent), and (c) those with very poor or no knowledge (14 per cent). It should be noted that this division is somewhat arbitrary. For purposes of research, it is a means of disclosing the correlations between knowledge of the law and various objective and subjective social traits, rather than a diagnostic instrument for determining the extent of general knowledge of the law in Polish society. Neither does the index pertain to specific legal regulations or ordinances.

The research findings indicate the following categories as possessing a relatively better knowledge of the law:

Males of the 35–49 age group.

Persons of a higher educational level (those with an elementary education show a better acquaintance with the law than those without any formal education; those who had completed secondary education know more than those with only an elementary education).

Persons involved in social service work.

Those with legal experience (criminal or civil) associated with appearance in court.

Persons who declared a past or present need for legal advice.

Persons interested in following press reports, radio or television broadcasts dealing with legal matters.

Knowledge of the law thus has an instrumental character. It is characteristic of those better situated socially. Greater knowledge, it may be assumed, facilitates their adaptation to complex and changing social reality which requires more elaborate functional patterns of personal behavior. *Knowledge of the law is a means for effective action under the conditions of intricate social relations.*

The findings throw light on still another fundamental problem. Previous research had advanced the concept of differentiation of regulations and legal principles. Knowledge of legal enactments or regulations is understood as acquaintance with the tenor of legal texts based on the awareness of their obligatory nature, whereas knowledge of legal principles means cognition of the basic norms of right and wrong in relation to the spheres and conditions, in which a given type of behavior is permissible. The previous research assumed that knowledge of legal principles and legal regulations will shape up differently in different social circles and, in particular, that it will vary drastically as between ordinary citizens and administrators (controllers) of the law. Thus it was assumed that knowledge of legal principles is relatively well grounded among ordinary citizens while their acquaintance with legal regulations is comparatively weak. Administrators of the law, that is, professional legal practitioners who directly or indirectly control the behavior of others, were expected to differ more from the general population with regard to their knowledge of regulations than of legal principles.

The 1970 research on legal awareness verified the above assumptions to a considerable degree. Questions were formulated which, in line with the above assumptions, were regarded as indicators of knowledge of legal regulations. An index was prepared on the basis of the questions. An analysis of the findings of that index indicates a direction of correlation identical with that of the knowledge of legal principles. But, as anticipated theoretically, a good knowledge of legal regulations is highly associated with a higher educational level and with mental work. Correspondingly, a weaker knowledge of legal regulations is strongly related to a lower educational level and agricultural and unskilled occupations. The direction of correlation is similar with respect to whether the professional position occupied by the subject is managerial or rank and file, although this association is not clearly evident in the case of general knowledge of the law. A more detailed investigation among people with a legal education and those engaged in law administration would undoubtedly confirm that correlation on firmer grounds. Nevertheless, an important warning arises from the research in question: rules or directives addressed to the ordinary citizen in legal language will, in the main, leave him unresponsive. The questions will be effective only if, or to the extent that, they are interpreted into patterns of behavior, especially prepared so as to enable a grasp of the contents of the directives propounded by administrators of the law. The ordinary citizen is impressed primarily by clear and basic legal principles.

*Evaluation of the law*

A second fundamental problem (with which every legal system is supposed to be concerned) is the extent to which a given legal system is generally regarded as just or unjust. Again, we shall take the findings from the 1970 study.

The main item which attempted to explore this problem was the following:

Question: 'According to your judgment is the law in our country, taken on the whole, just?'

|  | Per cent |
|---|---|
| 1. Is just | 56·5 |
| 2. Is not just | 6·6 |

3. Qualified answers
    a  Partially    5·8
    b  Depends on realization    2·1
    c  Other    3·1
4. Difficult to say    25·4

Several categories of respondents showed a statistical tendency to declare that the law in Poland is on the whole just. These were younger people, those with relatively higher education, inhabitants of smaller cities and rural areas, and persons actively engaged in social service work. There does not appear to be any other correlation here with occupation, neither do personality variables play a visible role.

In the light of the data obtained it is clear that problems relating to evaluation should be elaborated in a more detailed manner in subsequent studies. Nevertheless it is apparent that the law has general support.

*Prestige of the law*

The prestige of the law is another crucial feature which is necessary for effective functioning of a legal system. The Polish study of 1964 throws some light on this problem. Popular views on observance of the law were distributed as shown below.

Question: 'There are different views on the question of the practical observance of the law. Please choose from the opinions listed those which appeal to you most, or write your own.'

|  | Per cent | |
|---|---|---|
|  | Urban | Rural |
| 1. The law should always be obeyed even when we think it is wrong. | 44·3 | 45·3 |
| 2. When one is confronted with a regulation one considers wrong one should only appear to conform to it, but in practice one should violate it. | 22·7 | 22·5 |
| 3. One should in general disobey laws considered wrong. | 17·7 | 18·8 |
| 4. I have still another opinion. | 4·7 | 4·1 |
| 5. It's hard for me to say. | 10·6 | 9·3 |
| N = 2,820 | 100·0 | 100·0 |

To summarize the findings in respect to the various factors influencing in one way or another respect for the law: people between the ages of 35–49 and those over 60, persons with higher education, white-collar workers, those whose families belong to the intelligentsia, people who feel secure,* people having stable and limited affiliations,† the rationally disposed (not dogmatic),‡ and those engaged in social service work (albeit with a somewhat more frequent inclination to circumvent the law) all tend—more than others—to respect the law even when it is considered wrong.

Correspondingly, the categories which more often than others declare a disposition to circumvent, ignore or violate legal regulations include the 25–34 year age group, those either having no education or with only elementary schooling, the offspring of strata other than the intelligentsia, unskilled workers (violation), skilled workers (circumvention), persons with feelings of insecurity,§ people with loose and transient affiliations, people with many social contacts, dogmatic individuals (circumvention), the inhibited (violation) (see footnote †, below), the frustrated, those with disordered systems of values, ¶ and, finally, people not engaged in social service work.

Additional data afford a possibility of some cross-national comparisons, although limited at this stage of the development of comparative studies. As W. Kaupen writes:[3]

> We start from the assumption that submission to the State authorities is more developed in Germany than in other countries. If this is right, we should find among our interviewees a greater number of those people who think that laws should be obeyed even if they are not right. This proves to be the case,

---

* The question included the following: No. 12: 'Do you think that people should be trusted?'
† Indication as to whether or not a person belonged to small primary groups was given by response 2 to item 13, which read: 'Apart from your family, do you know many people whose friendship and warm feelings you do not doubt? 1. No one, 2. Only a few, 3. A large number, 4. Don't know.'
‡ 'The indicator of mental inhibition was reply no. 1 to item 14 of the questionnaire, which read: 'If you are in a large company and someone who is very sure of himself argues for a view that is the opposite of your own view, what is your reaction? Do you 1. Give way, or withdraw your own view? 2. Show that he is wrong? 3. Carry on the conversation and find out during the discussion who was right? 4. Don't know?'
§ The question included the following: 'No. 12: Do you think people should be trusted?'
¶ Dogmatism is indicated by response 4, and an unintegrated system of values by response 3, to item No. 20 which reads: 'There are people who find it easy to judge the behavior of others as good or bad, while other people have doubts about such judgments. Do you ever have such doubts? 1. On the whole I have no such doubts, 2. Sometimes I do have doubts, 3. I often have doubts, 4. I very often have such doubts, 5. Don't know, 6. I never think about such things.'

comparing our data with those gathered in Poland* and in The Netherlands.†

TABLE 5.1  *Attitudes towards the law in Poland, Holland and West Germany*

| Question (Statement) | Poland | Holland | W. Germany |
|---|---|---|---|
| The law should always be obeyed even if, in your opinion, it is wrong. Agree | 45% | | |
| Do you think a law should be obeyed, even when you feel this law is unjust? Yes | | 47% | |
| You should obey the laws, even if you do not think that they are just. Agree | | | 66% |

The findings on knowledge of the law, evaluation of the law from the point of view of its ethical justification, and prestige of the law give in general a fairly consistent picture. This general picture, at least in Poland, is that the law on the whole is accepted and, additionally, that 'those at the top' more than 'underdogs' express a tendency to support the law.

It seems useful to distinguish three levels of acceptance of the law and basic moral norms. The acceptance can be either (1) lip-service declaration (purely vocal manifestation of certain values often presented to meet perceived social expectations); (2) internal acceptance (commitment to internalized values which are sometimes not externally expressed, for example in cases where the values could be regarded as deviant or where commitment is not strong enough to elicit corresponding behavior); or (3) behavior that is consistent with the accepted values.

The techniques used in the studies described above give some warrant that the attitudes of acceptance reflect some degree of commitment.

Several problems remain that need additional clarification. One is: what sociological category of the general population is especially prone to accept the law? The studies show in a preliminary way that this category is comprised of—on the basis of objective factors—the

---

* The comparative data for Poland have been taken from the author's article, 'The prestige of law (preliminary research results),' *Acta Sociologica*, 10, 1966, pp. 81–96.
† The Dutch results have been collected by P. Vinke, 'Inner acceptation of legal rules,' mimeographed paper, Leiden, 1969.

so-called 'intelligentsia'; that is, people with a secondary or higher education, whose family background is intellectual, and who are white-collar workers. As for subjective factors, these are also people who do not show signs of insecurity; they are rational (not dogmatic), have bonds within their own group, and engage in voluntary social-service work. Even if we apply a correction to allow for the possibility that they wished to make an impression by their replies, it should be noted that after all this is a stratum of people who by their very jobs are predisposed to carry out the law on various levels of the state administration where the law is applied either directly or indirectly; no doubt (in contrast to the general opinions one hears every day) this occupational routine does have an important effect on their views regarding respect for the law.

If one went by daily observation and experience, lessons taken from history, and views often expressed on the subject, one might think little respect for the law would be found in the general population. Surprisingly enough, however, it turns out that the most frequently chosen response (44·3 per cent of the urban population, 45·3 per cent of the rural population) is that the law should be respected in all circumstances. A possible explanation is that the population as a whole takes a Socratic view of the law, a collective attitude that differs from the attitude of the individual. Socrates, as we know, respected the law even when he did not respect the judges who applied the law to his case. His guiding principle was that the system of law as a whole should always be respected, even though it may be a bad law and be wrongly applied in certain individual cases and contexts, and although it is possible to despise some detailed versions of its application. This attitude is the result of long centuries of society's collective experience which has been forged in the course of many complicated and contrasting situations. This capital, consisting of respect for the law, which has been collected and absorbed by society despite seasonal changes and upsets (the proximity of events destroys perspective and suggests that pathological deviations are much more marked than they are in reality and blinds one to the vast reservoir of society's accepted attitudes), cannot be easily shifted because it is weighed down and anchored by the ballast of its historical traditions.

But there are other somewhat more complicated and puzzling questions: what is the source of the relatively good general knowledge of the law? Why, despite several traditional and historical factors, does respect for the law seem to be relatively high? Why, in spite of the high respect for the law, is the rate of criminal and deviant behavior, especially in the area of economic activities, also relatively high and, in some areas, steadily rising?

It is not easy to give satisfactory answers to these questions.

Relatively good knowledge of the law is a somewhat spurious indicator. Usually behind a legal norm there exists and operates a corresponding moral norm. Due to the complicated processes of socialization, moral norms are quite deeply internalized; they underlie and support legal norms. If this is the situation, then when a problem concerning knowledge of the legal norm arises the internalized moral norm prompts the response.

Probably the processes of legal socialization are more complicated than is usually perceived. These processes apparently operate on the levels of declarative acceptance of and commitment to legal norms. But strong counter-motives might operate at the same time and neutralize legal values at the time that the appropriate behavior is supposed to emerge. So the junction between accepted legal values and actual behavior could be disrupted by the intervention of additional external factors. Pressures of various kinds could appear, such as urgent needs, frustrations, blocked opportunities, neutralizing ideologies, and sub-culture values (including sub-cultural violence). All these factors could operate and may be regarded as a generalized excuse which suspends the functioning of the values in the face of a pressure situation.

These attempts to provide answers to puzzling questions may elucidate the complicated problem in some way; however, they do not solve it. In order to give a full, or at least a more satisfactory, answer, it is necessary to consider additional elements of a psychosocial character. Personality traits can enter here as variables. There are complex situations in which any known explanation seems useless. In a criminal sub-culture with blocked opportunities, frustrations, and all possible neutralization devices available, some people would still behave in a way prescribed by pure legal and moral values, and some would behave in a way which disvalues the law.

Thus, one possible explanation could be: different personality variables may change the interplay of social and sub-cultural factors. In fact, such personality traits as insecurity, maladjustment or dogmatism could modify attitudes toward the law and subsequently legal behavior in a substantial way. But are they sufficient for an adequate explanation?

### Invisible factors

The additional elements that can be introduced in order to suggest one more step toward an adequate theory of the functioning of the law could be described as invisible factors. At least three types of invisible factors can be operationally defined and empirically isolated: principled and instrumental attitudes, social and individualistic orientations in ethics, and directions of affiliation.

## Principled and instrumental attitudes

The 'principled attitude' can be defined as a direct, spontaneous acceptance or rejection of some rule relative to projected or actual behavior. The 'instrumental attitude' is, according to the proposed definition, one where the acceptance or rejection of projected or actual behavior is dependent upon specific calculation of different possible alternatives of behavior and the evaluation of their effects.

It seems that this sort of distinction between attitudes representative of various types of human behavior, and particularly those concerning legal and moral behavior, may prove especially fertile. For instance, the long-lasting and intricate dispute on egoism may be solved comparatively easily by stating that egoism is a conglomeration of notions, eclectically composed of two features: orientation toward narrowly defined personal enjoyment, and the instrumental attitude. Thus, political double-dealers might be presumed to show mostly instrumental attitudes, while political ideologists display principled attitudes. One is bound to assume that in stabilized political systems the principled attitudes will prevail, reflecting, as it were, order in the social structure (where everyone is allotted his own position, part and role, and where these are comparatively well fixed within the existing *status quo*). In changing systems, on the other hand, the instrumental will prevail as being more adequate to continually shifting circumstances. An overwhelming predominance of principled attitudes may be a symptom of stagnation in a given social system; it may be an indication of a pathological stagnation hampering or even preventing altogether the growth of developmental trends. On the other hand, one may also note that an overwhelming preponderance of instrumental attitudes may be a pathological situation as well, depriving the system of a basis or a reserve of autonomous social force indispensable (as a core of elementary social values and ties) for the realization of the basic functions of that system. Thus, a principled attitude is conceived as one having reference to some general and binding principle in a situation where a new stand must be adopted in view of new circumstances, conflicts, changes of roles, etc. Consequently, an individual with a tendency to adopt a principled attitude will, in an unexpected situation for which there are no direct standards, patterns and solutions, look for some general rule among those known to him—a rule which would be applicable to that particular situation. The case is supposedly different with instrumental attitudes. An individual with instrumental attitudes, when faced with a new, difficult and unexpected situation, will be inclined to consider it upon the basis of his own individual store of knowledge: what the results are likely to be of this or that alternative action, and which alternatives would be profitable for him. One can assume that

98

individuals better adapted to life would, as a rule, react with principled attitudes (it seems, as it were, more economical in the long run to react at once—in an engaged situation—according to rules specially prepared by relevant experience, rather than entangle oneself time and time again in teleological deliberations); while those whose social or psychic adaptation is not as good would react according to instrumental attitudes.

What relation do these theoretical expectations have to available empirical data? Some of the propositions were tested in the study of legal and moral attitudes of the Polish population in 1966. A more detailed study of the same problem was conducted in 1970 (in connection with research on knowledge of the law). Several questions of the questionnaire were designed to test some of the anticipated hypotheses. An index was constructed to enable a synthetic analysis of eventually forthcoming data. Below is one of the more basic questions upon which this index was built.

Question: 'Some people have firm moral principles, and they are true to them regardless of the result—others strive above all to attain their goal. What is your opinion on the subject?'

| | Per cent | |
|---|---|---|
| | Urban | Rural |
| 1. One should always be true to one's principles in behavior regardless of the result (principled attitude). | 22·5 | 22·3 |
| 2. If conformity to principles were to bring undesirable results, it would be better to think over one's principles and adapt them to the situation (mixed attitude). | 39·3 | 32·8 |
| 3. Rigid principles are altogether superfluous; one should behave so as to obtain the desired effect (instrumental attitude). | 31·2 | 31·6 |
| 4. I am unable to decide. | 6·7 | 13·0 |
| (in research of 1966, N = 3,178) repeated in research of 1970, N = 2,197 | 99·7 | 99·7 |

A summary of the major findings is as follows:
1  The principled attitude increases with age.
2  Increase in the level of education basically increases the instrumental attitude, but a college education changes this tendency into

99

acceptance of an attitude which is a compromise between the principled and instrumental.

3  Leadership position is linked with either the principled or compromise attitude.

4  Qualified workers and craftsmen are predominantly instrumentally oriented; white-collar workers are oriented toward compromise.

5  Insecurity and lack of good life-adjustment are related to the instrumental attitude, while the principled attitude seems to be correlated with security and good life-adjustment. Further analysis also shows that rural inhabitants tend to have principled orientations, while city dwellers are more instrumentally oriented.

Without going into a detailed analysis of these results, it can be said that the possibility of empirical demonstration of attitudes of a special type has been shown. It should also be emphasized that these attitudes are not perceived as personality traits, or as economic, religious or political attitudes. While they are invisible, they presumably exist, and act to modify in a consistent and systematic way not only individual but also collective behavior.

## Social and individualistic orientations in ethics

Again, this facet of the study on legal and moral attitudes of the Polish population in 1966 could be regarded as a special type of pilot study (although this research had a pilot study of its own) for the main research conducted in 1970, in connection with the research on knowledge of the law.

By individually oriented ethics we mean a set of norms regulating social behavior, of which the predominating ones are those which prescribe behavior toward other members of small, more or less informal groups. Thus, in general, individual ethics condemns thieves, killers, adulterers, frauds, and false witnesses; that is, those who inflict harm on others in 'face-to-face' relationships. Even if examples of such behavior do not actually occur in some narrow circle of people who know (or could know) each other, evaluations still remain generalizations of experiences of this kind. Consequently, underlying the norms of individualistic ethics are various elementary types of behavior approved or condemned in narrow human contexts.

On the other hand, norms of socially oriented ethics refer to the social roles and positions which are, or can be, occupied by an individual. The predominant aspect of this type of ethics is that it does not evaluate the personal qualities of an individual or the ways he conducts himself, but rather the effects caused by his occupying a certain position in the social structure. Let us take, as examples, some questions from the above studies which were intended to deal with these problems. The questions are taken from the study conducted in 1966.

Question: 'Would you regard a person who is conscientious, a good colleague, a good father to his family, but who was a member of the Nazi party in Germany (before and during the war), as a decent person on the whole?'

|  | A. If he was active in the organization | B. If he was not active in the organization |
|---|---|---|
|  | Per cent | |
| 1. Yes (he could be regarded as a decent person) | 13·0 | 46·4 |
| 2. No | 65·4 | 25·8 |
| 3. Difficult to say | 20·7 | 26·1 |
| 4. Lack of data | 0·9 | 1·7 |
| N = 3,167 | 100·0 | 100·0 |

An index of individualistic and socially oriented attitudes with statistically calculated correlations, based on the following and similar questions (from the 1970 study), illustrates the different traits characteristic of the two attitudes:

*First question:* Assuming that some institution has to reduce its staff by discharging an employee and the choice is between the two persons described below, which of the two should be discharged?

Candidates for dismissal:

A   a poor and not quite suitable worker, but with very difficult financial and family conditions,

B   a capable and professionally suitable worker in a favorable financial situation and with some family support.

Which would you discharge?

|  |  |  |
|---|---|---|
| 1 | the first | 31·0 per cent |
| 2 | the second | 46·8 per cent |
| 3 | I can't make the choice | 21·8 per cent |

101

*Second question:* If there were a choice between the two following candidates for the position of manager,

A  one who shows concern for his subordinates, is sympathetic and friendly, but at the same time weak professionally and unable to cope with his responsibilities,

B  a good specialist and organizer but not concerned with people, ill-natured and disagreeable in his relations with others.

I. On the whole, which of them do you value more highly?

| | | |
|---|---|---|
| 1 | A | 49·7 per cent |
| 2 | B | 27·0 per cent |
| 3 | Hard to say | 22·2 per cent |

II. Which of the two would you prefer to work under?

| | | |
|---|---|---|
| 1 | A | 61·2 per cent |
| 2 | B | 21·9 per cent |
| 3 | Hard to say | 16·4 per cent |

*Third question:* Which of these two do you rate more highly as a man? Mr S, warm-hearted, on whose help people in trouble can count but who is inefficient in his work and little devoted to his obligations.
Mr T, a highly skilled and model worker but entirely indifferent to the cares and affairs of others.

I. Rated higher as a man:

| | | |
|---|---|---|
| 1 | Mr S | 60·8 per cent |
| 2 | Mr T | 21·7 per cent |
| 3 | Hard to say | 16·7 per cent |

II. Preference as a workmate:

| | | |
|---|---|---|
| 1 | Mr S | 59·3 per cent |
| 2 | Mr T | 25·5 per cent |
| 3 | Hard to say | 14·8 per cent |

A general analysis of the findings clearly suggests that the individualistic predominates over the social orientation. A statistical analysis discloses the following additional correlations.

The individualistic orientation relates to: a comparatively lower educational level, rank and file position, symptoms of an insecurity feeling, poor adaptation to life, non-engagement in social-service work, instrumental disposition, declared friendliness as a personality pattern for others, and the trait of more sharply condemning transgression against private than against public property.

The social orientation is linked with the following traits: comparatively higher educational level, managerial position, lack of insecurity feelings, better adaptation to life, involvement in social-service work, principled attitude, declared industriousness, honesty and social-service work as a personality pattern for others, and the trait of more sharply condemning transgression against public than against private property.

Dry figures once again reflect a clear picture: those in less favorable situations (rank and file positions), people who feel insecure, and the maladjusted are disposed to regard the world defensively. They orient toward the individualistic attitude and are disposed to defend their petty goods (objectively or subjectively assessed). Such personalities also attempt to make use of the instrumental attitude in order to gain more—if they can. Those who display the social attitude behave accordingly. They think (objectively or in the light of their subjective evaluations) in categories of the greater good of society, since it may be assumed that their basic needs have been satisfied (statistical data bear out here a kind of philosophical skepticism concerning human nature). The present study provides a basis for the assertion that the social orientation is likewise a pro-legal one. For the fact that the legalistic attitude and the disposition to a social orientation are linked with similar determinants justifies the assumption that the two converge.

The skeptic may ask: But what is the link between legal awareness (which is understood as a knowledge of the law and of legal attitudes) and the types of attitudes distinguished here? The answer is relatively simple. First of all, as pointed out above, the empirical data suggest that the legalistic attitude is linked precisely with the social orientation, and the anti-legalistic with the individualistic. Second, mere observation will show that the place of work has become for many people a second home, and in many cases a first. If that is so, the simple reflection suffices to realize the effects of transferring the disposition to an individualistic orientation—applicable to the conditions of family and neighbors—to the impersonal, dehumanized relations geared to effectiveness, which, according to the principles of efficient functioning, should dominate in the production plant. If this diffusion also means the penetration of the individualistic attitude into a sphere where there functions a co-ordinated system of socially oriented attitudes, cannot this process bring about the skirting of or violation of the law?

## Directions of affiliation

Involvement in the society, affiliation with the basic values of society, and degree of anomie are recognized as essential elements of the attitudes that could favor or oppose the law. Nevertheless, the affiliation could have many directions: it could take as a target the social system as a whole, a nation which is part of this system, a class, a given social stratum, a specific type of social group, a given social group. The legal system usually represents the interests of the entire social system, but an affiliation with this or that group does not necessarily mean that the intensity and direction of this affiliation will at the same time strengthen an adherence to the global social system and consequently produce support for its legal system. Affiliation with a group that is in opposition to other social groups or to society as a whole could produce the reverse effect. This type of affiliation might produce attitudes which are anti-legalistic. The processes which take place in the social system as a whole should not hide the interactions that take place in relatively small social systems: organizations, institutions, factories, corporations, etc. An affiliation with a given sector or branch of an organization does not necessarily mean there are inherent ties with the core of the organization. Often such adherence could initiate or strengthen a separatistic drive and movement.

The available empirical data from Polish studies in 1964, 1966, and 1970 show that affiliations with some groups that are attached to a given social system generate additional subsidiary pro-legal sentiment. Therefore the existing evidence should be treated, at the present stage of investigation, as an indication that this direction of inquiry could be regarded as fruitful. If so, types of affiliations, the types of groups which become the targets of these affiliations, and the intensity of the affiliations should be studied. Not only would a more accurate understanding of the function of the affiliation emerge (the affiliation could be understood as a type and degree of dependency and type and degree of protection which a given individual has toward a given social group), but more precise studies, as a basis for inquiry into the roots of legal and moral norms, could subsequently be carried on.

To sum up the major findings of the Polish research, we have tried to point out that:

1 Paradoxical as it may seem, the more complicated studies of legal systems, if put into effect, could be more fruitful than some spuriously regarded simple studies which aim to compare isolated legal institutions.

2 Prestige of the law, as one of the most important elements of legal awareness, should be understood as manifested on any of

various possible levels—declaration, acceptance and commitment, basis for behavioral motivation.

3 Three-step hypothesis on the functioning of the law should be more fully developed.

4 Different variables which affect the functioning of the law should be more carefully studied not only for their possible determinations of the observed social behavior but also in their mutual interplay and interrelations.

5 Additional factors (described above as 'invisible factors') should be introduced as necessary elements for the understanding of pro-legal and anti-legal behavior.

Despite an abundance of rhetoric and stale verbiage, structuralism has been unable not only to explain more complicated elements of social structure but also to give even a vague definition of its own approach. None the less, failure to clarify existing versions of structuralism does not necessarily mean that this approach is pointless. The sound intuitions that exist behind the vague semantics of structuralism could possibly be grasped and organized by introduction of the notion of invisible factors. Indeed, these factors are not reducible to social variables; they are also not in the nature of personality traits. Still, they interrelate social and subjective variables in a consistent and systematic pattern. Thus they could be regarded as set, and as the fabric of social interactions.

If the concept of invisible factors has some explanatory power, in what way might it be useful in explaining the previously mentioned contradictions? In what way, especially, could this concept possibly solve the paradox of good knowledge and acceptance of the law, and at the same time increasing deviant and criminal behavior? In the light of the foregoing remarks, the explanation appears relatively simple. Socio-economic factors are not sufficient to explain the contradiction, neither are factors inherent in the sub-culture. Neither do personality factors taken exclusively present the possibility of a full explanation. Interrelations among all these factors afford some useful approximation: undesirable conditions and the situation of being an 'underdog' could push one towards crime; nevertheless positive influences in the sub-culture could work to counteract this pressure. But is this approximation adequate? The introduction of the notion of invisible factors seems useful at this stage of analysis, enabling us to take an explanatory step forward. For while the combination of poor social conditions and anti-social personality traits might indeed be countered in some way by the sub-culture, what kind of outcome would emerge from this opposition? If such factors as an instrumental attitude, individualistically oriented ethics and lack of affiliation enter the picture, then the positive impact of the sub-culture could be easily corrupted and wiped out by rationalizations

105

and neutralizations. If a principled attitude, social orientation in ethics and strong social affiliation were to support the influence of the sub-culture, then the forces due to bad social conditions and an anti-social personality could be outweighed.

By the same token, good knowledge of the law and respect for the law can be outweighed when elements of a negative social condition combined with 'negative' personality traits are further strengthened by the influence of such invisible factors.

## Comparative investigations on legal and moral attitudes

Historians and economists have clearly set forth the diversity of the social determinants of various legal systems. It has become obvious that those systems can be extremely dissimilar and that they are instrumental in character with respect to the social structures within which they operate. Now it is hardly conceivable that any legal precepts or institutions could be compared with others belonging to a different social system, without their peculiar social, economic and political contexts and their divergent roles being taken into consideration.

The achievements of jurisprudence in this field should be reconsidered again. Even if we dismiss momentarily the objection that the insights contributed by anthropological investigations have been neglected, it still remains true that comparative analyses of legal norms have constituted almost the sole type of theoretical consideration. For whenever the historical and economic approaches are more or less lost sight of, unsystematic impressionism slips in, which consists of taking certain arbitrary assumptions for granted and illustrating them by biased empirical findings, or else of a mere exegesis of the compared writs of law.

There have been undertaken, however, a series of complex investigations designed to compare attitudes toward similar legal and moral issues in different societies. It is not claimed that the results obtained will be final or definitive. The main intention of the project is to test the utility of certain intra-systemic research techniques and to build up a systematic basis for further empirically testable macro-systemic studies.

While we consider our data to be tentative only, any objection that conclusions are drawn which extend beyond the empirical data must be rejected as either naïve or mischievous. For, in the first place, there is a general methodological principle that a generalization based upon sound empirical data, even if they are incomplete, is better than one which is based on no data at all. Second, two levels should be discerned in our set of generalizations: conclusions drawn from the actually available data and working hypotheses for further investigations.

Any study can be considered as a pilot inquiry with respect to any subsequent ones devoted to the same problem. There had been quite a number of such pilot studies prior to our initial investigations on moral and legal attitudes in Poland. The Scandinavian studies on the social sense of justice[4] and the Finnish investigations[5] can be considered to be such introductory inquiries to the 1966 survey on legal and moral sentiments of the Polish population.

In turn, the Polish 1966 survey has stimulated similar ventures in the Netherlands, Belgium and Brazil. The Dutch investigations, most elaborate of all the foreign endeavors, concern mainly the issues of tax regulations,[6] but they also deal with some problems which are central for the Polish program. At the time of writing, the researchers are now in the final phase of analyzing the findings. The Belgian study (under the direction of I. Van Houtte) is in the phase of data collecting and no generalizations can yet be made. The Brazilian project[7] is still mostly in the planning stage.

The common feature of all these ventures is that they are focused mainly on what is usually called the legal sentiment, i.e. opinions about and attitudes toward legal and moral norms. The fact that the recent research objectives—in particular the Scandinavian and Polish studies on prestige of the law—are closely related, led us to assume an approach which can be defined as 'co-operative comparative study.' Independent studies on similar problems are undertaken in various countries, with due consideration for the specific systemic, economic, legal and political peculiarities of each of them. Such programs have a number of advantages: they provide diagnostic knowledge on the several societies; they allow for comparisons of selected aspects of the investigated populations; they permit the focusing of the independent researches on specific problems; and they promise to bring out a core set of research hypotheses which may eventually become the tested analytical basis for subsequent inter-systemic designs centered in a single research institution.

Before reporting some results which are available in the present phase of the research work, I would like to discuss, by way of what may seem a digression, some notions concerning comparative studies in general, and comparative studies of legal systems in particular.

What we call 'federalistic' investigations may be opposed to what can be defined as the 'a-prioric-centralistic' approach. Within the latter, some preconceived research conception is taken for granted. Referring to prior knowledge, various social systems are selected for comparative analyses, and detailed hypotheses to be tested in those systems are derived from the a-prioric general theories. It must be remarked that this kind of approach involves at the outset an extensive risk of failure. For it may well turn out in the course of the research that the investigated social systems cannot be compared at all (in terms of the generally accepted hypotheses); or that various additional factors (left out in the initial phase of defining the research strategy) are significant, which the preconceived and petrified working assumptions do not allow us to grasp with sufficient precision; or that various obstacles which had seemed to be of superficial character have turned out to be methodological problems which are difficult to solve; or that the results of studies based on a-prioric assumptions are vague and not interesting enough for a comparative analysis of different social systems.

These methodological difficulties can be magnified by another significant consideration. In the recently developing methodology of comparative investigations there is insufficient clarity as to whether this kind of study (if we put aside those in which control groups are investigated for additional comparisons) can be applied to the social systems defined by nations, states or even social-political camps. Moreover, various comparisons between social systems can be related to sub-systemic investigations. Thus, for example, studies on the functioning of various legal systems could be compared with data on several sub-cultures within a given social system which tend to support or oppose the legal principles.

There are still more methodological troubles involved in federalistic investigations. For in such investigations of various social systems the factors selected as the dependent variables (i.e. those which are influenced by some other factors) can be either homogeneous or not. A legal system is a homogeneous or uniform variable because it is always a uniform and adequate formal system produced by a society. Similarly, different social settings (such as nations) evolve their peculiar national characters which are unique syntheses of various historically determined political, social and economic influences and qualities.

Federalistic studies concerning such problems as the family, work, local authorities, leisure, etc., are in a situation which is methodologically less advantageous than studies of the law. For example, the model of the family can be shaped in various ways in different social systems not as a mere result of differences in the political systems in which the several types of family function, but also as a result of other influences, such as the prevailing economic, social, demographic conditions, etc., and their peculiar modifying combinations; thus we have to contend here with a greater variety of independent variables influencing the dependent ones.

In this connection, diagnostic and theoretical federalistic investigations must be distinguished. A study of the diagnostic type can disclose the diversity or similarity of certain characteristics such as, for example, family models, leisure habits, and types of functioning of the local authorities, in various societies. However, nothing more than that is provided. It is simply put forth that in a given social system there are monogamous families or that nuclear family units prevail, while in another society there are more polygamous or patriarchal families. Theoretical federalistic studies differ from the diagnostic in that they attempt, besides fact finding, to verify definite relationships. As already mentioned, verification of theoretical relationships at various levels is only possible when the studied variables are uniform in character; since the legal systems and their elements are marked by the uniformity required for comparative analyses, analytic comparisons of legal systems are particularly valuable, as they can not only provide diagnostic data but also form a basis for formulating adequate hypotheses concerning more general regularities.

However, the a-prioric-centralistic approach to comparative analyses of legal systems suffers serious limitations, in spite of the broader opportunities opened up by the comparative method. An illustration of such shortcomings can be seen in the investigations by W. Evan, a comparative study of non-socialist legal systems.[8] Two types of data were juxtaposed: various features of social systems such as urbanization, industrialization, religion, level of economic development, etc. on the one hand, and data concerning the functioning of the investigated legal systems on the other. Here are some of the findings:

1    There is a positive correlation between the level of bureaucratization, industrialization, urbanization, professionalism and the number of lawyers employed in the society.

2    There is a positive correlation between the growth of bureaucracy and the number of legal faculties in universities functioning in the society.

3    There is a positive relationship between the number of legal faculties and the number of faculty members who participate in legislative activities.

4    The role of the police can be conceived in two ways: either as an institution whose major task is to maintain and support the legal order, or as an agency of political patronage. If we accept this distinction, we can see that the role of guarding the legal order is related (in terms of the data of the described study) to high levels of industrialization, urbanization, and professionalism. Political patronage is connected with low levels of industrialization, urbanization, and professionalization.

As in the above example, results of studies of this type tend to be rather vague. It can also be objected that several of their basic concepts, such as the number of persons engaged in legislative activities or political patronage, do not mean the same things in various social systems. Hence it can be doubted whether basic characteristics that are ambiguous in their meaning can be reasonably compared at all.

Investigations we have labeled as federalistic aim to avoid the disadvantages of the a-prioric-centralistic approach. While federalistic investigation makes use of the results of prior investigations, treating them as pilot studies, it is a two-phased endeavor. During the first phase the study analyzes *legal constructs* peculiar to the investigated social systems, and looks for similar constructs within the range covered. In this phase the following problems are the main focus: analysis of the cases of similar functioning of different legal constructs within similar social systems, and analysis of eventual legal cases of similar functioning of different legal constructs in dissimilar social systems. The information collected during this first phase of the co-operative investigation is indispensable for devising a common, synthetic research tool (a questionnaire), for clearing up the basic concepts, for preparing comparable statistical procedures and techniques of coding of the data, etc., thus forming a starting point for the second phase of the design.

The second phase can be devoted to a more systematic study of *legal systems*, accounting for their peculiarities (determined by their traditions) and similarities (such as, for example, between the legal systems of socialist countries), and any eventual identity of legal constructs or basic norms in dissimilar social settings (we can risk the guess that there is no such identity, except for issues of minor social importance, such as incest, though a tendency toward a greater global uniformity is remarkable, as is illustrated by, for example, the Charter of Human Rights).

The Polish, Dutch, Belgian and Brazilian surveys should be considered as an attempt at international co-operation in collecting information for the first of the two phases here distinguished. We shall discuss some of their results, with references to earlier endeavors treated as pilot studies.

The investigations so far have been devoted to what is called the legal sentiment prevailing within various social systems and consequently they are based mainly on analyses of verbal declarations. In this context the recurrent problem of the relationship between declared opinions and actual behavior arises again. A pertinent and simple model (already mentioned on p. 95) of the involved mechanism has been offered by Z. Sufin.[9]

It turned out that [the declared attitudes and behavior] towards some values have been consistent, while towards others they have not. A number of explanatory hypotheses were tested, leading to a general model of interpretation.

110

The postulated values  The general model of valuation
. . . . . . . . . . . . . . . . . . . . . . . .

| Declarative Acknowledge-ment | Acceptance Inter-nalization | Acceptance The need of realization |

The model is based on the assumption that there are three distinct types of link between the postulating of a value and its realization. The attitude towards a value can be marked by various degrees of involvement, expressed by a mere verbal acknowledgement, an acceptance (internalization), or a need of realization of the value . . . due to external conditions.

The difficulties posed by verbal deduction can be overcome by various methods. For example, topical problems can be selected which are apt to be emotionally highly significant for the respondents, thus inducing them to express their real views; however, this occurs more readily if the issues tackled in the questions are not too close to a respondent's personal situation. Special experiments can be designed in which the declared attitudes, e.g. of rigorism v. tolerance, are compared with the actual behavior corresponding to the declarations.[10] Yet another strategy, employed in the federalistic investigations, consists in introducing special populations of various kinds, such that the attitudes of the respondents are peculiarly, systematically and continuously biased by their broader situation in life. Thus, besides the average population (representative samples of adult populations, 3,000 respondents in Poland and 1,200 in the Netherlands), supplementary control populations are introduced. As noted earlier, in the Polish survey such populations were (a) judges, as those who systematically and professionally inculcate law into social life (in the Dutch research the corresponding group were tax officers) and (b) recidivists who had been habitually breaking the law (both countries). Though such methodological devices do not guarantee that there is no discrepancy between the declared opinions or judgments and those which are the actual basis for behavior, still the above (and other) tools allow us to grasp and assess with reasonable reliability the eventual distance between the two.

The comparative studies on various social systems, supplemented by sub-systemic inquiries (studies of sub-cultures, specific populations, etc.) make possible a tentative formulation of the following observations.

I When violation of the basic norms of social interaction is involved, the average population tends to condemn it more strongly

111

and to demand more severe legal sanctions than do officers of the law. Thus, the judges in Poland and in Finland and the tax officers in Holland are in general inclined to be somewhat more lenient toward cases of violating elementary principles of social interaction than is observed among the average population. The explanation for this interesting finding is not that officers of the law are less exacting, but that they are more aware of the inadequacies of coercion as a tool of social engineering, and are in a position to assess more realistically the possible range of applications of more severe condemnations and penal sanctions.

II The average population condemns violation of the basic norms of social interaction only slightly more strongly than do those who break the law themselves.

Both the Polish and the Dutch data reveal that the basic social values are fairly strongly internalized by the whole population and that those who repeatedly break the law (the recidivists) differ but slightly in the intensity of their moral indignation against the breaking of generally accepted rules. Supplementary studies of various legal sub-cultures, in particular negative ones, such as, for example, that of professional delinquents, would probably show that professional delinquency leads to a drastic lowering of the intensity of moral condemnations. However, even while such studies are still lacking, we can refer to the investigations of the recidivist subpopulation to modify proposition II along the following lines: even a slight lowering of moral indignation is related to a very significant lowering of demand for legal sanctions.[11] Thus, whenever moral condemnation lessens a little, legal condemnation lessens very much. This proposition appears to shed important light upon the moral origin of legal condemnations and leads us to observe attentively the store of moral values which may seem irrelevant to the law but still are likely to hinder or support its functioning very significantly indeed.

III In questions of procedure and order officers of the law more strongly condemn cases of misbehavior than does the average population, which in turn more strongly condemns them than do those who break the law.

The Polish and the Dutch average populations alike are marked by fairly strong negative attitudes toward violating the principles of social order. However, significantly, in both countries officers of the law, as if in the nature of their profession, always more strongly condemn this kind of misbehavior, while the recidivists, as if in the nature of their trade, always have less respect for such norms than does the average population.

IV A legal condemnation entails a moral one.

Before we undertook the Polish survey we had supposed that there were some types of behavior regulated by administrative and technical prescriptions which were morally indifferent; i.e., it was supposed that the breaking of these prescriptions would entail no moral condemnation. Surprisingly, it turned out in the Polish research, and it was confirmed by Dutch data, that a legal condemnation (inclusion of a behavior into the class of those legally regulated) brings about a tendency to view the given behavior in terms of moral judgment. It is remarkable that this relationship has been confirmed as well by subsystemic inquiries among social subgroups functioning within the larger whole. Thus the Polish study on recidivists revealed that this population, much as the national sample, tended also to condemn morally behavior which in their own opinion should be condemned by law.

v A high level of moral indignation together with its formalization in regulations of the penal law brings about the demand for legal sanctions; a high level of moral indignation which is not formally confirmed by law does not bring about such a demand.

This proposition results from a comparison of the Polish and Dutch data on attitudes toward adultery. It is strongly condemned in both countries (70·3 per cent of the Polish national sample and 81·8 per cent of the Dutch national sample). However, in the Netherlands the prevalent sentiment is formalized and adultery is considered a crime (though the relevant paragraph of the penal code is 'dead' and no longer applied in practice). In Poland there is no law against adultery. As a consequence 53·3 per cent of the Dutch population and only 16·7 per cent of the Polish sample want to have penal sanctions against it.

VI The higher the education the more reformation is considered to be the main function of punishment, rather than retaliation. Comparative data from both the Polish and the Norwegian investigations (the latter in this context being considered as a pilot study) confirm this relationship.

The findings (mainly diagnostic in character) have found confirmation in various social systems. However, not all of the tested hypotheses have been confirmed by the data. For example, the Polish data gave no confirmation to the proposition supported by Norwegian results that, regardless of education, women tend to be more severe than men in their condemnation concerning issues of morality (except for women who are big-city dwellers and those who are materially well-off), while men tend to be more severe concerning trespasses against property rights.

VII Pure rigorism bears an inverse relation to the level of education; pure tolerance increases with the level of education. However, rigoristic attitudes with respect to violation of the basic norms of social interaction and trespasses against minor regulations and

113

against property are more marked in the better educated respondents.

It can be seen from the above findings that some theoretical expectations find supplementary support in the systemic-comparative analysis, while others do not or are modified. Moreover, comparative studies of the co-operative type provide interesting information of yet another character. Thus it was found in a preliminary investigation prior to the survey proper that certain legal and moral attitudes typical for Polish society did not appear to a significant degree in the Netherlands. For example, social orientation in ethics (the tendency to appreciate an individual with reference to the social consequences of his role-performing or social position, rather than to his personal qualities) is marked among the Polish population, but hardly so among the Dutch. Among the Poles condemnation of a person for having been a Nazi generally takes precedence over whatever his personal merits are. In Dutch evaluations the private qualities would determine the overall balance. Similarly, Poles believe that for social reasons cultural relics in the possession of private persons should be protected against unlimited use of the rights of property. The Dutch declare the primacy of the right of an individual to dispose of his property at will.

In sum, co-operative investigations allow the peculiarities of various social systems and of the legal systems functioning within them to be grasped more systematically and with greater precision.

### Attitudinal studies on parental authority: USA and Poland

As noted earlier (p. 111) the subject matter of any specific study should be emotionally arousing enough to elicit definitive answers from the respondents, but on the other hand should not involve their interests so closely as to produce a tendency to systematic biasing of their answer. It also ought not to produce feelings of inferiority in the respondents. An investigation of legal sentiments should concern problems which are not too remote from the everyday experience of respondents and the problems must be amenable to formulation in simple everyday language.

It seems that parental authority is an issue of the right kind to be used in a survey of public opinion. Two such surveys will be reported below: an American and a Polish one.

The main aim of the American researchers was to investigate the following: (1) What are the consistencies and inconsistencies of the laws concerning parental authority and the society's legal sentiments on this issue? (2) Are those sentiments uniform throughout the population, or are they fragmented? (3) What, if any, is the influence of such factors as age, income, sex, education and religion upon the views concerning such law? (4) What motives and reasons are summoned by people to justify their views on parental authority? (5) To what degree do the results of sociological investigations justify the soundness of various specified legal prescriptions?[12]

The population studied (arbitrarily selected) consisted of the adult inhabitants of the state of Nebraska, with the exception of those detained in mental institutions and prisons. It was decided that one person per 1,000 adult inhabitants would be investigated, which meant 860 subjects. The questionnaire was prepared during the course of thirteen months. Its final version was elaborated after two pilot studies. The respondents were selected so that the sample of 860 persons would be representative with respect to the following criteria: rural or urban residence, race, nationality, income, number and age of children, property status, education, sex, age, profession, religion, and membership of associations and unions.

The survey was intended to cover three basic issues: (1) the tendencies toward either limiting or enhancing parental authority; (2) the degree and nature of the child's autonomy; and (3) whether support for the family should be the responsibility of its members or of the state. A number of detailed legal issues were located which could shed light upon these problems. The following considerations determined the selection of the legal cases employed: (1) the possibility of predicting exactly the court's verdict in the given lawsuit;[13] (2) cases which had concluded with final verdicts; (3) cases in which the legal opinions conflicted; and (4) such issues as would be likely to elicit controversy or towards which the collective attitudes would not be unanimous. Technical and statutory legal issues were excluded. Seventeen cases were selected with which to investigate the general problem of consistency or inconsistency of statute law with general public opinion.

The research revealed a consistency between the law and general opinion in only 5 cases; discrepancies were found in 10 cases, and in the remaining 2 an unambiguous interpretation of answers was difficult (opinions were sought on such issues as whether parents should be authorized to control their children's incomes, what the minimum age for marriage should be, and whether a child should be entitled to sue third parties responsible for disruption of the family).

Besides the detailed findings, some general results were arrived at. One achievement of the survey was the finding of discrepancies between the law as written and the views and opinions as to what it should be. Another was the discovery that the problem of the so-called 'age of adolescence' has not been legally regulated. As the authors report, while the period of adolescence and its peculiarities are clearly distinguished and recognized by the respondents, still the law of the USA does not construe it as a distinct legal category.[14]

115

An analysis of research results brought up the basic question: is the legal sentiment of a society essentially diversified depending on background characteristics of its various groups? The implicit answer, surprising to the investigators and constituting, as we shall see later, a starting point for studies of the problem of the prestige of law, was: no, it is not. Opinions concerning the investigated issues were relatively consistent; there were no serious differences between the views of men and women, of the young and the old, of those with higher or lower incomes, of country and city dwellers, etc. Wherever there were differences of opinion, they concerned details of the issues. Thus it can be said that there is something over and above individuals and groups which unites a society in its common attitudes towards fundamental problems. It can be predicted, however, that in other legal matters, more related to economic issues, extensive differences in legal sentiments of various social groups and classes would appear.

A comparison of the views expressed by men and women revealed that the differences, even though distinct, concerned only a few minor issues. Thus, men were more ready to limit parental authority with respect to the child's marriage, problems of religious education and health; women were more ready to accept such limitations with respect to the child's career choice, education, management of the child's property, etc. While the available data do not permit a definite statement that the views concerning parental authority of the two sexes differ, still they allow for a tentative hypothesis to the effect that representatives of each sex are less inclined to accept limitations set upon parental authority in respect of those matters with which they are most concerned. Indeed, in the life of American families it is the women who are more preoccupied with health, religious education, and marriage of their children than are most men. Consequently, the women are less inclined to accept limitations of parental authority with respect to these particular domains of family life.

Differences were evidenced also between the views of men and women concerning financial aid for needy members of the family, either by its other members or by the state. Men are more eager than women to have the burden of aiding the family transferred to the state rather than to its other members. To account for these differences, three explanations were offered by the authors of the study: (1) men are more willing to accept a child's emancipation and they acknowledge the rational consequences of the fact, whereas women feel more deeply related to their children, and their emotions reach beyond formally acknowledged emancipation; (2) since men are traditionally expected to support the family, they are more sensitive to the burdens of aiding its extra members; and (3) as has been indicated by other studies as well,[15] women are in general more conservative, and men more liberal.

What differences in opinions are there in terms of rural *v.* urban residence? The problem of who is and is not a 'city dweller' arises at once under American conditions. What are the criteria defining an area as an urban or a rural settlement? To distinguish between town and country inhabitants, the authors decided to consider the following factors as characteristic for the urban settlements: more impersonal and anonymous social interaction, more ethnic and religious variety among the inhabitants; greater occupational specialization; more obvious differences between job and family life; and greater differentiation of incomes.

What we know about urban and rural life in general would lead us to expect that it is the town dwellers who will be more apt than the country folk to hold the state responsible for aiding their needy family members. The results were quite surprising: it turned out that it is the rural population which believes that in such cases the state rather than the family should provide aid. As explanation the authors offered two hypotheses: (1) Rural migrants more frequently return from towns to their villages than city dwellers come back to the town of their origin; thus country folk appreciate more realistically the burden that falls upon a family when its 'prodigal' member comes back home. Cumulative experiences of this kind can bring about a negative attitude toward the prospect of supporting such kin and the desire that this responsibility be passed on to the state. (2) There is a well-established opinion (and much evidence in its favor) that country dwellers are more conservative than urban inhabitants. However, this view may no longer be valid, since so many changes have apparently occurred in the rural environment that one can hardly speak now of an overall conservatism of the country population. More researches are necessary to test to what degree this hypothesis remains plausible.

The professed religion also modified views on parental authority, or at least on some of its aspects. It was found that Protestants are more likely to accept limitations on parental authority than are Catholics. Thus, for example, 31·2 per cent of the investigated Protestant population opted for the exertion of parental authority if a child decided to change religious affiliation, and 54 per cent would keep their right to intervene if a child wanted to abandon religion altogether. Among Catholics, 54·7 per cent wanted to retain their right to intervene in the case of a shift of religious affiliation, and 73·0 per cent in the case of his abandoning religion entirely.

The investigators offered the following explanation for these discrepancies. The traditional type of family and of parental authority, with its frequent authoritarian character,[16] seems to be more

117

strongly supported by the Catholic than by the Protestant clergy. Besides, it is known from other sources that Catholic priests have more contacts, both formal and informal, with their parishioners than do Protestant ministers, and thus it is in the Catholic church that views and opinions are more efficiently propagated through personal interaction.

Another interesting question concerned who is likely to grant more freedom to their children: those with high school education or those without it. The general answer is: persons with high-school education are less willing to have their parental authority limited and to increase the autonomy of their children than are persons without such education. As is known, people with high-school education usually belong to the middle class of American society. It is also known that this class is marked by a very persistent urge to improve its social standards, mainly by raising the social positions of its children. Middle-class parents do their best to guarantee their children an education that will permit them to advance socially. This tendency, however, comes into conflict with an opposite one. Persons with high-school education are usually more liberal in their pedagogical views and are more ready to allow for, and to consider with understanding, views which are different from their own. In the domain of parental authority this would be expressed as a tendency to grant more freedom and autonomy to the children at the expense of the parents' rights. According to the authors of the research, the opposition of the two tendencies can be explained as follows. Educated people are likely to extend full parental authority mainly to younger children whose prospective careers have not yet been defined, while their liberal propensities come to be asserted when the child reaches adolescence and has formed some idea as to his future professional and social roles.

Also compared were views concerning parental authority held by those who have their own children and those who do not. Interestingly, those who did have children were more willing to accept limitations of parental authority than those who had none. The following explanation was offered. Those who do not have children tend to give more unqualified and peremptory answers to questions on parental authority, whereas those who are or have been parents themselves have learned from experience that it is more beneficial to a child's development and training that parental authority be subject to some limitations.

A summary comparison of a number of socio-demographic characteristics (sex, income, education, etc.) with opinions concerning parental authority led the researchers to formulate a general statement on the view of the investigated American population. Parental authority is modeled so as to be exerted to the child's advantage (even though this may sometimes be conceived in peculiar terms). Old-fashioned views construing parental authority as an authoritarian institution, occasionally based on a belief in the 'natural rights' of parents *vis-à-vis* their children, do not find many adherents. Parental authority is treated as a means to certain pedagogical aims rather than as an aim in itself. The general opinion would support statutory intervention so long as it provided for the appropriate rearing and education of children. It is apparent, too, that general opinion tends to support more autonomy for children than the laws actually grant.

Besides the topical conclusions concerning the scope and specifics of parental authority, the investigators found grounds for further generalizations. Seeking to explain why there is such an extensive discrepancy between legal sentiments and the positive law, they noted that family law is not exposed to any particular pressure-group activities. It is well known that American legislators are vulnerable to pressures exerted by various social and political vested interests represented by what are called pressure groups,[17] which would attempt to direct the legislative initiative in such ways as would be most advantageous to them. Better organized, wealthier and more active groups can often gain the upper hand over others which may represent much more essential social values. The fact that there is a remarkable internal consistency in the positive law regarding parental authority, despite the lack of legal sentiment to back it, may be accounted for in part, according to the research authors, by the absence of appropriate pressure groups. And as we know, in American law the system of precedents is remarkably developed and judges are apt to be intensely attached to traditional ways in the teaching and administering of law. Established procedures and routines are strongly resistant to change.

In comparison with other types of cases, there are relatively few lawsuits concerning parental authority. Conflicts between parents and children rarely end up in court. Since the cases are few, and hence so are papers, verdicts, glosses, appeals and discussions on these issues, other legal problems take precedence in legislative activities. The frequently deplorable consequences of court verdicts concerning the relationships between parents and children are simply no cause for alarm among legislators.

These considerations lead to a general hypothesis to the effect that the efficiency of the working of legal precepts is proportionate to the degree of support they find in the legal sentiment of a society. This idea was formulated in rather extreme terms by Bertrand Russell, who wrote:[18]

the Law is almost powerless when it is not supported by public sentiment, as might be seen in the United States during

119

prohibition, or in Ireland in the '80's, when moonlighters [and moonshiners in the USA—author] had the sympathy of a majority of the population. Law, therefore, as an effective force, depends upon opinion and sentiment even more than upon the powers of the police. The degree of feeling in favour of Law is one of the most important characteristics of a community.

A remarkable achievement of this American investigation is the finding, emphasized by the authors, that a supportive legal sentiment is not the only factor enhancing the efficiency of positive law. Another such factor is an acceptance of law through inertia. This was quite apparent in the discrepancies between the legal sentiment and the precepts concerning parental authority. However, law does work on the basis of support through inertia; conflicts requiring formal solutions do not materialize because the initiative to bring them out is lacking, and inertia is conducive to accepting the *status quo* rather than resisting it.

An acceptance of the law may thus have any of various origins and degrees of intensity. It can be an emotional acceptance based on a deep identification of the legal sentiment with the law; it can be supported by mainly rational considerations; or it may result from social inertia. In each case the degree of acceptance enjoyed by the law is apt to be different, and consequently the given law will be greatly or little respected, or somewhere in between. This kind of general statement underlies the studies on the problem of the prestige of law, which is strategic for its functioning.

Related to the American research is a Polish survey of opinions on parental authority, carried out in 1963 by the Center of Public Opinion Studies (Ośrodek Badania Opinii Publicznej) under the supervision of the author.[19] From a representative sample of the adult population of the country, divided into rural and city dwellers, 2,723 responses were obtained, comprising about 90 per cent of the initial sample of 3,000. The sample was drawn from indices of the *Statistical Yearbook* for the year 1961.

The Polish survey, taking advantage of earlier experiences, focused upon only a few problems which seemed to be the most significant. It included one aspect which had not been tackled at all by the American scholars—the problem of familiarity with the law. First, familiarity with legal principles was distinguished from familiarity with precepts of law. By legal principles were meant norms which are consistent with the basic legal notions; usually they refer to the shape of the basic rights and obligations and the basic categories of the allowed and the forbidden. On the other hand, precepts of law are mainly technical and procedural in character; they describe the available methods of realization of the objectives determined by legal principles. This distinction made possible a general finding that the knowledge of legal principles was fairly good, while the knowledge of precepts of law was relatively poor.

These findings seem to confirm the supposition that legal principles promulgated by legislators can be received by the population in various ways. Norms involving legal principles usually reach the people by a long practical training. They are learned in the context of observation of life, knowledge of legal events, patterns of personal and family experiences, etc. From the legislative point of view, internalization of legal principles is a long and complex process. Its expected outcome is acceptance of the enacted principles.

In the case of legal precepts the picture is different. These are most often worded in esoteric juristic terminology and are addressed chiefly to the guardians of the law, i.e. to those who execute the claims of the legal system, and who are professionally trained to comprehend such information. They know how to interpret legal language and are familiar with the procedures of applying it in practice. Hence it should be supposed, by way of a general hypothesis, that the average citizen becomes familiar with the law either through a long process of internalization of legal norms which are eventually transformed into legal principles, or else through imitating recurrent models of behavior of the executors and supervisors of law. As a result, the orientation of the citizens to the current form and contents of law depends not so much on their immediate access to its sources, but rather on their reading of law from the behavior of its officers.

The Polish legal system is based on different principles from those of the American one. By the time of the investigation in 1963, certain aspects of family life had been regulated by the Family Code of 1950. While its stipulations were changed to some extent by the 1964 Code, the investigations showed that the precepts of the 1950 Code were essentially accepted by the community.

Stipulations concerning the age at which civil rights are granted, effecting a change from the pre-war situation, were among those enjoying community acceptance. The open claiming of civil rights on the part of the young apparently reflects their strong desire for these rights and their wish for early participation in social and political life. It would appear to point, in any event, to great potential energies among the young generation, even if this does not necessarily always reveal itself in civic and political activities. It should be remarked, too, that it was in the educated groups that more people believed that civil rights should be granted at the age of 18, rather than the pre-war limit of 21 years.

A comparison of the Polish and American findings, even if the data are not directly comparable, is interesting in several respects. Opinions

E

121

on whether support of needy family members should be given by the family or by the state were distributed differently in Poland from the distribution in the USA. For example, in the case of the illness of a parent, among country dwellers with a rural background 67·9 per cent expected the help to come from the children and 28·4 per cent from the state; among the urban intelligentsia, 49·4 per cent favored support from the children and 45·3 per cent from the state. It should be remarked that the traditional view that in such emergencies the children rather than the state ought to provide help is still rather deep-rooted in some social categories. Urban inhabitants with rural backgrounds revealed an attitude rather similar to that of country dwellers: help from children, 55·9 per cent; help from the state, 38·9 per cent. The rural population of peasant origin favored help for the aged: from children, 64·0 per cent; from the state, 32·3 per cent. On the other hand, the urban intelligentsia favored placing the burden on the state: 40·9 per cent expected support from the children and 53·1 per cent from the state. Here, too, relics of parochial attitudes can be seen; the urban inhabitants with rural backgrounds, are attached more to their childhood or adolescent beliefs than to the opinions of their urban neighbors: 50·6 per cent believe that the children should help and 43·5 per cent view it as the state's obligation.

Thus the investigations carried out in Poland suggest rather than prove different findings from the American research. The Polish country folk still believe that the obligation to support needy family members should be *charged upon* their relatives (children) rather than on the state's agencies. The following explanation can be offered. The rural population (as well as town dwellers of rural origin) is still apt to think in terms of mutual help within the family or neighborhood, rather than of a businesslike way of solving problems by resorting to administrative agencies and institutions. This type of thinking induces one to depend first of all upon the narrow circle of people linked by family ties or material relationships, rather than on remote institutions where strangers often play incomprehensible bureaucratic tricks. An even more extensive generalization might be made that a comparison of Polish and American social environments reveals that in America human interaction is dry, businesslike and marked by a rational bent toward formal solutions even in private and family matters, while in Poland the predominating style is more emotional and humane.

As noted earlier, the following hypothesis was formulated by the American researchers: members of each sex are less likely to accept a limitation of their parental authority on issues which concern their own sex more than the opposite one. The American survey showed that men were more ready to limit parental authority with respect to a child's marriage, religious and health problems, while women were more ready to accept limitations concerning the choice of a child's career, his property, and his education. Polish investigations confirmed this finding to some slight extent with respect to property and financial matters (men's domain) and in still lesser degree with respect to religion (women's domain). In Poland, much more uniformity of opinion concerning parental authority was found, perhaps because in that country women are equal to men not only in their formal rights but also in their actual social and economic status.

Another American generalization, that people with their own children are more likely to accept a limitation of parental authority than are childless persons, was not confirmed. Polish data even point in the opposite direction. Again, the diversity of the two cultures might offer an explanation. Perhaps the finding that childless persons demand more parental authority is not a generalization valid for all of mankind but is related to the peculiar social setting. According to other studies,[20] children in the USA exert strong pressure upon their parents, and hence the lenient attitude of parents simply reflects their reconciliation to the hard facts. Cases are reported of parents not wanting to buy a TV set, being aware of the detrimental pedagogical effects of TV programs, but eventually having to give in under the impact of the children's demands—particularly when the children had troubles at school because they were not familiar with the current TV culture. Thus the attitude toward parental authority among persons who have children of their own can well be a consequence of the pressure exerted by the juvenile sub-culture, as well as by the larger community, i.e. by reference groups which advance a viewpoint, now fashionable in America, favorable to the extensive autonomy of children. It may be expected that the differences in this respect between Polish and American societies will tend to diminish because of the increasing claims and pressures of the juvenile sub-culture in Poland, too.

As has already been noted, both the American and the Polish studies on parental authority revealed a significant tendency to conceive of law as a single, structurally coherent pattern. It was also shown that the efficiency of law is proportionate to its support by the legal sentiment. Research on parental authority has thus contributed some valuable experience to opinion surveying, showing it to be a useful method for analysis of the extent of acceptance of positive law. Nevertheless, an important limitation on the methodology of opinion surveying must be kept in mind. Namely, it is difficult to determine how far the answers can be taken seriously. We cannot know the degree to which an answer is sincere and reliable, or to what extent it is mere verbalizing or self-serving. This intrinsic limitation in polling (offset as much as possible by various devices such as

123

control questions, or indirect questions, etc.) calls for supplementary studies by other methods. These methods should provide means to determine the degree of validity and objectivity of the results of opinion polls. The experiences described in this chapter might be applied in later investigations using opinion surveying.

# 6 The monographic method

When we study a social institution by the monographic method we try to grasp its functioning in all possible aspects, so as to assess its specific and peculiar character. There is much to be said in favor of this method. Its main advantage is that an analyzed social institution is intensely and deeply studied, and for the very reason of its specificity it is particularly useful in producing policy recommendations. However, it has a deficiency too; the conclusions it offers cannot very easily be generalized and applied to apparently quite similar situations.

There are two varieties of the monographic method. Traditionally, it consists of investigations of some specified institution. Various techniques can be applied: participant observation, interviews, questionnaires, document analysis, or even historical inquiries into the origin of the institution. Its other variety deals with abstract constructs rather than with actual institutions, such constructs being embodied in several actual structures each of which has its own peculiar features. The objective of this variety of the monographic method is not to gain insight into the functioning of one existing institution, but rather to study a general type which allows for many concrete modifications.

A study by P. Blau can serve as an example of monographic research of a legal institution by participant observation. Blau was placed as a clerical worker in a USA administration agency for a period of a few months, in order to study as fully as possible the functioning of the unit in which he worked and to describe the social and job profiles of his colleagues, their attitudes toward superiors, and the attitudes of the latter to their subordinates, and of the whole institution to its clientele. His investigations led him to the following generalization: if there are friendly, informal relationships between the employees of an institution, and if their official activities are isolated from their personal concerns and obligations, then the

125

institution works efficiently as an administration agency. Moreover, clerical workers who are very little appreciated by their colleagues tend to be highly punitive and aggressive toward the clientele. Of course, those generalizations refer to only a certain type of administration and they may not be valid in other administrative systems, or in specific agencies such as, for example, military administration. In the latter case, the element of formal orders is apt to come to the fore. The picture is also likely to be different in some peculiar situations, such as when the administrative workers are poorly paid.[1] Investigations by means of participant observation are relatively easy when the researcher who takes a job or enters into an environment is not very different from the other members of the studied community. However, quite frequently, cultural or professional barriers impede the observation of social behavior, which is fully possible only when the researcher is accepted by the researched group without reservations. In spite of this difficulty, the technique of participation is particularly valuable, since it provides access to all the details of the studied environment. 'Participation in the group life of factory workers permits learning their habits, the social norms accepted by them, the structure of informal groups and their social behavior, in their natural form.'[2]

I shall present below two examples of the use of the monographic method. The first will be an analysis of the situation of lay assessor judges. This example illustrates a standardized technique of monographic study, which aims at collecting data permitting a description of the situation of the assessor judges as a whole. The second example refers to what is called the 'second life,' which is widespread in a number of closed reform institutions. The term refers to a peculiar informal structure, essentially unknown to those who are not within it and having many features which are evaluated as socially negative.

## Investigation of lay assessor judges

Sociological investigations can be based either on verbal declarations of opinions, judgments or attitudes, or on the actual behavior of individuals or groups, observed in experimental situations. The studies which analyze verbal declarations are exposed to the charge that it is difficult to assess the relationship between the declarations and the actual behavior (if the latter occurs) in real situations. On the other hand, in experimental settings it is difficult to tell to what extent the awareness that the undertaken behavior is not real—even though it is of a kind that would at some time be experienced in real life—changes the behavior. In sum, researches on opinions deal with declarations without knowing whether they are consistent with behavior, whereas in experimental studies types of behavior are observable but are modified to an unknown extent by the awareness that they have been artificially evoked.

A general hypothesis can be proposed to the effect that discrepancies between behavior and verbal declarations concerning social activities occur only when people have some special reasons to conceal their real judgments, attitudes or opinions; if, for example, they have some private motives, or if they are professionally biased by the pattern of their social roles. In principle, however—and this is why the anxieties about the discrepancies between opinions and behavior seem to be exaggerated—people tend to reconcile what they do and what they say. This statement corresponds with the general theory of cognitive dissonance. It says that 'the incompatibility of beliefs acts as a punishment, and a reconciliation of two incompatible beliefs is felt as a reward';[3] when people act against their beliefs, they are threatened by cognitive dissonance. On one hand they pronounce certain opinions and accept certain norms concerning a definite behavior, while on the other they are more or less aware that their behavior is inconsistent with what they believe to be right.

For these reasons sociologists greatly appreciate any opportunities which allow them to learn what factors influence real and not faked behavior. The scope of such opportunities is rather limited, since social and ethical considerations forbid the manipulation of people's behavior without their knowledge and consent. Only on rare occasions is it not felt to be immoral to disregard this limitation.

In sociological-legal investigations there are additional problems. These are brought about by the fact that in law as in morality it is not possible to establish norms 'not in earnest,' if only because law tends to be universal; thus it is somewhat incongruous to make the range of its functioning dependent upon some ulterior reasons, such as scientific ones. Given this situation, sociological-legal researches which permit of gaining a direct, genuine and not pre-arranged insight into the process of the functioning of law are indeed something exceptional.

The investigations of the lay assessor judges belong to this category. They are remarkable not only because the actual events occurring within the investigated institution (the court) could be observed, but for other reasons as well. They were so designed that the views and opinions concerning the functioning of the institution, investigated alongside its actual functioning, could be confronted with the observed behavior of the people active within the institution.

Studies on lay assessor judges, i.e. assistant judges in criminal trials, began in 1964; they were carried out by a research team acting within the Institute of Legal Science of the Polish Academy of Sciences. The members of the team, led by S. Zawadzki, were: J. Bafia, M. Borucka-Arctowa, J. Kowalski, M. Rybicki, W.

Skrzydlo, A. Turska, Z. Ziembiński and A. Porgórecki (scientists); and A. Frydecki, Z. Kubec, Z. Krause, W. Kleniewski, and J. Wieczorek (judges). L. Kubicki acted as scientific secretary.[4]

The institution of lay judge is relatively little known in spite of its significant social function. There are now about 50,000 citizens in Poland who perform this function. Lay judges participate in about half of all the cases heard by the courts.

If we consider that during 1965, i.e. during the period of the investigations, courts of the first level heard almost 430,000 cases, as a result of which 222,323 adult persons were sentenced, among them 165,687 to terms of imprisonment, and educative and reformatory measures were applied to 29,730 juveniles, we can assume that those courts decided in more than 200,000 cases with lay judges as their members.[5]

The lay judges enjoy all the rights of judges, and have the same obligations as professional judges do. They are denied only the capacity to preside at trials and conferences. There are two lay judges and a single professional judge on the jury, so that the social strata represented by them are in the majority, except for those cases when a single judge is assigned or when only professional judges are admitted. Both the professional judge and the lay judges are entitled to express an opinion differing from that of the majority, in the form of the so-called *votum separatum*. The intention of the legislature, when the institution of lay judges was first established, was to introduce an element of everyday experience into court procedure. Another function of the lay judges was to disseminate the legal awareness gained and shaped by them in the court among their original social and occupational settings.

Thus, the lay judges, according to the legislature's intention, were expected to become societal judges, performing the function of liaison between the courts and society, and a *sui generis* factor of social control over the courts of law.

Though the lay judges have been active for almost two decades, our knowledge of the efficiency of their activity, the degree of their acceptance of their duties, and the attitudes of the wider judicial community and of their original occupational environments towards them has remained rather small. Perhaps as a consequence a number of opinions are current which are in many respects incompatible. According to some views, the institution of lay judges is a spurious device, i.e. one which appears or claims to fulfill its assigned role but whose actual social role is in fact negligible. According to others, the lay judges are a very important element of the socialist legal order, and their influence upon the apparatus of justice is extremely important from the political point of view.

The investigations were expected to provide answers to these questions as well as to describe the institution in its many aspects. The study was based on a questionnaire addressed to lay judges,[6] on interviews with them, on questionnaires addressed to professional judges, solicitors and public prosecutors, and on interviews with them. Elections of lay judges to their posts were observed and, finally, a peculiar technique was employed consisting of secret observation of the actual behavior of lay judges during the performance of their role. Thus the methodological technique noted earlier was applied in practice.

One of the main techniques of such a monographic method is the observation of human behavior and comparing this with the relevant opinions and attitudes. Sometimes the observation is under cover of a role performed within the group. E.g., a sociologist is employed in the court so as to enable him to become familiar with environment in some specific respect.[7]

The technical and operative routine of investigations carried out by secret observation was as follows. Court secretaries, graduates of legal faculties who were personally known by a member of the research team, were invited to collaborate. They were asked to fill out a detailed questionnaire (thirteen pages of print) concerning the course of the trial and the judges' conference in cases heard by penal courts of the first level. The main concern of the questionnaire was the actual influence of the lay judges upon the outcome of the trial.[8] The task of the applicant was to fill in the questionnaire carefully and in detail after the trial, and to supplement the objective data from the files. The questionnaire did not contain the names of defendants, witnesses, experts, etc., or those of the judges, and it was established in advance that it would be the duty of the applicants to keep these names secret if anyone asked about them. They were expected to refuse to reveal names even if some member of the research team requested them, for whatever reason. This stipulation had been made in order to insure the principle of anonymity for the study. Thus the investigated subjects were not to learn that they had been exposed to observation. On such an assumption official permission was obtained to carry out the project.

The study covered district courts in regional cities (64·2 per cent of the total number of judges), district courts in district towns (31·9 per cent), and regional courts (1·6 per cent).

The investigated cases were mainly those of crimes against the legally protected individual values (health and life), and of theft of public and private property. The defendants were mostly men (86·4 per cent) and most often in the age bracket of twenty-five to forty years. Their occupations were quite varied, but the majority were skilled workers employed outside agriculture, and the next largest group were unskilled workers. Their most frequent educational level was elementary; married persons prevailed, and those who were married and had more than two children comprised 20 per cent of all the defendants.

The main research problems, however, related to the social situation of lay judges and to their behavior during the trial proceedings and the conference for a verdict. They were mainly white-collar workers, the second largest group being skilled workers. Their educational level was most often high school. Most of the investigated lay judges were performing this function for the first time. A relatively smaller group (about 30 per cent) were in office for their

TABLE 6.1 *Lay judges interested in cases prior to day of the session*

|  | % Yes | % No* |
|---|---|---|
| Education: |  |  |
| elementary | 7·0 |  |
| high school | 8·7 |  |
| college | 15·2 |  |
| Term: |  |  |
| first | 7·0 | 91·7 |
| second | 15·7 | 83·0 |
| Court: |  |  |
| district town | 3·9 | 84·0 |
| regional city | 14·6 | 78·7 |

* In this and the following tables certain percentages do not add up to 100 per cent because some categories (such as 'no data') have been omitted.

second term, and a very small number for their third term. The bulk of lay judges were members of the PZPR (the Communist Party).

The investigated professional judges were mostly men between twenty-five and forty years of age. The second largest group were men between forty-one and fifty-five, and then women between twenty-five and forty.

The lay judges were assigned to cases in the ways normally accepted in their courts, i.e. they were not specially selected according to their qualifications, requests, the judges' requests, or in any other special manner. Their attendance record was very good, though it should be remarked that the data concerned only those trials that did take place, omitting those which were deferred or for some reason did not take place. In general, the lay judges were not reluctant to attend; such an attitude was reported in only 4 per cent of all the cases.

The lay judges were usually not interested enough in the cases they were expected to judge to look through the files before the day of the trial. It can be seen from Table 6.1 that those who reveal more prior interest in the subject matter of the cases are those with relatively higher education, those performing their service for a second term, and those assigned to district courts for districts which are part of regional cities. Not shown in the table is the remarkable finding that the lowest level of prior interest in the cases was revealed by women lay judges in the age bracket of twenty-six to forty (92 per cent 'No'). Lay judges have very little information or knowledge about the offenses or crimes to be judged by them from sources other than the court, and in general they do read the files on the day of the trial.

The behavior of professional judges is also interesting. They rarely

TABLE 6.2  *Lay judges showing interest during court proceedings*

|  | % Yes | % No |
|---|---|---|
| Men | 44·6 | 11·6 |
| Women | 50·9 | 7·3 |
| Education: |  |  |
| elementary | 37·5 | 9·4 |
| high school | 40·7 | 7·7 |
| college | 56·1 | 3·0 |
| Occupation: |  |  |
| unskilled worker | 32·1 | 28·6 |
| skilled worker | 46·3 | 5·6 |
| professional | 57·7 | 3·8 |
| Term in office: |  |  |
| first | 44·9 | 8·4 |
| second | 50·9 | 5·9 |

give the lay judges any information about the cases on their own initiative. It is also only on rare occasions that a professional judge explains to the lay judges the legal aspects of the case. He is not likely to give them any directives aimed at stimulating their active participation in the trial.

As can be seen from Table 6.2, lay judges do display interest during the course of the trials. These data reveal that women lay judges show more interest in the trials during their course than men do (the reverse of the showing prior to the trials). Persons with more education show more interest in the trials than the less educated. By occupation, the most interested are the lay judges who work in the professions (including the scientists in this category), followed by the skilled workers. Those in office for their second term show somewhat more interest than those in office for the first time.

The lay judges interfered very little with the course of the proceedings. Rarely, if at all, did they ask questions. However, when they did, it was usually to the point. Their attention appeared focused mainly on the evidential materials and then on the person of the defendant. They showed relatively little interest in the injured parties, though under this latter heading many of the questionnaires were left blank.

Men focused their attention—mainly and to a greater extent than women—on the evidence; the women showed more interest in the defendants. The evidential material was most likely to attract the attention of professionals; less interested were the white-collar workers, and unskilled workers the least so. Questions asked by lay judges during trials were usually unrelated to their occupations; the judges for the most part did not reveal their attitudes toward the case; and although the percentage of questionnaires with 'no data' under the relevant heading is fairly high, the lay judges appeared to follow very well the meaning of the motions made during trials.

The behavior of the presiding judge toward the lay judges was generally indifferent. In about 25 per cent of the cases he suggested that they might wish to ask questions, though he often did this in a very formal and cursory manner. According to the observations, the lay judges did not impair the authority of the court during a session, but rather tended to enhance it. However, here again 'no data' was a frequent answer.

It turned out that there was extensive agreement between the feelings of the lay judges and those of the professional judge as to the guilt or innocence of the defendant. This agreement, however, tended to be much less as to the legal ramifications. Here a unanimity of viewpoint was recorded in only about one-third of the cases. In about half the cases with verdicts of guilt the imposed punishment was suggested by the professional judge; in about a quarter it was based on the lay judges' initiative. When the latter hesitated or got confused, it was the professional judge who formulated the suggestion (in a number of cases, at least). In some cases the imposed punishment was the unexpected result of a conference. The lay judges, it was found, tend to favor less stringent punishment.

If there was a controversy during the conference for a verdict, it was settled in one of three ways. In about half of the cases there was no controversy at all. In roughly one quarter of the cases a settlement was imposed by the judge, and in the remaining quarter, compromise was arrived at by discussion. Less educated lay judges yielded relatively more often to the professional judge's views. First-term lay judges did so more often than second-termers, but at the same time they more frequently tended to voice disagreement with the professional judge. The lay judges played no direct part during the trial in about 65 per cent of the cases. In roughly a third of the cases they helped the professional judge, and in only a few cases did they appear to be an annoyance to him.

Several interesting relationships are revealed by correlating the actual role of lay judges with their various characteristics. From the data in Table 6.3 it can be inferred that: men influence the course of a trial more often than women and in fewer cases play no active

TABLE 6.3    *Estimation of the actual role of lay judges*

|  | Helped the judge % | Annoyed the judge % | Played no role % |
|---|---|---|---|
| Men | 33·7 | 1·2 | 62·9 |
| Women | 23·7 | 2·7 | 70·9 |
| Men: |  |  |  |
| 25–40 years |  |  | 60·1 |
| 41–50 years |  |  | 64·1 |
| more than 50 |  |  | 65·3 |
| Women: |  |  |  |
| 25–40 years |  |  | 69·8 |
| 41–50 years |  |  | 75·7 |
| Occupation: |  |  |  |
| unskilled worker | 28·6 |  | 71·4 |
| skilled worker | 40·7 |  | 57·4 |
| professional | 50·0 |  | 38·5 |
| retired |  |  | 74·1 |
| Education: |  |  |  |
| elementary | 30·5 |  | 65·6 |
| high school | 29·5 |  | 65·2 |
| college | 39·4 |  | 59·1 |
| Term in office: |  |  |  |
| first | 29·5 |  |  |
| second | 34·0 |  |  |

role; older people are more likely to be passive; professionals (including scientists) collaborate with the professional judge more than do skilled workers; retired people tend to play no role in a trial, and unskilled workers do only a little better; collaboration with the professional judge and an active role in the process are positively correlated with higher educational levels; second-term lay judges collaborate with the professional judge more than do first-termers. The observers estimated that the activity of lay judges during the trials had in most cases no discernible influence upon the outcome;

133

in a few cases it appeared to bring about a more severe verdict, but in more cases whatever influence there was manifested itself toward the lenient side.

The most interesting point in the research is of course a comparison of the actual role of the lay judges, as revealed by the observations, with expressed opinions and evaluations regarding it. Such a comparison enables one to assess the extent to which lay judges (and others who have professional contacts with them) objectively perceive the role performed by them. Moreover, factors determining the functioning of the institution can be identified. The study of a legal institution which is relatively young and which, based on new political and social values, has been introduced in the pursuit of democratic and socialist goals, can easily be thwarted by all kinds of normative biases. Declarations concerning the acceptance of such an institution and evaluations of its role can be biased by the atmosphere surrounding it. It is the task of research to reveal the extent to which those verbal declarations are or are not consistent with reality.

The data on declarations show that the lay judges strongly believe they do influence the verdicts. Thus 69·2 per cent among them believe that the judge never decides alone. While 17·7 per cent admit that this is sometimes the case, only 4·3 per cent declare that decisions are made by judges only. This belief of theirs is incompatible with the observations, which clearly show that lay judges do not play a direct part in the process in roughly two-thirds of the cases.

Even more interesting in terms of comparison are the declarations of various groups of professional lawyers. According to the statements of 85·4 per cent of the solicitors (out of 464 solicitors questioned, 103 or 22·2 per cent answered)[9] only very few lay judges actually influence the decisions of courts. Opinions of prosecutors were similar. According to 73·7 per cent of them (out of the 400 questioned, 194 or almost 50 per cent answered) only a few lay judges influence the verdicts. However, and this is most remarkable, only 46 per cent of the professional judges declare that lay judges do not influence verdicts (of the 386 judges asked, 107 or 28 per cent answered the question).

A reasonable conclusion would seem to be that the general role of lay judges should be defined as a passive one, contrary to their own image of their role. However, various other indices, such as that they are rarely absent from court, are interested in what is going on, ask matter-of-fact questions, systematically tend to make the verdicts less harsh, and get involved in controversies with professional judges, warn us that such a conclusion would be rather rash.

Resort to a general sociological theory will help us to understand the problem better. Sociologists distinguish various types of what they call 'reference groups.' The *positive* reference groups are those to which an individual aspires or strives to belong; they determine the behavior of the individual since they are the main source of the rules and values accepted by him. The *negative* reference groups are those which an individual actively or passively avoids. He would dislike being associated with them in his own eyes, and even worse in the eyes of others. The *comparative* reference groups are those to which an individual does not aspire, but their standards provide him with convenient criteria for evaluation of his own and others' behavior. J. Kubin has suggested that the concept of a fictitious reference group can be construed by introducing the criterion of actual empirical existence or the non-existence of the imagined group. According to this idea, sometimes a visible social group capable of satisfying an obvious social need is lacking. Fictitious groups created by the TV and other mass media are then used for comparing actual behavior with some perceived standard.

For the study of lay judges it seems fruitful to introduce another theoretical concept. It may also serve as an illustration of how the extensions of the concerns of general sociology into narrower fields can sometimes feed back upon the language of social research. This proposed theoretical concept is the *control reference group*.[10]

> By control reference group I mean a group whose evaluations of the principles of behavior are taken into consideration; though it is an object neither of aspiration nor of avoidance, the fact that its presence is acknowledged or taken for granted modifies behavior toward an adjustment of one's own relevant criteria to those which are known to be respected by the control group.

The lay judges, even though they may remain passive, carefully observe the course of the court proceedings in all its phases. Thus the professional judge is apt to be constrained by the two pairs of insistent eyes (often trying hard to see through the muddled procedure); it must be remembered that the lay judges are only in a formal manner subjugated to the presiding judge, for they remain independent of him along organizational lines. While the presiding judge is continuously active, the lay judges have only to remain passive onlookers—thus, even more attentive ones. When occasionally they do intervene, their remarks are business-like contributions. The judge cannot be unaware of the vigilant attention of his two monitors, and must be quite conscious of the limitations imposed upon him by their very presence. An experimental study—e.g. based on tapes of the same kinds of trials adjudicated by a team of three (a presiding judge and two lay judges) and by single judges—would indicate the extent of such limitations and whether or not the decisions of a judge are notably different if he is left alone.

From the various descriptions of conferences on a verdict (the questionnaire contained an open question calling for extensive description of the conference and the way it was handled) it can be inferred—and the quantitative data confirm the conclusion—that lay judges tend to represent the more lenient attitude, while professional judges are rather more rigoristic. This rigorism can be accounted for not by the judges' personalities or their professional routine and lack of sensibility, but by the peculiar institutional conditions. In fact, various suggestions and demands on the part of the administration and pressure from their superiors can induce judges to more severe attitudes than their personal propensities would incline them. Thus, whatever the final verdict, it would appear to be a net result of various tendencies interacting within the group of three. The observations of trials and of conferences on a verdict can therefore be summarized in the form of a general remark: lay judges are a peculiar control reference group for the professional judge within the judicial panel.[11]

It seems that we shall be closest to the truth if we say that at present it is the function called by our research team the 'function of social control' which tends to come to the fore. It consists mainly in the fact that the very presence of lay judges in a judicial panel influences the course of the proceedings, whatever the behaviour and attitudes of the parties involved might be. This function, expressed by the participation of lay judges in trials, even though it be wholly passive, has been tentatively called during the research 'the latent function.'

Among the objectives of the research, besides analyzing the actual social function of the institution of lay judges, was the advancement of sound practical working recommendations. These have been formulated by S. Zawadzki as follows:[12]

Several legal institutions seem to demand improvement. There are also several technical problems which have to be taken care of, such as:
(a) lay judges should be required to give up their positions after several terms, so as to secure actual rotation of duties;
(b) they should be assigned to trials by a system excluding the possibility of special or intentional selection;
(c) all lay judges elected for the given term must participate actively in the verdict-making;
(d) facilities must be provided permitting them convenient access to the files before a trial;
(e) there must be an institutional provision for the lay judges to present their views during the conferences on a verdict

independently, i.e. before the presiding judge expresses his opinion;

(f) the lay judges should be exempted from all redundant activities and obligations related to the presentation of their views, in particular from the obligation to write a justification whenever they outvote the presiding judge;

(g) the obligatory participation of lay judges in the first-level proceedings (simplified and executional motions) ought to cover a wider scope of cases;

(h) it should be reconsidered whether it might not be reasonable to introduce the social agent (i.e. the lay judges) to the second-level or appellate courts;

(i) lay judges should be institutionally guaranteed immunity on behalf of performance of their duties; and

(j) additional legal protection must be secured for them relating to the performance of their functions.

## Investigations of the 'second life'

All scientific investigations have several stages, from a formulation of the problem to the final conclusions that can be drawn from the results. The first phase is the identification of a theoretically or practically important problem and the defining of it in empirical terms so as to make it open to research. The next phase is the development of the problem into a series of questions that have to be answered and of hypotheses which must be tested. It is only at this stage that a research method can be selected which promises to answer the questions that have been asked and to collect the relevant data for testing the hypotheses that have been ventured. Field work then starts and, following this, its results are arranged and described, and generalizations as well as explanations of the discovered facts are tentatively offered. In the social sciences, the last phase of the research work consists in the formulating of directives for social engineering, intended to change some undesirable situation or to introduce improvements in some aspect of social or civic life.

Thus, a scientific method is the net product of many interrelated and complex factors. Its selection must depend on the starting point, as well as on the expected results. In the investigations of the so-called 'second life' it was the monographic method which seemed to be the most adequate for an analysis of this complex phenomenon.

In Polish scientific literature, the problem of the second life was formulated for the first time by S. Jedlewski. He wrote:[13]

I shall now consider more extensively the problem of second life in a reformatory and its consequences. The phenomenon simply cannot be avoided, inasmuch as the inmates, not screened with respect to their degree of demoralization, interact and influence each other continuously and steadily. Aggregates are formed, composed of individuals or of small or large groups, professing incompatible systems of social, ethical and cultural values, and even attempting to rule their conduct by such systems. Individuals and groups are unable to adjust to this type of situation, and may become completely disintegrated.

The disintegration of the community of a reformatory as a result of the activity of negative leaders is apt to eliminate the educative influence of the institution, i.e. the formal influence of teachers and administrators. If individuals or groups are out of the control of the reformatory institution, delinquency is of course enhanced. It must also be remarked that phenomena of this kind are related to psychoneurotic or even psychotic disorders, by no means rare inasmuch as the juveniles sent to reformatories are not properly screened.

What is called 'second life' in various types of correctional reformatory and penal institutions exists independently of the official life that is displayed to the outside world, and which is prescribed by the general norms of society and by the specific educational practice pursued within the institution. Its existence, as well as some of its features, had been known, but full knowledge of it was still lacking. It was not so much theoretical curiosity as practical need that induced us to undertake the complex study. To do so we chose, along with the monographic method, a few of the correctional, reformatory and penal institutions within which second life was most probably fairly developed.[14]

A number of basic questions emerged after a scanning of the relevant literature on second life: Is second life brought about by certain fallacies of the educative process? Or is it formed as a result of a faulty selection of stubborn and delinquent juveniles for reformatories? Is it perhaps an expression of the lack of didactic skill on the part of the personnel? Is second life a product of 'human nature' in a situation of particular oppression? Is it a result of some peculiar social processes occurring under isolation, limitation of personal freedom, and accumulation of reciprocal aggression?

The study of second life began with two monographs elaborated by S. Małkowski.[15] It was found that the inmates of non-penal, correctional institutions[16] are stratified. Their life is divided into two basic areas: official life related to school *and* controlled activities and, on the other hand, the hidden second life, governed by its own laws. The essence of second life consists in a peculiar stratification which can be reduced to the division of inmates into 'people' and 'suckers.' The 'people' are independent and have power over the suckers. The 'people' are all equal; they differ only in their degree of acceptance of the patterns of behavior that comprise the second life rituals. The daily routine of second life is strongly ritualized. The body of these rituals is called 'grypserka' (from 'gryps'—a slang word designating a letter smuggled into or out of a prison); Małkowski defined it as 'the inmates' language and its grammar.' In this language certain normally innocent words (as well as some that are not) are insulting and noxious to either the speaker or the one to whom they are addressed. In the first case it is said that someone 'belches out to himself'; in the latter he 'belches out to another.' A belching can be canceled and made innocent by saying 'with a big-cat' (original Polish: 'z kiciorem') or it can be rejected from another by saying 'with a return,' to which the belcher's retort is 'back to you again' (Polish: 'z abarotem,' with the hint of a Russian word meaning 'reverse' or 'turn'), throwing the belch again to the 'opponent' who then says 'with a windlass'; thereupon the belcher: 'up to you' and the opponent 'hi-cats' by saying 'with a hi-cat,' or else, if he wants to enjoy the belching for a moment, says 'up to you with no return,' so that it is not he but the original belcher who must 'hi-cat' (cancel out) his own belch.[17]

The most severe offense in the inmate community is tattling or informing on other 'people'. The preceptors, who are considered as 'zekses,' i.e. 'non-people,' cannot be in any manner informed about the elements of the inmates' life. 'Suckers' do not belong to the community and thus they can be tattled on; such a tip is not considered as informing. An inmate would be an informer only if he were to tell the preceptor about anything concerning a 'man.' A 'man' is one who is recognized as such by the other 'people.' It is also the 'people' who decide whether and when someone has 'suckered down' himself. One can sucker down oneself, or become a sucker, by:

1  informing on 'people' to the preceptors;
2  indulging in passive homosexual practices;
3  raping a 'man' or forcing him to wash his or someone else's socks;
4  washing someone's socks or feet;
5  taking food or cigarettes from a sucker or taking anything that a sucker has had in his mouth;
6  giving a hand to a sucker or defending him;
7  repeatedly belching out against 'people' or against himself, or not answering the belchings of others;
8  smoking a cigarette picked up from the floor in a lavatory;
9  drinking water in a lavatory if the door is open;
10  breaking one's word of honor (Polish slang: 'skrzywiać

zastawką'; literally 'to bend the bar,' but other interpretations are also possible);

11   eating from a sucker's plate; drinking from a sucker's cup; drinking water from a tap touching it with the mouth; rubbing oneself with a sucker's towel;

12   picking up a spoon or a fork from the wrong end;

13   maliciously refusing to learn 'grypserka' (the language);

14   sleeping in a sucker's bed;

15   eating in a lavatory;

16   barking (literally, acting like a dog); or

17   selling the secret language to the police.

It can be seen that one can become a sucker by a simple lack of due care. The 'people' then have the right to 'straighten up' such a sucker. This is proposed in particular if the suckered one has formerly been accepted by 'people.' The ignominy can be purified by flogging —but only once. The ritual demands that the 'straightened' must endure ten strokes with a belt from each of the 'people.'

The preliminary research formed the basis for further monographic developments. Investigation of another reformatory institution was thus undertaken.[18] Here it was found that the stratification of social positions was even more complex than had been expected. The inclusive category of 'people' was further subdivided into 'gut people' (Polish: 'git ludzie'; 'git' is a slang adjective of general approval, with a hint of the German 'gut', i.e. 'good'; 'ludzie' means 'people') and plain people. 'Gut people' are those who come from big cities, have experienced much, especially along criminal lines, have committed a number of offenses, have contacts with the underworld, and are marked by such qualities as cynicism, boldness, cunning, etc.

The 'suckers' are classified into three essential categories: first, 'clean suckers' who still have the chance to come back to the world of the 'people,' as they have not been disgraced by informing or by passive homosexual practices; second, 'clean suckers' who have informed on 'people' and therefore can never again be accepted as 'people'; and third, the 'dirty suckers,' the passive homosexuals who remain on the bottom of the social ladder and for whom there can be no return to the 'people.'

An individual coming to a reformatory or a correctional institution for the first time has to pass a test; he is in the phase of 'catch as catch can.' He is observed by the 'people' and after some time is included in the category which they find proper for him. If he had already been a 'sucker' in some other institution, he cannot rise to a 'man's' rank in the new one.

In the two correctional institutions studied earlier by the Team for Studying Social Norms and the Pathology of Social Life, the proportion of 'people' and 'suckers' was more or less equal. The inmates of this type of institution are directed there by tutelary courts, special agencies of national councils, etc.; they are 'difficult' juveniles, but in principle they are not delinquents. The situation was quite different in the reformatory that was subsequently studied by the team. A reformatory is a penal institution to which juvenile delinquents are sent by criminal courts. They cannot stay there once they have passed the age of twenty-one. A reformatory sentence is a rather severe one; usually recidivists are placed there. The stratification in the reformatory was different from that of the non-penal institutions: most of the inmates were 'people.' A later investigation undertaken in the same reformatory, since the discovered proportion of 'people' and suckers seemed to be doubtful when confronted with the earlier

TABLE 6.4   *Proportion of inmates*

|  | 1st study | 2nd study |
|---|---|---|
| Gut people | 10 | 11 |
| 'People' | 15 | 20 |
| Catch people | 1 | 0 |
| Clean suckers, eligible for straightening | 1 | 1 |
| Clean suckers | 1 | 3 |
| Dirty suckers | 1 | 4 |

results concerning correctional institutions, revealed that there was indeed an essential disproportion in the number of 'people' and suckers. The proportion remained constant between the two studies, though the investigated population was to some extent changed in the meantime. This is illustrated in Table 6.4.

In an attempt to explain the phenomenon of 'second life' the hypothesis was set forth that 'second life' was a product of prison and that it had been transmitted to correctional and reformatory institutions by various criminal contacts. To test this hypothesis, a study was made in a prison for recidivists. B. Zielińska conducted very intensive interviews with a selected group of recidivists over a period of two months.[19] Summarizing her results she wrote:[20]

The position of an individual in the system of informal relationships is a net result of many overlapping variables, each of which represents a certain hierarchy of prestige in the jail.

(a) the variable of age accounts for the classification of the 'youngsters' (under 21 years), the 'zgreds,' and the 'petty zgreds' (past middle age).

141

(b) The so-called 'bix' (the pattern of prestige among the youngsters) has the 'cwels' at the bottom, then the 'suckers,' then the 'men' (or 'people') and, at the top, the 'urkas.'

(c) The social and regional background distinguishes the 'people' from the 'yokels.' (At prison N, in which most inmates are from Warsaw and its suburbs, 'yokels' are those from remote regions of the country, betraying themselves by dress, accent, quiet behavior, and sometimes also by particular types of offenses.) . . .

(d) According to the type of offense, the following groups are distinguished: the 'thieves,' who are traditionally the jail elite, the 'bandits,' and the 'hooligans.'

(e) the prison standing is also important; first and second-termers are treated differently from the multiple recidivists.

The second life in prison is influenced mainly by the 'bix,' i.e. by the pattern of conduct related to the juvenile delinquent sub-culture, chiefly hooligan; the 'bix' is most conspicuous among the juvenile prisoners, the 'youngsters.' . . . The older recidivists and those who wish to appear 'reformed' to the jail administration usually prefer to stay away from second life. The 'old' thieves can even afford to be loyal to the administration and to refuse to participate in the excesses of second life, without risking the disapproval of the common opinion, because their reputation is sufficiently established. However, they by no means condemn second life. It is only their own interest and convenience that induces them to withdraw.

Second life is not a 'product of the prison,' since it is not observed among criminals sentenced for economic offences (offenses against state-owned companies—author's note). . . . Neither is second life a product of the prison conditions of life, for had it been so it would have been homogeneous in its extent, whereas the hierarchy of prisoners actually depends, in the prisoners' awareness, on the type of crime or offense committed. It should rather be supposed that second life is 'brought' into prison from the outside world by the underworld groups, among which the hooligan gangs are perhaps the most influential. . . . The extra-prison origin of second life can be evidenced by the fact that the position of an individual in the informal jail hierarchy depends on his criminal past and on his way of life in freedom, as well as on his position in the free underworld. For example, one can be accepted as an 'urka' in prison if he had been a notorious criminal before being sentenced, but the 'urking' or 'bixing' in prison alone, not supported by a genuine criminal experience, would not increase the status of an individual in the second life system.

Further investigation, also carried out by the monographic method and covering forty prisoners, sought to find out to what extent the principles of second life discovered in correctional and reformatory institutions functioned among the imprisoned belonging to the youngest age group.[21] The results essentially confirmed the earlier findings and added some new ones. Thus, according to the data collected in this study, the test period during which the position of a new inmate is decided is expected to last for about three months. However, this period can be much shorter, because:[22]

(a) The newcomer is quickly defined and classified; it can be felt what sort of person he is and he comes to be liked; (b) he (or his reputation) is known by some of the other prisoners and he may know them; (c) the knowledge of prison ways can be decisive (one who is well oriented need not undergo the test); (d) the test period is for the weak only; and (e) he may not have been able to go through the whole period because of being moved to another cell block.

The investigations shed light upon the functioning of second life and revealed many of its characteristic features. They also demonstrated that the existing second life stratification had many marks of cruelty. The question arises—why is this so? Analogies between human interrelations and some animal behavior may explain these phenomena to some extent, but are such explanations sufficient? Do they explain the complex stratification of second life and its basic line of division between 'people' and 'suckers'?

Various hypotheses were ventured to account for the phenomenon of second life discovered in the investigations. One is as follows:[23]

The second life of juveniles . . . is a social structure and a system of symbols associated with it, guaranteeing a continuous division into active and passive homosexuals, providing the former with moral justification for the sexual exploitation of the 'suckers' and allowing them to maintain a feeling of their own purity and morality.

'Second life' so conceived is a hidden mechanism setting in motion the social activity within one of the two distinct areas of life and institution. The system, in which two levels can be discerned—the symbolic one with the model division into two sexual castes, and the level of actual behavior—seems to be one inherent in sexual isolation. But then it can be supposed that elements of 'second life' are present not only among juvenile delinquents, or among young people with criminal propensities, but wherever the freedom of heterosexual contacts of young males is limited, i.e. in certain military regimes or in the system of boarding schools. The British system of fagging might be seen as an example of such an institution which has grown into a respectable tradition, a moral norm and a pragmatic vindication. However, the school situation creates different conditions because of the fluctuation of the age groups. Fagging also used to be a system consisting in unconditional domination and subordination, an asymmetric system with its peculiar folklore and with homosexual undertones which can be heard behind the reminiscences, but the element of inter-caste mobility was added to it. Each fag knew that after some time he would have his own fag. This is a different model, with different psychological tensions and moral attitudes from those in the closed and essentially unchanging structure of the 'second life' of penal and reform institutions.

This hypothesis seems to be too narrow. In the first place, second life involves inmates who, because of their age (sometimes only eleven or twelve years) hardly seem motivated by the sexual drive to the extent that it would be the predominant element of the social structure to which they aspire, and second, other factors seem to play more significant roles here.

All those who are inmates of punitive and isolative institution (correctional, reformatory, custodial, penal) can be called—for convenience and after A. Kojder—'imprisoned.' Thus according to our basic hypothesis aiming to explain the functioning of second life, it is not isolation that is the basic oppression for the imprisoned, but the cumulation of punishments resulting from the interpersonal patterns in which they must live because of the isolation. Obviously, the imprisoned are deprived of several vital rewards which are enjoyed by people in normal situations. They are devoid of fancy or individualized food, sexual relations, convenience, opportunities to pursue individual interests, ability to move without limitations, privacy, etc. They are also deprived of an extensive sphere of the imagination. The gray everyday world in freedom, not to mention the luxurious festive days, seem to be superbly gorgeous and interesting in comparison to the monotony of isolation. When the normal world is beyond access, not only does the stock of stimuli become poorer, the world of associations emaciated, and the continuously repeated emotional feelings less and less differentiated, but—and above all—there is an enormous increase in the number of repulsive, conflict-bearing or frustrating situations, mutual aggressions, distrust, suspicions and claims, clashes of incompatible habits, tactless remarks, and practical jokes.

The imprisoned are exposed to all the oppressions of isolation. Their frustration certainly tends to be taken out in some manner on the representatives of the resocializing process, i.e. on teachers, guards, psychologists, administrative personnel, etc. However, the aggression directed against this category of people is moderated, for the administration has the real power. Still the overt aggression does not disappear or become neutralized, but remains intense, though hidden, as experience increases. Such accumulated aggression requires some vent, or a reward which is typical for an artificial situation. Such a paradoxical reward can be aggression against one's mates. For a group subject to pressure there are several ways to strive for inner reintegration. One is through a re-emphasis of the group's solidarity. This usually happens when there are certain supra-personal ties, such as a common task. Another is the transfer of aggression toward the group as a whole or to its individual members by mutual interaction. A third way is the building of a 'second life' of the group.

The imprisoned are isolated from the outer world. The visible representatives of this world are for them the prison functionaries. In their eyes, the functionaries are their main oppressors. However, since any action against them is risky and dangerous, it is convenient and attractive to transfer the aggression against the other inmates, thereby multiplying it. However, the prison world is not a world of continuous aggression and total chaos. Even the informal community of the imprisoned requires some amount of order. Mutual aggressions are thus arranged in certain patterns. They are regulated by the structure defined by second life. It is a system which transforms the universal reciprocity of punishments into a pattern of punishments *and* rewards, arranged by the principles of stratification. Some members of the community are in the position to transform the punishments into rewards.

How does the transforming mechanism of second life work?

In the normal world, where there is virtually no isolation, human interaction is essentially a source of mutual gratification. The increasing dryness of human relationships which appears in various social systems induces a tendency to look for substitutes, such as drugs. However, where there is intimacy as well as social distance available, people seek contact with each other because they find emotional rewards. They tend to accept each other spontaneously without any instrumental reasons: interaction as such is rewarding for them. In the situation of isolation, however, interaction is a source of punishment. Individuals reject each other. But the rejections cannot possibly break the system within which they occur, for it is a closed system in which people are condemned to live together; thus, rejections come to lose their essential character. They become instrumental. A man is no longer an object in himself, but becomes a means to something else, namely to secure substitute rewards.

In consequence, second life consists in an artificial but rigoristically observed social stratification. Being pushed to a lower position in the rank order is a punishment, while advancement in it is a reward. Thus, in a world in which there are no real things, a man is reduced to the status of a thing by being pushed to a low position in the rank order and within a system which has no extra-personal tasks to be realized by its members. One of the essential human features is dignity. To be able to maintain it, a man must not be humiliated, i.e. he must be in a position not to agree to others' behavior which he feels is humiliating for him. When a man becomes a thing, he is thereby continuously humiliated. Homosexualism, if it does not derive from an inner need, is an objectification and instrumentalization of the body. Since in general people feel that their body is an integral part of their person, its instrumentalization is also a reducing of the person to the status of a thing. The perverse world in which reducing others to things is a source of gratification, by transforming a punitive situation into a rewarding one, can also be seen as a desperate attempt to rescue and reintegrate one's own person against the cumulative oppression which threatens to disintegrate it. Thus second life is even more sinister, as it can be interpreted as a defense and a means of reconstruction dependent on the total disruption of the personality by others.

Such a general mechanism seems to account for several phenomena. It can be expected that second life will be more developed in populations whose members are apt to have less personal integrity. In fact, the researches point out that it is more widespread among the younger than among the older. Second life would contain more magical elements when ways of behavior relating to practical life are less developed. In fact, older prisoners, with some experience of work and life behind them, reveal less ritualization than the younger; for example, they tend to reject the principles of 'grypserka' (secret modes of communication). Factors which favor the escape into second life are the compulsive mechanisms of school in correctional and reformatory institutions, and the lack of work in prisons. Girls and women, who usually put the main emphasis in their private life on the family and who in general find less gratification in the outer, objectified patterns of human relationships, tend to suffer less when those patterns are transformed into a source of punishment and, by building various substitutes for family life, seek escape into the second life world less frequently than men do.

Such are the tentative explanations of the detailed findings. Here is the eventual general correlation: in social systems and situations in which the essential type of human interaction consists in acceptations and in gratifications which are brought by them, there is no ground for an emergence or development of the phenomena of second life; in those social systems, however, in which the pattern of instrumentalism and exploitation predominates in human interrelations, second life finds favorable conditions for its development.

A general question thus arises: what should be done to get rid of both the symptoms and the causes of second life, or at least to reduce them to the possible minimum? The basic factor that promises to do away with second life is the finding of such ways of modeling the informal interrelations as are apt to be more attractive than whatever is guaranteed by the second life pattern. However, this general directive involves complex problems related to its practical realization, or to translating it into detailed recommendations.

To this point I would like to direct the remarks by A. Krukowski in his tentative synthesis of the problems of the sociology of reformatory institutions.[24]

Three factors have to work together in order to suppress second life: (1) the formal organization of the institution (i.e., of both the personnel and the inmates) should be so changed as to maximize the essential objective of a reformatory, i.e., resocialization, by means of satisfying the genuine psychosocial needs of the imprisoned. (2) 'Grypserka' as a social system should be controlled and then eliminated. One of the means to accomplish this can be the disintegration or breaking up of the groups of 'grypsers' by making them less attractive for a number of their members, manipulating the rivalry of the leaders, organizing the existing antagonisms or conflicts between the group members or various statuses, eliminating the antagonism between the 'suckers' and 'people.' One type of such manipulation may consist, as J. Włodarek suggested, in transforming informal groups into semi-formal and formal ones, e.g. by organizing educative teams adjusted to the interests and needs of the imprisoned, controlling their task performance, rewarding or punishing such teams as wholes so as possibly to bring about a shift of their objectives and norms or even their disintegration. . . . (3) The relationships between the inmates and the personnel should be so shaped as to produce a climate favorable for the processes of resocialization; a genuine contact consisting in partnership ought to arise between the two groups.

This means above all that the way of treating the imprisoned which has been typical for the traditional prisons ought . . . to be radically changed: the repressive and reluctant attitude of the functionaries must give way to a cultured and friendly approach, marked by respect for the human rights and needs of the prisoners and by a readiness to help them in anything that is reasonably their due.

147

As to the postulate of the changes in the formal organization of reformatory institutions, two issues have to be stressed: (a) the social isolation of prisoners ought to be reduced (this need not mean more lenient conditions of life inside; for some categories of criminals conditions may well remain quite severe); and (b) prisoners ought to be properly classified and distributed.

Even though some of these proposals might be open to discussion or doubt, still they can provide a starting point for considerations on how to remedy the present deplorable situation in some reformatory institutions. For by means of the monographic method of research, an interesting descriptive diagnosis has been produced, a theoretical explanation has been offered, and suggestions have been made which could contribute to the lessening or elimination of some of the undesirable phenomena.

# 7 The experimental method

The application of sociological methods in legal research is particularly useful in three basic types of situation. First, when a need arises to gain an insight into the existing state of affairs and to arrive at a diagnosis of the forces and factors which determine the studied section of social reality. Second, when the objective is a testing of certain assumptions and hypotheses upon which legislation is or could be based. The task consists then in formulating clearly the underlying assumptions, either expressed or tacit, and in determining to what degree they are valid. And third, sociological methods of research can disclose whether enacted legal precepts have attained their intended effects, and whether or not they have also brought about any unexpected and undesirable effects. Data secured by these methods are likely to be more reliable the more quantitative they are (provided that the methods themselves are valid) and the more opportunities there are to apply the experimental method. However, it must be remembered that the experimental method can be conceived and applied in one of two ways: rigorously or loosely.

An experiment can be said to consist of the testing of a hypothesis concerning the interdependence (or its lack) of two or more variable factors by manipulating one of them in such a manner as to be able to observe changes in the other factor or factors.[1] The procedure runs as follows: a hypothesis concerning the relationship between two factors is formulated; a real empirical situation is arranged in which one of the factors is involved; this factor is manipulated and it is observed how the other factor is modified, if at all—i.e. whether the changes are or are not consistent with the hypothesis. If changes in the manipulated factor are followed by changes in the observed one, it can be stated that there is an empirically identified relationship between the two.

149

This method, though quite fruitful, presents many methodological difficulties. One of the most troublesome problems related to experimenting in the social sciences is to keep constant the factors associated with an experiment. Real social settings are so complex that it is very hard indeed to build up situations in which the additional factors remain at least approximately unchanged. Thus the primary and more rigoristic meaning of experiment refers to a situation which has been deliberately arranged so as to identify the relationships among the factors involved in it by manipulating them or making them influence each other.

Sometimes, however, the meaning of 'experiment' in the social sciences or in considerations of social practice is construed differently. We speak of an 'experiment' when we have arranged a situation, or introduced some new type of social link, or a model or pattern of behavior, and then try to evaluate the effects of the newly introduced factor. In this case it is a general judgment that is our objective; it is pursued by observing various consequences brought about by the new institution, or new pattern of behavior, in the course of its actual functioning in social reality. This is obviously a broader and more liberal usage of the word 'experiment.'

In what follows I shall present and discuss investigations of so-called 'social courts'[2] considered by official initiators as a social experiment. In this context I shall thus speak of an experiment in the latter of the two meanings of the term. It should be noted, however, that here it is the legislators who were doing the experimenting, with sociological researchers independently formulating the hypotheses and carrying out the investigations.

A number of initial hypotheses were formulated before the investigations on social courts were undertaken. They were:

1 conventional means of penal repression are often insufficient and do not discourage certain types of socially negative behavior;

2 the pressure of public opinion exerted by the job environment is in many cases more efficient than the nuisance of a criminal procedure;

3 the influence of public opinion in a given job environment depends on the integrity of the employee community;

4 an immediate repression is more efficient than a delayed one; and

5 socialization of the means of production leads to the emergence of new forms of legal sentiment related to the use of these means and to the distribution of their products.

Besides these theoretical issues, several diagnostic problems also arose. The main impulse for undertaking the studies on social courts, as well as their basic objective, had been the need to describe the institution of social courts and their actual functioning, in matter-of-fact rather than impressionistic terms, so as to form a clear image of their emergence and working.

In consequence, the following problems were set forth for study: 1 Is the judging by social courts, i.e. forcing a company employee to face his colleagues who would collectively condemn him, an efficient means of preventing petty offenses and trespasses? 2 Is it or is it not true that leaving certain cases to social courts rather than sending them to normal courts leads to the emergence of double justice—one for the citizenry at large, and another for those who happen to be employed in companies in which social courts are functioning? 3 Are social courts approved by the employees of the companies in which they exist? 4 Is the selection of cases submitted to social courts proper with respect to the types of cases, the institutions which submit them, and the persons of defendants? 5 What is the influence of the legal regulations concerning social courts upon their actual working? 6 Do social courts, besides their direct effects in the suppression of petty offenses, bring about any other consequences which are positive for company managements? 7 What if any, unintended negative effects have been noticeable in the activity of social courts? 8 Can the present functioning of social courts be improved, and in what manner and degree?

The above list is by no means exhaustive, but the questions noted are the most essential ones, and the answers to them concern the factors most significant for the success of the experiment of social courts.

Investigations were carried out in several phases. Here I shall report mainly the basic research, carried out in the initial phase of the project. This phase, lasting for three months, covered a limited territory (only the voivodship, i.e. region, of Wrocław), and the early period of functioning of the social courts (last three months of 1960).[3]

The research techniques employed were: interview and questionnaire, document analysis, content analysis of press materials, and participant observation. The use of various techniques promised more objective results as they could be cross-controlled. The following factors were taken into consideration: the size of the companies in which social courts were operating; the size of the towns in which companies with social courts were located; and the size of these companies (number of employees), sex distribution of their employees, type of production, and degree of training of employees. In the questionnaire inquiry among employees, the quota sample technique was used.[4] The criterion of selection was the type of job, three job groups being distinguished: clerical, skilled workers and technical personnel, and unskilled workers. The interviews were made by means of questionnaires prepared in advance. Another group of respondents were divided into three categories and a separate questionnaire was prepared for each. The first category consisted of social workers (who were interested in establishing social courts), such as party activists and union workers sponsoring the social courts on behalf of the town, district or regional authorities; judges of courts of law and prosecutors; social, party and union activists of companies with social courts; representatives of the workers' self-government agencies; and judges and secretaries of the social courts. By means of the questionnaire and a number of supplementary conversations 64 interviews were carried out with this group. The second category, consisting of the employees of companies in which social courts were functioning, yielded 151 interviews. The third category, defendants in the social courts, yielded 11 interviews.

Analyses of documents and materials were limited to the scrutiny of documents which recorded the organization and functioning of social courts. These were: regulations for social courts; 'directives' for social courts elaborated by the regional (voivodship) court; an eighty-page report of a conference of the lawyers of Wrocław on social courts; a memorandum to the regional committee of the PZPR (Communist Party) concerning the activity of social courts; a prospectus of a bill on social courts elaborated by the Ministry of Justice, together with its justification; and a few others. The most ample research materials were provided by protocols of trials held in social courts. Out of approximately 70 trials carried out, 48 protocols were obtained and analyzed. Documents concerning the ways in which social courts were summoned in some companies were also considered. One trial in a social court was directly observed. A questionnaire was sent to the managements of all the companies in which social courts were active, asking for quantitative data concerning offenses against their property—before and after the introduction of social courts. A separate source of information were the reports of research team members who sometimes succeeded in obtaining various data extending beyond the scope covered by the questionnaires, interviews, and data contained in documents. Some supplementary materials on the social factor in the system of justice could be obtained from scientific and press publications, rather scanty at this time.[5] The results can be briefly presented in the form of summary answers to our eight questions.

*Re* 1 As to the efficiency of social courts, the data show that in the general opinion of employees they are an effective means of suppressing theft in the enterprises. Thus, out of 112 respondents, 83 considered social courts to be an efficient means, 9 persons believed they were not, while 20 had no opinion. The opinions of social workers also can be interpreted as affirmative in this respect.

An objective evaluation of the efficiency of social courts was attempted as well. A questionnaire asking about the number of thefts before and during the six months following the introduction of social courts was sent to sixteen companies in which the courts were functioning. Only four companies responded and their answers do not permit of stating with any degree of certainty whether the number of thefts had actually dropped. However, decrease in the number of thefts cannot be the only measure of efficiency of social courts, for in some of them hooligan offenses and family conflicts also are solved, and it is difficult to evaluate in numerical terms the success of the courts in these kinds of case.

Some responses can serve as indices of the deterrent effect of social courts: (a) in one company a defendant declared that if his case was sent to the social court he would commit suicide (the case was judged without admitting an audience); and (b) many workers declared that trials in social courts had a very strong deterrent influence because of the fear of shame. One of the research findings was that men are probably more vulnerable than women to the punishment of being publicly shamed, whereas women fear fines (which impair the situation of the whole family) as a more severe repression.

*Re 2* The question of whether the existence of social courts leads to double justice and creates feelings of injury can be answered as follows. In general, the legitimacy and authority of social courts were not questioned either by the majority of employees or by the defendants at the time of the research. As far as we learned, none of the defendants had quit his job after the social court's verdict; only one defendant failed to appear in the court and only one pleaded not guilty. All 11 defendants considered their verdicts as essentially sound but only 3 accepted them without reservations, 8 objecting to some points. The objections can be grouped into three categories: 1 a feeling of being singled out: 'Why was it just me who was picked by the social court?'; 2 the feeling of disproportion between the committed offense and the 'punishment' (e.g. theft of an object worth 20 zloties—i.e. less than one dollar or 40p—and the shame of having to face the whole personnel of the company); and 3 the social court can lead to double jeopardy: 'What authority can a social court have if a case judged by it then goes to a court of law?' (One such case was noted.) Most employees, as well as social activists, consider the verdict of a social court as a punishment rather than a mere opinion.

*Re 3* There is considerable evidence that social courts are accepted. The question of whether punishing by shame is right, just and effective was answered 'yes' by 110 employees, 'no' by 2, and 'I don't know' by 6. Those asked about the attitudes of their colleagues toward social courts gave 99 favorable answers and 8 negative ones, while their own opinions were favorable in 117 cases and negative in 9.

Among the social activists, to the question of whether they found critical attitudes toward the institution of the social court, 53 per cent answered 'no,' and 36 per cent, 'yes.' Those answering 'yes' commented that a few negative opinions criticized the courts as being incompetent; some cited opinions against judging workers only. In general, the answers indicated that the critical opinions referred to details rather than to the institution as such. Analysis of a control question confirms the sincerity of the answers. Of all 122 respondents, 20 answered 'yes,' 96, 'no' and 6, 'I don't know' to the question: 'Would you like to be elected a judge of a workers' court?' The high percentage of 'no' answers is to some extent accounted for by the respondents' belief that they were not qualified to be judges. Of 147 responding, (some identical questions were addressed to social activists and employees) most believed that suitable persons had been elected to be judges of social courts.

*Re* 4   One of the essential problems was proper selection of cases sent to social courts. First, what types of case ought to be dealt with by these courts; second, who (what agencies or individuals) should send them there; third, on what basis should those be selected who are to be judged by these courts.

Most social workers favored sending to social courts cases of theft (mainly petty ones); 30 per cent wanted to have hooligans judged by them, and about 10 per cent declared that minor suits of libel and insult ought also to be included. Analysis of forty-eight protocols of trials revealed that petty thefts accounted for somewhat more than 50 per cent of all the cases.

Cases directed to social courts were, in fact, selected by several overlapping criteria. The main criterion was simplicity of the deed, the fact that guilt seemed well established, a relatively low value of the article stolen, and an unambiguous social evaluation of the offense. Simple cases were selected so that the judges, newly elected and inexperienced in legal subtleties, could easily handle them. In selecting the cases, the personality and background of the defendant was not always taken into account—in one case, as already mentioned, trial in a social court had to be conducted without an audience because the defendant threatened to commit suicide if the trial were public. Various data lead to the conclusion that offenses committed by persons who are known as not very scrupulous about the company's property or who do not enjoy the good opinion of others are rarely dealt with by social courts. The fact that cases for social courts are most frequently selected according to type of offense, so as to make the procedure as easy as possible, means that some categories of people—among them the administrative and managerial personnel—whose cases tend to be more complicated are not directed to the social courts; this has led to the feeling of 'workers' courts and courts against workers' (at the time of the study the institution was called 'workers' courts').

*Re* 5    It is only since 1965 that there has been a bill regulating the legal status of social courts. At the time of the study such regulations were lacking, and this caused a certain skepticism toward these courts, above all among professional lawyers. However, skepticism was felt among the workers as well; the stability of the institution was doubted. Such feelings were reflected in some of the answers to our questionnaire and also in statements made by judges of these courts.

*Re* 6    In general, the answer to the question of whether social courts, besides their role in suppressing offenses, had led to other positive effects in the social and administrative work of companies was affirmative. However, such positive effects were not felt everywhere. In three companies of the four responding it was found that social courts had actually contributed toward improving the company's operation. For example, due to the court's suggestions:

a    It was decided to prevent the stealing of a particularly expensive washing powder by distributing it from a dispenser in liquid form. A relevant order was issued by the administration.

b    It was arranged that when supplies were dispensed, their description and quantity was recorded so as to avoid cheating or fraud.

c    Arrangement was made to catalogue the items in the dining-room and to control the supply.

*Re* 7    Several unintended and undesirable effects of the functioning of social courts were also discovered by the research. Among them were:

a    In two cases it was found that persons not belonging to the panel participated in a secret conference of the judges, which was a violation of the elementary principles of the procedure and led to negative opinions as to the pressures exerted upon judges in the phase of formulating their verdicts.

b    In one case the competence of a social court was not properly defined and the case, after it had been judged by this court, was sent to a normal court of law. This brought about a sudden decrease in the number of those (spectators) present at the next trial and gave rise to generally negative attitudes toward social courts. However, in this particular instance the negative reaction could have had a unique and independent cause. In that factory social property was rather frequently stolen and there was a fairly 'sentimental' mood about the fact (the product manufactured was alcohol), so that latent negative attitudes toward the social court could already have been present, needing only a rationalization such as the case already judged by the social court being later sent to a regular one.

c  It was found that, against the intentions of the organizers, in many cases only those employed in the same section of the company as the defendant were interested in his trial, rather than all the employees as a body.

d  As a result of the activities of social courts it was revealed that some workers did their own personal work in the factory, particularly when they could not do it elsewhere. Frequently they just wanted to use the factory's tools and facilities. Summoning people to social courts for this kind of trespass was not well received by the workers.

*Re* 8  The research suggested that the organizational pattern of social courts which existed at the time could be improved by considering the following:

a  Too frequent court sessions lead to a decrease in interest among the employees. Too rare sessions, however, require exceptionally careful selection of cases; moreover, it allows people to forget about the existence of the court. Selection of cases ought to be based on open, commonly familiar and accepted criteria, so that defendants would not get the feeling of being singled out unfairly. Such a criterion could be, for example, repeated breaking of the law or regulations in the same company, such as the fact that a similar trespass by the same person had already been handled by the company's administration.

b  If social courts were authorized and obliged to conduct the investigations, the whole procedure might be improved and made shorter. As it is, the investigations are made by the factory guard, the management, the police, the prosecutor, and the management again, and it is only after all this that the social court enters. But it has been observed that a trial in a social court exerts stronger impact and its 'social resonance' is greater when the interval between the offense and the trial is not too long.

c  In some instances, mainly where it has won sufficient authority for itself, the social court can not only crystallize opinion into condemnation of antisocial behavior but also act as a tutelary institution. An offender may prefer being judged by the social court to being fired from his job.

d  A determination should be made as to the openness of trials in social courts. Should they be open to the general public, or only to the employees of a given company? When would non-employees be admitted? In what cases should the trials be held without an audience? Can the trials be publicized by the mass media? And so forth. During the inquiry, mixed procedure was admitted.

e  At the time of the investigations it was not clear what punishments, if any, could be inflicted by social courts and, consequently, what their competence was as compared to regular courts of law and penal administrative collegiums. The research led to the recommendation that until the proper legal regulations were enacted, the courts of law and the police and prosecutors' agencies should respect the verdicts of social courts.

f  The research gave support to the frequent postulate that the defendants be entitled to make appeals against the verdicts of the social courts.

An analysis of the data showed that in several cases, particularly those of petty theft of public property, the traditional means of repression had been insufficient and that new modes were useful. The impact of a trial in a social court was often strong and its discouraging effect quite efficient. The means of repression hitherto generally employed had been relatively slow and without much effect on prevailing opinion. On the other hand, what a person believes others think of him, or the 'reflected ego,' as F. Znaniecki used to label it, is one of the most personal, intimate and precious values cherished by anyone. If the opinion of a group is mobilized in order to show that it disapproves of a person who up to then had believed he was positively valued by others, the person censured can experience a real shock. It can be said that in self-evaluation we rely more on others than on ourselves. A prison term or a fine does not necessarily influence the image of the reflected ego; public condemnation can exert a much stronger impact.

A further finding was that mobilization of public opinion was by no means always easy or possible. In those companies in which there was a peculiar negative sub-culture in the form of a 'sentiment' for theft, it was difficult to evoke strong collective condemnation against it. Therefore, influencing by public opinion depends on whether it is possible to mobilize sufficiently active nuclei of such opinion in the given environment.

One of our hypotheses was that the discouraging effect of a punishment is proportional to the immediacy of its being inflicted. This relationship was confirmed by the data. Trials in social courts held after too long a period since the offense was discovered did not evoke interest, neither did they find any extensive 'social resonance.' Public opinion is more easily focused on hot items.

The nationalization of the means of production has given birth to the belief that these means are, to a great extent, left at the employees' disposal. This belief underlies the feeling that workers are entitled to use the company's facilities to their own private advantage. Attempts to punish workers for using the nationalized means of production for their individual, non-income needs are inconsistent with this legal sentiment, and thus it is impossible to consolidate collective opinion to condemn such behavior.

157

In addition to the above partial verifications of the hypotheses, the research permitted a diagnosis of the functioning of a legal institution newly introduced as a social experiment. It turned out that it was possible to carry out inexpensive, thorough and reasonably quick sociological inquiries which were valuable to the legislator, since they provided him with information concerning the effects of his legislative actions. Thus theory was soundly related to practice: sociological-legal investigations were geared to recommendations *de lege lata*.

After the phase of the basic research, further investigations on the functioning of social courts were undertaken.[6] Questionnaires were sent to the presidents of all the social courts active at the time, to the presidents of voivodship courts and to voivodship prosecutors, as well as to the voivodship commissions of the trade unions. Letters of inquiry were also sent to the directors of the companies in which social courts were active. Only a small percentage of all these groups sent the inquiries responded. The questionnaire dealt with the following issues: is the existence of social courts at all purposeful? Is it possible to run them on an experimental basis before a proper bill is enacted? What is the scope of their competence and what educative means are at their disposal? How are they controlled? On whose initiative are they established? What are the causes of their failures if they do not function properly? To what extent do professional workers of the agencies of justice participate in the preparatory works of these courts or in training their functionaries, and what other help do these agencies offer? How can the functioning of social courts up to the present time be evaluated and what are the prospects for their development? Which of their experience are useful for the future? And finally, what has been the influence of social courts toward decreasing the number of petty offenses within the companies?

Further studies of a monographic type were also undertaken. The functioning of a selected social court was observed and analyzed, and particular attention was paid to various social, organizational and economic activities related to the work of this court. The author of the study conducted interviews with a number of the company's managers, as well as with representatives of social organizations active there and with functionaries of the court. He also analyzed the distribution and mobility of the personnel of the company, and examined the files of the trials held by the court.[7]

These supplementary researches did not add much new material to the findings of the initial basic phase, though the monographic study did perhaps succeed in undermining to some extent the optimistic official view as to the prospects for the development and work of the social courts system.

On March 30, 1965, a bill was enacted regulating the legal matters relating to social courts. According to the stipulations of the bill, social courts can be called forth on the initiative of employees. They are to be controlled by the trade unions, and regular courts of law are obliged to help them (particularly in interpreting the binding law). Social courts are authorized to judge cases:

related to the breaking of the principles of social coexistence or of social order, in particular neglect of the citizen's obligations, neglect of obligations toward one's family or toward one's employer, improper attitude toward other workers, infringement of order and quiet at the place of job or residence, neglect of the rules of safety and hygiene at work, trespasses against public property or against the principles of its protection, illegitimate use by workers of the facilities belonging to a socialized employer, quarrels resulting from common residence or use of common facilities, or neighbor relationships in the countryside.

The bill stipulated that social courts cannot judge directors or their deputies. The courts are to be called forth as a result of a motion by the company's council (i.e. the local trade union presiding body), by a resolution of the conference of the workers' self-government (a collective body representing various organizations active within the company and its management), or by a general meeting of all employees. A decision to call forth a social court must be confirmed by a voivodship trade union commission. A judge on a social court can be any citizen over the age of twenty-six, never sentenced by a court of law, enjoying the respect and confidence of his colleagues, and with a proper experience in social life. A suit can be submitted to a social court by any citizen. Sessions of a court are to be open, but the court can exclude any specified parties from its session. A social court cannot inflict punishment; it can impose only educative means. These include: an obligation to apologize to the injured party, an obligation to compensate for any damage, an admonition, a condemnation, and an obligation to pay an amount not exceeding 300 zloties (i.e. an equivalent of about $10 or £4) to a charitable cause. Social courts should strive to reveal and hence discourage the sources of negative phenomena which underlie the cases considered by them, and it is their duty to suggest appropriate measures for improvement. The verdicts of social courts are not subject to any appellate procedure, with the exception of a prosecutor's intervention if a justified social interest has been infringed.

The institution of social courts is particularly interesting to legal science. It has been functioning for some time as an experiment, enabling accumulation of the experience necessary for giving it its optimal legal shape. But the sponsors of the eventual bill regulating

159

the legal status of social courts had available not only the various observations made by practitioners, for the series of sociological-legal researches presented above provided objective data concerning the functioning of these courts. Hence, a general problem arises concerning the influence of science upon legislation, which can be reduced to the specific question: to what extent did the sociological-legal investigations influence the contents of the bill?

To answer this, we compared the recommendations suggested by the researches with the forces known to have influenced the legislators. To do this, a peculiar type of analysis was carried out consisting of a parallel observation of two processes: the mutually supplementing sociological-legal investigations and the several legislative moves undertaken.[8] Consequently, various sources of information concerning the factors influencing the actual shape of the bill were analyzed. It was found that the significant elements to be considered were: the several versions of the bill, together with the justifications appended to some of them (six such versions were consecutively elaborated); various remarks, suggestions and objections submitted by various institutions when asked their opinions concerning the version proposed by the Ministry of Justice; notes about workers' courts excerpted from reports by presidents of voivodship courts; and political assumptions concerning the institution of social courts, containing the general principles for the functioning of the social courts system, with particular emphasis put upon its separate character with respect to the other institutions of justice.

Analysis of the legislators' moves showed that they never referred to any results of the sociological-legal investigations when elaborating the projected regulations of the bill. This means that the legislators do not consider science as an institutionalized partner to which they should turn for opinions in those instances where scientific researches might shed light upon the problems of interest to them. Of course, the fact that sociological-legal investigations concerning the functioning of social courts have not been referred to does not at all mean that their results were actually considered by the legislators. It only means that, on the one hand, sociologists have been unable to translate their results into recommendations which could have been directly assimilated and accepted by the legislative agency, and, on the other, that the legislators, undertaking the difficult and complicated task of giving legal shape to a new institution, might seek help mainly from their traditional partners. This finding requires that both sides, scientists and policy-makers alike, try to evolve the relevant 'relay roles,' whose task it would be to translate the results of social researches into a language familiar to the legislators, as well as to inform scientists which problems are actually significant and vital for the lawmakers. Though such a function is now performed in some measure by those administrative officials who are at the same time active scientists, still it is essential that these roles be performed systematically and within institutional frameworks, rather than only when a lucky coincidence allows for it.

We still have no unequivocal answer to the basic question of whether or to what extent the final contents of the bill on social courts was influenced by the results of sociological investigations. In general it can be said that in certain instances the bill and the recommendations approach each other, while in others they seem incompatible. The two are similar in that: social courts are authorized to deal with a broader scope of cases than the petty theft of public property; the bill permits summoning to these courts persons in managerial positions (with the exception of company directors and their deputies); social courts can hold sessions which are closed to the public if it is deemed necessary; they are charged with the obligation to look for the sources of the negative phenomena and to suggest appropriate improvements; and the verdicts of social courts in principle cannot be reconsidered by regular courts of law. However, there are incompatible points, too. The judges of social courts have not been provided with the symbols of authority necessary for the effective performance of their function (e.g. the judges are searched at the exit from a factory like the other employees, which severely undermines their authority); the bill stipulates clearly, and in opposition to the recommendations of the researches, that social courts shall consider cases of illegitimate use of a factory's facilities by its workers. Though these discrepancies do not have the character of essential incompatibilities, they seem to have resulted from insufficient attention devoted to the research data. If the institution of 'relay roles' suggested above had existed, we could expect that the discrepancies would have been reduced or reconsidered by the lawmakers in their justifications of the bill.

From the point of view of justice and effectiveness, it is obvious that social courts are an example of a dubious social situation. But it is equally obvious that sociological-legal investigation can be used to help implement socially harmful elements as well as to unmask such institutional elements or attempts at their implementation.

# 8 The statistical method

There are two types of research which make use of the statistical method: those for which the securing or interpreting of quantitative data is the main objective, and which are based on official or other evidence or on materials collected by specialized agencies; and those which are essentially carried out by other methods and which make use of statistics as an auxiliary. In social research the statistical method is also employed as an auxiliary meta-method (or as a higher-level procedure). Thus, for example, investigations which use the questionnaire or files analysis as their main tools sometimes can, or even ought to be, exposed additionally to a statistical analysis. On the other hand, monographic studies are hardly subject to quantitative elaboration, though not without exceptions since some auxiliary determinations, such as sociometric analyses, may be applicable.

The statistical method is particularly useful for social research when sequences of events are studied and when some general hypotheses about these sequences are formulated and call for verification. An example of this kind of problem can be the functions and dysfunctions of punishments applied throughout extensive periods of time. In this instance statistical analysis promises to determine the effects of punishments in relation to the frequency of their infliction or their modification or abolition.

As we know, legal sanctions are applied because order must be preserved. There is a traditional belief that deviant behavior should be punished, in particular when it violates law and order. This is because, among other reasons, it discourages people who have not broken the law but might otherwise do so, thereby ensuring not only that offenders are punished but that law and order will be maintained. It can therefore be said that there is a general relationship between the need for social order and the system of punishments evolved by a given society.

Generally, if the social need for order begins to be seriously threatened there is a tendency to develop further the apparatus of control, which in turn strengthens the pressure toward obedience to law; there is also a tendency on such occasions to call forth institutions which are extra-legal and incompatible with the accepted legal order, but which begin to perform the roles which are normally expected to be played by law. This general proposition could be translated into a number of more detailed ones, so formulated as to permit their empirical verification. It is only at this phase that the statistical method can be applied at all, for it does not enter the realm of applicability until the analyzed problem is ready for quantitative elaboration.

Let us consider a concrete example. If a legal system is incompatible with the concept of law and order prevailing in a given society at a given moment, institutions emerge spontaneously to assume the task of guaranteeing order. After East Pakistan won its independence in 1947, the British administration was, as we know, removed from the territory. Several districts obtained their own police forces. However, it soon turned out that the police were insufficiently trained and that their functionaries were tied by very strong family, neighborly and other links to the regions they served. For these and other reasons the population very rarely resorted to the police in cases of robbery, theft, murder, and other crimes. Those policemen who did actively engage in investigations soon fell into disrepute in their territories, which made it difficult for them to perform their duties. This situation led in a number of regions to an urgent need to protect the basic personal and social values by any means, including armed vigilantes. In this context Newman made a number of observations which can be summarized in the form of the following relationship: the less respect there is for the efficiency of the apparatus of justice, the greater is the need for vigilante institutions; conversely, the more respect there is for that apparatus, the less need is felt for vigilante institutions. However, it can be supposed that this relationship is likely to hold only when both parties, i.e. those who value the efficiency and integrity of the executive authorities and those who have the power, recognize the same basic social and ethical values.[1]

The above considerations lead me to suggest an even more limited proposition, namely: abolition of capital punishment brings about an increase in the number of lynchings. However, a reservation must again be made that this proposition is likely to be true only in certain special circumstances. If, for example, after the Second World War capital punishment had been abolished in some countries formerly suffering from German aggression, it is quite probable that the number of lynchings in those countries at that time would have increased.

163

Perhaps it was in the expectation of this kind of consequence that in 1945 Belgium invoked the death penalty for collaborators, although this punishment had not been applied since 1863 (even though it was provided by law).

However, the proposition that abolition of capital punishment is apt to lead to an increase in the number of lynchings is difficult to prove. For according to it, we should expect relatively more lynchings where capital punishment has been abolished or is not applied in spite of the fact that certain social forces demand its use. And yet the available data do not confirm this expectation. For example, in the USA the number of lynchings decreased from 107 between the years 1900 and 1904 to a mere three between 1945 and 1949. Besides, lynchings usually occurred in those states in which capital punishment was legally applied. If we consider Arizona as an example, we find the following:[2]

> 1915–16—7 lynchings (capital punishment in force)
> 1917–18—7 lynchings (capital punishment abolished)
> 1919–20—13 lynchings (capital punishment restored).

Now, a question arises as to what factors determine the number of cases of 'lynch law'? In the third century A.D., Tertullian remarked a strange though fairly regular coincidence of events: 'If the Tiber floods the city or if the Nile expands its waters too far, if the skies remain unmoved, if an earthquake occurs, if there is a pestilence or a famine, then an outcry arises, "Throw the Christians to the lions!" '

Seventeen hundred years later the sociologists Raper (in 1933) and Hovland and Sears (in 1940) made another observation: 'If the price of cotton per acre of land in the southern United States is low, the number of lynchings of Negroes is high in this region.'[3] How can we account for this kind of relationship?

In the case of the Christians the matter is relatively easy. Many people at that time believed it was the 'crimes' of the Christians that caused great natural calamities. However, we can hardly suppose that the people in the southern USA today believe that the Negroes are responsible for the low prices of cotton. How, then, shall we explain the observed regularity?

The twentieth-century sociologists cited above offer an explanation with reference to the general proposition of the theory of frustration. These are:

1  The extent of frustration depends on three factors: (a) the strength of the reaction caused by failure in the pursuit of an end; (b) the degree of psychological disturbance caused by the reaction to the failure; and (c) the number of such reactions.

2   The intensity of aggression depends directly on the extent of frustration.

3   Aggression is directed in the first place against a person or institution which is supposed to be the source of the frustration.

4   Inhibition of an aggressive action depends directly on the severity of the expected punishment for the aggression.

5   Inhibition of the immediate act of aggression is a painful frustration, causing the aggression to be transferred to other available persons or objects.

6   An act of aggression constitutes a *catharsis* (a release) which reduces the propensity to further acts of aggression.

Considering the above general regularities, the phenomenon of aggressive assaults against Negroes can be tentatively explained as follows: the harvest is bad; such a disaster causes frustration and anger in the farmers and trades people; it would be absurd (and dangerous) to direct these feelings against the authorities or against God; awareness of this results in inhibition of direct aggression against the authorities, God, or the forces of nature; the aggressive tendencies are displaced towards those who are the weakest members of the community and who give no ground to suppose that they could defend themselves successfully; in consequence, aggression is released on the Negroes, who are the scapegoats; this aggression assumes the form of 'lynch law,' i.e. spontaneous and illegitimate killing. Of course, the explanation would be incomplete if we did not consider the racialist, intolerant and discriminating attitudes of the southerners toward Negroes; an explanation in terms of frustration-aggression mechanisms can only signify an already existing apparently widespread social approach to this problem.

Let us now turn to the question of the efficiency of capital punishment as a deterrent. First, against the common belief, the model of ethics records several exceptions from a principle that is seemingly universal and allows no exceptions, the principle 'thou shalt not kill.' According to M. Ossowska:[4] (1) suicide is rather generally accepted without ethical condemnation. (2) Homicide in defending one's own life or that of another is called homicide in the situation of 'higher necessity.' (3) The norm of not killing ceases for many people to hold good during war. (4) People tend to allow, though there is no universal agreement on this point, that it is admissible to inflict death out of pity, upon another who requests it; euthanasia in the proper sense of the word. In view of the many births of teratoid children following the use of thalidomide, there has been a tendency to extend the notion of euthanasia to such children, who are denied the chance of a normal existence. In this case it is assured that death is painless, but the condition that it be requested by the afflicted cannot be applied. (5) Induced abortion is thought by some to be a

165

form of homicide. (6) Finally, there is the exception that is our specific concern here, the inflicting of death by a legitimate sentence, i.e. capital punishment.

The problem of capital punishment in Poland, though it is extremely significant theoretically, does not apply to any large category of persons. Though it continuously stimulates serious disputes among scientists, and though the penal code of 1969 (in effect since January, 1970) treats capital punishment as an exceptional (language of criminal code) penal means, there are very few instances of its actual application (see Table 8.1).

With reference to the scientific controversies concerning the efficiency of capital punishment, it is worth while to consider first the basic arguments for and against its application.[5] Subsequently I

TABLE 8.1

| Year | Adults sentenced | Capital punishment |
|------|------------------|--------------------|
| 1961 | 302,045 | 14 |
| 1962 | 276,628 | 6 |
| 1963 | 253,100 | 8 |
| 1964 | 182,474 | 6 |
| 1965 | 207,976 | 3 |
| 1966 | 248,447 | 9 |
| 1967 | 271,796 | 4 |
| 1968* | 220,520 | 5 |

* Data from *Statistical Yearbook*, 1969, p. 582.

shall present numerical data to illustrate the use of the statistical method in the analysis of this complicated, important and historically ramified problem.

The functions of punishment are usually listed as: isolating a criminal from society, reforming the criminal, discouraging potential criminals, and retaliation. In the case of capital punishment, reformation obviously does not apply. Isolating from society those who have disrupted its orderly functioning consists in making it physically impossible for them to take part in communal life. This purpose is served by the institution of prisons. It is the deterrent function, however, which seems to be the most important from the point of view of social life as a whole. It means that not only will the crimnal himself be made to ponder the consequences of socially unacceptable behavior, but above all, others who witness the application of punishment will consider what is in store for them if they break the law. The argument that capital punishment has a deterrent effect is foremost among those adduced in support of its use. The function of retaliation raises complex problems. Though few people would admit it now, the desire to make the criminal suffer for his misdeeds is still for many an important motivation to apply various punishments, including death.

To bring some order into the multitude of arguments concerning capital punishment, we can distinguish, after T. Sellin, dogmatic and empirical arguments in favor of maintaining or abolishing it.

The dogmatic arguments in favor of capital punishment are: (1) it is the only kind of punishment (according to the advocates of retaliation) that makes a murderer atone for his deed; all other penalties are incommensurate with his guilt; (2) capital punishment is the only just penalty for murder; and (3) the death penalty is more humanitarian than a life term in prison (the penal code of 1969 abolished life imprisonment in Poland).

Dogmatic arguments are also employed against capital punishment: (1) no one has the right to deprive another of his life (religious persons would add that since life has been bestowed upon us by the Creator, no man should take it away); (2) retaliation is not a justified ground upon which to build a system of penal law; and (3) capital punishment is unjust.

In empirical arguments other considerations come to the fore. Those who are against the death penalty are apt to justify their position in the following manner: capital punishment is not a sufficient deterrent to bring about a decrease in the incidence of crime. Its abolition, in those countries that have tried it, has not caused any increase in the number of crimes formerly punishable by it. A death sentence cannot be reversed, making it impossible eventually to compensate for an injury done by a mistaken verdict. It is only the abolition of the death penalty that offers effective protection against the possibility of such tragedies. A death sentence makes re-education of the criminal impossible, whereas the primary aim should be to rehabilitate the offender.

Empirical arguments in favor of the death penalty hold that it discourages people from committing deeds they would otherwise commit were it not for the ugly awareness of so severe a sanction. The idea of being put to death has a particularly strong effect upon people with certain mental disorders, and it is just these people— according to the advocates of this argument—who are to be most frequently found among murderers. Awareness that a death sentence might be forthcoming prevents the criminal from killing those who chase him in his flight from the scene of a crime. Abolition of the death penalty would tend to encourage lynch law; therefore it is better to protect people from wantonness and to consider such cases within the limits of a severe but objective court procedure. Some advocates of the death penalty would also offer such arguments as: it is more economical in that it does not involve the expense of maintaining a criminal for life; it safeguards the security of society by eliminating the criminal once and for all; and it prevents the proliferation in the human population of those who may have hereditary antisocial propensities.

It is not difficult to see that the most serious of the arguments favoring the death penalty is that which emphasizes its deterrent effect. The eugenic argument can be easily dismissed since sterilization, while less drastic than death, would be no less efficient in this respect. As to the economic anxieties, prison labor can be so organized and utilized as to have the inmates pay for their subsistence.

Comparing the dogmatic and the empirical arguments, it can be remarked that the former are immune to any scientific discussion. They can be accepted or rejected, but we cannot possibly discuss them in rational terms. From the point of view of a reasonable legal policy, i.e. one which proposes to consider the eventual effects of the existing legal regulations and the potential effects of those which could be introduced or modified, the essential questions are: does the death penalty restrain people from committing those crimes punishable by it? Does it entail any negative effects which go against the generally accepted social values, or which outweigh any positive effects? Do mistaken death verdicts occur, and how often? Does the existence of the death penalty perhaps provide a motive to commit homicide?

To be able to give sound answers to these questions we must know certain things concerning the influence of legal measures upon social life. We must formulate the basic general hypothesis, viz: the death penalty discourages people from committing the crimes punishable by it. The next step is to derive from this hypothesis a number of detailed suppositions that can be empirically tested and are subject to statistical analyses. Thus (1) in countries with similar social, political, economic, historical, and geographical conditions, and differing only in whether or not they have the death penalty, what differences are there as to the incidence of such crimes as murder, kidnapping, rape, treason, robbery, etc.? (2) Does the incidence of crimes subject to capital punishment change significantly in countries where it has been applied and then is abolished? (It usually happens that the death penalty is abolished, restored, and then abolished for the second time.) (3) Is the death penalty an efficient means of protecting the apparatus of justice, and, in particular, police functionaries, from attacks against them? (4) Can the death penalty itself be a stimulus to commit murder (this is said to happen when a suicidal person lacks the courage to kill himself and thus compels the hand of justice to do it for him)? (5) Has it been discovered that innocent persons have been sentenced to death and executed? (6) Does abolition of the death penalty bring about a tendency to lynch law? Finally, (7) to what extent if at all are murderers in prison a threat to other persons (prisoners, guards, etc.)?

The above problems and questions that are particularly important can be formulated (in accord with T. Sellin's suggestion) in the form

TABLE 8.2   *Incidence of homicides and executions per 10,000 inhabitants*

| | Maine* | New Hampshire | | Vermont | | Massachusetts | | Rhode Island* | Connecticut | |
|---|---|---|---|---|---|---|---|---|---|---|
| | homicides | homicides | executions | homicides | executions | homicides | executions | homicides | homicides | executions |
| 1920 | 1·4 | 1·8 | – | 2·3 | – | 2·1 | 1 | 1·8 | 3·9 | 1 |
| 1921 | 2·2 | 2·2 | – | 1·7 | – | 2·8 | – | 3·1 | 2·9 | 2 |
| 1922 | 1·7 | 1·6 | – | 1·1 | – | 2·6 | – | 2·2 | 2·9 | 1 |
| 1923 | 1·7 | 2·7 | – | 1·4 | – | 2·8 | 1 | 3·5 | 3·1 | – |
| 1924 | 1·5 | 1·5 | – | 0·6 | – | 2·7 | 1 | 2·0 | 3·5 | – |
| 1925 | 2·2 | 1·3 | – | 0·6 | – | 2·7 | – | 1·8 | 3·7 | – |
| 1926 | 1·1 | 0·9 | – | 2·2 | – | 2·0 | 1 | 3·2 | 2·9 | 1 |
| 1927 | 1·9 | 0·7 | – | 0·8 | – | 2·1 | 6 | 2·7 | 2·3 | 2 |
| 1928 | 1·6 | 1·3 | – | 1·4 | – | 1·9 | 3 | 2·7 | 2·7 | – |
| 1929 | 1·0 | 1·5 | – | 1·4 | – | 1·7 | 6 | 2·3 | 2·6 | 1 |
| 1930 | 1·8 | 0·9 | – | 1·4 | – | 1·8 | – | 2·0 | 3·2 | 2 |
| 1931 | 1·4 | 2·1 | – | 1·1 | 1 | 2·0 | 2 | 2·2 | 2·7 | – |
| 1932 | 2·0 | 0·2 | – | 1·1 | – | 2·1 | 1 | 1·6 | 2·9 | – |
| 1933 | 3·3 | 2·7 | – | 1·6 | – | 2·5 | – | 1·9 | 1·8 | – |
| 1934 | 1·1 | 1·4 | – | 1·9 | – | 2·2 | 4 | 1·8 | 2·4 | – |
| 1935 | 1·4 | 1·0 | – | 0·3 | – | 1·8 | 4 | 1·6 | 1·9 | – |
| 1936 | 2·2 | 1·0 | – | 2·1 | – | 1·6 | 2 | 1·2 | 2·7 | 1 |
| 1937 | 1·4 | 1·8 | – | 1·8 | – | 1·9 | – | 2·3 | 2·0 | 1 |
| 1938 | 1·5 | 1·8 | – | 1·3 | – | 1·3 | 3 | 1·2 | 2·1 | 1 |
| 1939 | 1·2 | 2·3 | 1 | 0·8 | – | 1·4 | 2 | 1·6 | 1·3 | – |
| 1940 | 1·5 | 1·4 | – | 0·8 | – | 1·5 | – | 1·4 | 1·8 | 2 |
| 1941 | 1·1 | 0·4 | – | 2·2 | – | 1·3 | 1 | 0·8 | 2·2 | – |
| 1942 | 1·7 | 0·2 | – | 0·9 | – | 1·3 | 2 | 1·2 | 2·5 | – |
| 1943 | 1·7 | 0·9 | – | 0·6 | – | 0·9 | 3 | 1·5 | 1·6 | 2 |
| 1944 | 1·5 | 1·1 | – | 0·3 | – | 1·4 | – | 0·6 | 1·9 | 1 |
| 1945 | 0·9 | 0·7 | – | 2·9 | – | 1·5 | – | 1·5 | 1·5 | 1 |
| 1946 | 1·4 | 0·8 | – | 1·7 | – | 1·4 | 1 | 1·5 | 1·6 | 3 |

* In Maine and Rhode Island there was no death penalty for homicide.

of hypotheses subject to verification by statistical procedures. If we postulate that the death penalty has a discouraging effect, then:

1 The incidence of murders ought to be higher in those states which have no capital punishment and which are otherwise similar to those in which it does exist.

2 The incidence of murders ought to increase after the death penalty is abolished, and should decrease after the penalty is reinstated.

3 The deterrent effect of the death penalty should be most conspicuous during those periods when public attention is focused on an execution.

4 Law enforcement officials should be more secure in those states having capital punishment than in those which do not.

*Re* 1 As we know, various crimes carry the death penalty in various countries. Among them are rape, kidnapping, high treason, murder, political subversion, etc. In order to determine the effect of the death penalty we should obviously investigate the increase or decrease in the incidence of crimes to which it is applied. Detailed scrutiny is made difficult by the multitude of factors which may be involved, and which vary from country to country. Therefore it is convenient (in particular because the relevant statistics exist and are available) when we are studying the deterrent effect of capital punishment to focus on the crime of homicide.

Analyses have been made with various types of indices. One example is a comparison of data collected in the New England states: Maine, New Hampshire, Vermont, Massachusetts, Rhode Island and Connecticut. All these states are similar in their social, economic, demographic and cultural characteristics. In Maine and in Rhode Island there is no capital punishment. A comparison of the number of homicides in these states between 1920 and 1946 does not reveal any significant differences (see Table 8.2).[6]

*Re* 2 There are also data concerning the incidence of homicides when the death penalty is in force and after its abolition. For example, in Maine, the death penalty was abolished in 1876, re-established in 1882 and abolished again in 1887. Table 8.3 gives the relevant data per 10,000 inhabitants.[7] They reveal the significant changes in the incidence of homicides during the alternating periods of abolition and re-establishment.

Saxony offers convenient materials for statistical processing of the official files, as there are available records showing names, sex, marital status, age, the years in which the crimes were committed, the years of verdicts, and motives.[8] The death penalty was abolished in Saxony between 1868 and 1871, and the results of investigations concerning sentences for murders and executions are shown in Table 8.4. These data indicate that neither abolition nor imposition of the death

TABLE 8.3    *Incidence of homicides in Maine per 10,000 inhabitants*

|  | Trials for homicide | Sentences for homicide |  |
|---|---|---|---|
| 1876–81 | 8·0 | 4·2 | death penalty abolished |
| 1882–6 | 6·8 | 5·8 | death penalty in force |
| 1887–91 | 6·0 | 3·8 | death penalty abolished |
| 1892–6 | 8·0 | 4·8 | death penalty in force |
| 1897–1901 | 3·4 | – | – |

penalty produced any direct or indirect deterrent effects. In particular, abolition did not influence the number of sentences for murder, neither does it appear to have had any significant influence upon the number of those committed.

Table 8.5 shows what are possibly the most systematically collected data, the numbers of convictions for murder in Sweden (excluding cases of infanticide). The same data (Table 8.6) show the incidence of homicides per 100,000 inhabitants.

Some reservations must be made in interpreting these data. Though the method of statistical analysis seems to be very strict indeed, still

TABLE 8.4

|  | Yearly average of sentences for murder | No. of murders per 1 m. inhabs over 18 | Yearly average of executions for murder |
|---|---|---|---|
| 1855–8 | 2·75 | 8·7 | 1·0 |
| 1859–63 | 2·6 | 9·8 | 0·6 |
| 1864–8 | 3·0 | 10·4 | 0·2 |
| 1869–73 | 1·2 | 13·2 | 0·0 |
| 1874–8 | 2·8 | 8·6 | 0·0 |
| 1879 | 4·6 | 4·0 | 1·2 |
| 1884–8 | 3·6 | 9·6 | 1·4 |
| 1889–93 | 3·2 | 7·8 | 1·6 |
| 1894–8 | 2·4 | 5·3 | 2·0 |
| 1899–1903 | 1·4 | 2·8 | 0·6 |
| 1904–8 | 2·2 | 4·1 | 1·2 |
| 1909–13 | 2·6 | 4·4 | 0·8 |
| 1914–18 | 3·2 | ? | 1·4 |
| 1919–23 | 5·2 | 8·2? | 0·0 |
| 1924–7 | 3·5 | 4·0? | 0·0 |

its basic fallacy is that it can lead to false conclusions if the assumptions on which it is based are not sound. The death penalty is a sanction that has been very deeply rooted in the culture of various societies since times remote. Throughout epochs it has been a means of socializing groups and individuals so as to insure the social order and obedience. It would be most naïve to suppose that a mere legal

TABLE 8.5

|  |  |
|---|---|
|  | *No. of* |
|  | *convictions* |
| 1913–17 | 23 |
| 1918–22 | 40 (death penalty abolished in 1921) |
| 1923–7 | 26 |
| 1928–32 | 29 |
| 1933–7 | 31 |
| 1938–42 | 17 |
| 1943–7 | 29 |

stipulation making this sanction either valid or invalid would be likely to achieve rapid and conspicuous results. Such a supposition would neglect the long-range educative influence of law and its basic function of inculcating and internalizing social values. What influences the people is above all the long tradition of laws and customs, which exerts continuous and strong pressure even when the detailed regulations of law are changed. Indeed, these regulations as such

TABLE 8.6

|  |  |
|---|---|
| 1754–63 | 0·83 |
| 1775–92 | 0·66 |
| 1793–1806 | 0·61 |
| 1809–30 | 1·09 (years 1814 and 1818 not included) |
| 1831–45 | 1·47 |
| 1846–60 | 1·24 |
| 1861–77 | 1·12 |
| 1878–98 | 0·90 |
| 1899–04 | 0·96 |
| 1905–13 | 0·86 |
| 1914–16 | 0·76 |
| 1920–32 | 0·53 (death penalty abolished in 1921) |
| 1933–8 | 0·46 |
| 1939–42 | 0·47 |

may not be widely known at all, and may reach the general population only after they have been transformed into principles.

*Re* 3 Data concerning the hypothesis that the deterrent effect of the death penalty should be most strongly felt during a period, or in a milieu, when executions claim much public attention can be found in some research done in Philadelphia.[9] Five cases were selected which had been widely known to the public and vividly described by the press, as well as not being in competition with other events evoking general interest so that the attention of the public could be focused almost exclusively upon them. The selected trials and executions took place in the years 1927, 1929, 1930 and 1932. By determining the number of willful homicides that had occurred during the 60 days before and the 60 days after each execution, it was found that during the 300 days before the five executions (60 days for each)

TABLE 8.7

| Days | Before the executions | After the executions |
|------|-----------------------|----------------------|
| 1–10 | 9 | 16 |
| 11–20 | 24 | 15 |
| 21–30 | 11 | 27 |
| 31–40 | 17 | 9 |
| 41–50 | 17 | 0 |
| 51–60 | 27 | 7 |
| Total | 105 | 74 |

there were a total of 105 days during which no homicide was committed, while during the 300 days after the executions there were 74 such days. Table 8.7 shows the relevant data plotted in ten-day intervals.

*Re* 4 Interesting investigations have been carried out in respect of the fourth hypothesis, that the executive agencies of law are safer when the death penalty is in force. For example, a questionnaire was sent to officials in 17 states in the USA asking about the number of assaults against police functionaries.[10] It was directed to police authorities in 6 states which had abolished the death penalty and in 11 contiguous states which had maintained it. The questionnaire asked first for actual data, and second for the opinons of police functionaries as to the efficiency of capital punishment.

The largest cities, such as Detroit, Minneapolis, New York, Cleveland and Boston, failed to answer the questionnaire, perhaps because they had too many other reports to make. Responding were 55 per cent of the towns in states which had repealed the death penalty and 41 per cent of the towns in those states which had retained it. It turned out that in towns in the states without capital punishment the percentage of assaults against police functionaries, in proportion to the number of their inhabitants, was 1·2 per cent, while in the towns of states having capital punishment the index was 1·3 per cent. Thus there was no significant difference between them at all. As for the opinions of police officials regarding the effectiveness of the death penalty, 89·9 per cent from the states with capital punishment answered that it was a factor protecting them against assaults by criminal elements, while 74 per cent from the abolitionist states answered that they did not believe in such a deterrent effect. The results point to a high degree of submissiveness of the functionaries to the norms of law which are binding for them; it is cause for thought to note the extent to which such norms are apt to blur the objective range of reality.

To sum up what has been said about the efficiency of the death penalty, I would quote the remark by E. Gowers:[11]

> If I had been asked for my opinion, I should probably have said that I was in favour of the death penalty and disposed to regard abolitionists as people whose hearts were bigger than their heads. Four years of close study of the subject gradually dispelled that feeling.

Polish investigations concerning the prestige of law[12] have given considerable attention to the problem of the death penalty. As a result of these investigations it was discovered that the majority of the Polish population favored the retention of capital punishment. Only a minority of both the urban population (32·7 per cent) and the rural inhabitants (31·8 per cent) expressed opinions against it. However, this clear approval of its use is not an argument in its favor for a lawmaker. That the population favors in principle the use of the death penalty is a significant social phenomenon, but the existence of some social fact does not necessarily mean it is rationally justified. In fact, the variables which in the Polish studies significantly correlated with the opinions concerning the use of capital punishment were all subjective in character. These had to do with such factors as feelings of insecurity, a dogmatic versus a rational attitude, authoritarian socialization in childhood, and the general level of social adaptiveness. Those who declared themselves opponents of the death penalty were more often free from symptoms of insecurity feelings, had been more leniently reared according to their own evaluation, and appeared to be enjoying life more, i.e. were better adapted to it.[13] Tolerant attitudes concerning the death penalty were coextensive with tolerance toward other problems.

To conclude our considerations on the death penalty let me share with you the thoughts of a Polish colleague:[14]

We can see that beginning with the epoch of the Enlightenment, the realm of sovereignty of the death penalty has been continuously shrinking. That eminent writers, social activists, advocates of progress, and champions of the rights and dignity of man have been opposing it. That at the present moment a great part of the civilized world does very well without this device. That international organizations, including the United Nations, appeal for its abolition. That no convincing and tested social reasons can justify it. And that it cannot be reconciled with the principles of contemporary humanism.

In this noble striving toward eradication of the death penalty the socialist world has its honorable share. It is the socialists who most often were the motivating force in abolitionist motions which have been voted by majorities in European parliaments. The Soviet Union abolished the death penalty, and in 1948 proposed abolition on a global scale. And if at present the socialist penal codes clearly announce the abolition of the death penalty and emphasize its exceptional character, they appeal not only to the judges for reflection. They also appeal to the lawmaker that he inquire at each opportunity whether it is really indispensable to maintain this measure.

It should be quite clear, then, that the use of even such a precise method as comparative analysis of statistical data cannot solve a problem which is extremely complex at its roots. A consideration of arguments pro and con in the matter of capital punishment would perhaps induce a judge or a jury, when it came to the final decision, to impose the death penalty, if at all, only in cases of mass murder, or genocide.

175

# 9 Analysis of legal materials

Data contained in various legal files can be a source of information about the functioning of law. These materials are particularly valuable as an analysis of legal files makes possible a critical and multiple scrutiny of the same, unchanging materials. However, it is very important to determine the proper techniques of selection of the available data. Any files offer a huge amount of information, some significant and some quite unimportant. It is thus a paramount task to determine at the outset what is likely to be of importance for the projected study. One peculiar difficulty inherent in the method of legal files analysis is that it must be supplemented by other methods of research. Since it is only on rare occasions that it is technically feasible to study the files and at the same time make use of the additional techniques, it is necessary to elaborate beforehand a strategy that will take into account the anticipated supplements.

In this chapter, as an example of the use of legal materials, I shall report a study on court suits against journalists. In Poland as in the USA and Great Britain, libel can be either a criminal act or the basis for a civil suit for restraint and damages. Nevertheless in practice the court suits in the USA and in Great Britain have an almost exclusively civil character, whereas in Poland they have a criminal character. From the methodological point of view, it was an objective source research. It was based on materials allowing for repeated analyses, i.e. on data which would not be exposed to change through the research process. However, it must be kept in mind that these materials are expressions of subjective attitudes of the persons involved in the lawsuits. Obviously, the arguments of the defendants and plaintiffs, and even sometimes the rulings of the judges, are determined by various psychological and external biases. Thus it can be said that the researches based on court files deal with objectified but essentially subjective materials.

A number of problems are raised by press suits and by suits against journalists relating to their jobs and publications. One of these is the question of whether such suits were perceived by journalists as a genuine danger to the news trade. But there are others, too. It must be determined what social factors such suits are related to, and what factors bring them about and influence their incidence, type, etc. It must be discovered what factors influence the court verdicts, both convictions and acquittals, and what is the proportion of the two types of verdict. Another problem is the type and range of the social values defended by means of the press suits. In turn, the situations must be defined which are conceived as caused by a newsman and which are likely to stimulate a defense by means of a law suit against him. On the other hand, it must be ascertained what is the scope of freedom of a journalist, i.e. his latitude for attacking publicly people or institutions without being actually vulnerable to a lawsuit. Finally, it is necessary to determine whether or not the legal precepts in force (in this case contained in or related to the 1932 Polish penal code) themselves raise doubts with respect to both their interpretation and their effects.

The study covered all the materials available throughout the entire country contained in the files of lawsuits ending in a binding verdict between 1956 and 1960 against journalists publishing their items in daily newspapers. The present author was responsible for the whole project.[1]

A number of difficulties arose at the outset. During the preparatory work on the project it was impossible to determine or even to predict roughly the overall number of press suits that would be encompassed. Thus at this phase one of the paramount problems was the technical task of how to locate the files, to determine their number, and to map out their geographical distribution.

The following research plan was adopted:

1 determine the essential problems;

2 prepare a questionnaire inquiring about press suits and distribute it to editors of all daily newspapers;

3 determine from responses to the questionnaire the number and distribution of the press suits;

4 determine the number and distribution of press suits learned about by other means;

5 systematize the data concerning the number and distribution of the press suits;

6 make a map of these suits, covering the whole country;

7 make a preliminary study of the files of a few press suits;

8 prepare a questionnaire for a pilot study;

9 carry out such a pilot study;

10 analyze and discuss the results of the pilot study;

11 prepare a final questionnaire;
12 carry out the essential study;
13 systematize the collected data; and
14 elaborate the results.

Essentially, the survey followed the plan rather closely. A questionnaire inquiring about press suits was sent to all the important daily newspapers in the country. However, in spite of our repeated urgings to some of the editors, the questionnaire failed to bring the expected abundance of data, the main reasons apparently being a lack of records and lawsuits against their employed journalists and the lack of co-operation on the part of the editors. In such a situation we had to seek supplementary means. For example, we asked the press concern RSW 'Prasa' (which sponsored the bulk of Polish newspapers) to check their financial records for payments for legal defense of journalists sued for activities related to their jobs.

Another source of data was news items concerning such cases, although the data were usually incomplete and did not always enable unambiguous identification of the persons, localities, courts, etc. Some information could also be gathered by correspondence with or visits to penal departments of courts. But this procedure had its deficiencies, too. The courts do not keep records in such a way that press suits would be in any manner conspicuous. Like any others, they are to be found in the so-called repertorium or in other types of files by the journalist's name under the defendant's heading or under the heading of the legal qualification, i.e. the relevant article of the penal code. However, there were so many cases entered under Article 255, paragraph 1 of the code that it was practically impossible to select the press suits among them.[2] Still another means of gaining some information was direct contact with a number of journalists, some of whom were able to supplement our data in some way.

It seemed necessary to collect the data on the number and distribution of press suits with utmost care, since it had been anticipated that our financial resources would enable us to study only a part of the identified files. Thus it appeared important to set up criteria of selection such that the files actually analyzed could be considered as optimally representative. However, contrary to these expectations, it turned out that the number of cases which had reached a verdict and concerned journalists employed by daily newspapers (i.e. excluding cases still in progress, discontinued, involving weeklies, etc.) was such that they could be almost entirely covered by the study.[3]

Table 9.1 shows the distribution of identified press suits in the period studied (according to date of filing). A map and a table of frequency were then plotted, and a few suits selected at random for analysis in Cracow and Warsaw. This introductory work allowed us to elaborate a questionnaire which was designed, after minor modifications, to serve as the basic research tool. Following a number of tentative pilot studies, the questionnaire was given the finishing touch.

The research team, having participated in the discussions on the questionnaire construction and after receiving appropriate instructions, set out to do the field research in accord with the plotting on the map. As noted above, virtually all the press suits identified throughout the country were studied. The few exceptions were justified on the one hand by the very small number of suits in some cities, and by the high cost of traveling to them, on the other; e.g. Olsztyn was omitted for this reason. The accumulating materials were systematically arranged as they came in.

Before the collection of materials was completed an additional project was undertaken. The investigations had revealed that the

TABLE 9.1

| Year | No. of press suits |
|-------|--------------------|
| 1956 | 7 |
| 1957 | 16 |
| 1958 | 11 |
| 1959 | 7 |
| 1960 | 2 |
| Total | 43 |

press suits were essentially cases coming under Article 255, paragraph 1 of the penal code, i.e., they belonged to a type of case very frequently brought into the courts. Thus it seemed reasonable to investigate a random sample of Article 255, paragraph 1 cases litigated against others besides journalists. A control group representing the average population was introduced to the research scheme because, while the collected materials on press suits shed light on court practice *vis-à-vis* journalists, these cases are in various ways peculiar in character. It seemed that their peculiarities would be easier to grasp if they were compared with other lawsuits of the same general kind, i.e. where the defendants were not distinguished by their type of job.

The aim of our study was to obtain answers to questions of various types. Some were an attempt to secure diagnostic knowledge, or a better insight into the existing situation. Others expressed suppositions as to the factors controlling various elements relevant to press suits. Still other questions were asked to learn whether the actual regulations affecting the press fulfilled the role of defending both the interests of journalism as a trade, and social welfare. The basic questions were: (1) Are press suits so frequent as to be a threat or a nuisance to the trade? (2) Is there a tendency on the part of the courts to convict rather than to acquit the journalists involved in such suits? (3) What factors appear to determine conviction or acquittal in a press suit?

Our suppositions concerning the essential regularities relating to press suits had been, before final analysis of the results, the following:

1    The more reliable the published materials, the less the probability of a court conviction.

2    The more respected the social values attacked by a publication, the greater the probability of a lawsuit.

3    The higher the social position of that which is attacked, the greater the probability of a lawsuit.

4    The higher the social position of that which is attacked, the more probable it is that the public interest (an institution, an office, etc.) will be involved in the suit.

5    The more strictly a newspaper observes the principle of preserving the anonymity of informants, the greater the number of lawsuits against the journalists employed by it.

The research results provided clear answers to some of these problems. The question of whether press suits are frequent enough to be a serious nuisance to the trade must be answered decidedly in the negative. Roughly forty lawsuits over a five-year period is a negligible number, given the number of journalists employed in the country and the frequency of their publications. In the year in which the study was made (1963), about 4,000 persons were active in the profession, according to the data of the Association of Polish Journalists.

So how could it happen that there was a common and firm belief that press suits were a plague to the journalist profession? The problem can readily be explained in the sociological concept of the 'boomerang effect.' The journalists had been misled by themselves. It is one of the newsmen's tasks to publish interesting and topical events and thus to give them publicity. The fact that journalists are professionally interested in court cases in which their colleagues are involved leads them to overplay their coverage and thereby convince themselves that the extent and frequency of these cases is greater than it actually is. The journalists created a myth which in turn began to haunt them. However, for several reasons to be discussed below, this myth is not dangerous.

Now, the first result of the research was the finding that the press suits were by no means a frequent phenomenon and that the publicity enjoyed by them was brought about not by their abundance but rather by the peculiar features of the journalist profession itself.

The press suits are, with only a few exceptions, litigated on private motions (private suits). Table 9.2 shows the overall number of private suits brought into the courts during the years 1956 to 1960. It could be estimated that 92 to 94 per cent of these cases referred to the same articles of the penal code which were relevant in the press suits. Thus, comparing the 750,880 libel and defamation cases litigated with the mere forty-odd cases of press suits we can see the extent of the social backfire caused by publication of an item of news, if the few cases could win such great publicity.

The power of printed matter—which journalists tend to overestimate when they are involved themselves and to neglect when others are the subject—comes even more conspicuously to the fore when we consider the results of the question of whether the courts tend to convict rather than to acquit journalists in press suits. Out of 39 investigated cases, the defendant journalist was acquitted in 31,

TABLE 9.2

| | |
|------|---------|
| 1956 | 164,620 |
| 1957 | 193,713 |
| 1958 | 147,329 |
| 1959 | 127,058 |
| 1960 | 118,160 |
| Total | 750,880 |

and convicted in 7, and one lost his case in a civil suit. The corresponding data for the control group (cases in which the defendants were not journalists) are: 32 convictions (including 7 settlements out of court) 8 acquittals in appellate courts. Thus the proportion for journalists is exactly the opposite of that for other groups of society. In other words, if a suit is brought against a journalist, there is a high probability (more than 75 per cent) that he will be acquitted; in a similar situation, a defendant who is not a journalist will most probably be convicted (the odds here too being above 75 per cent). However, it must be remembered that the journalists involved in press suits are essentially championing what they perceive to be the public interest, while non-journalists sued for offenses against Article 255, paragraph 1 are usually motivated by private interests.

An interesting side effect of press suits, by the way, is the by no means negligible positive function of these suits for defendant journalists. Information about the proceedings is usually played up in the newspaper which employs the journalist, and the story is echoed by other media. As a consequence the name of the defendant journalist becomes widely known (often not until then), and this name-recognition factor is quite important in the trade. Thus, the balance of advantages (resultant publicity) and disadvantages (a small chance of conviction) does not seem at all bad.

How then, do we account for the relative impunity enjoyed by journalists in their work? To provide an explanation we must consider what factors lead to a conviction and what factors tend to result in acquittal in a press suit. Analysis of the justifications of verdicts (and of convictions in particular) reveals that several considerations influence the judges in their evaluations of the charges.

The hypothesis had been set forth that the more reliable the published material is, the less the probability of an adverse verdict. In the light of the collected materials, though the judicature is not quite uniform in this respect, this hypothesis appears as rather banal and not quite sound. In all the investigated cases except one, the courts took it for granted that the journalists' targets concerned social interests, and thus we need give this no further consideration. Since it is not discussed at all in the process of decision-making by the judge, the crucial point becomes the problem of the 'good faith' of the defendant. However, is it actually possible to prove that a journalist had acted in 'bad faith'? In the only recorded case in which the judge resorted to the charge of subjective bad faith, it was not actually proved by the court and in the last analysis it was reduced to the finding that the facts publicized by the journalist had been false. In a court proceeding, good or bad faith is a matter of evaluation and not of fact, and other than psychological tests can hardly be conceived. Anyone can claim his good faith, and there is no means of telling a true declaration from a false one if someone's convictions are the reference.

Our second hypothesis was: the more respected the social values attacked by a publication, the greater the probability of a lawsuit. What we learned bears out this hypothesis only with due modifications. A comparison of the two sets of data, those concerning the press suit and those concerning the control group litigations, reveals that the essential difference between them is in the type of values at stake. In 'normal' suits the main struggle is for personal values; in press suits, while this kind of value may be involved, too, the main emphasis is on those having social and professional ramifications. The following types of values were distinguished in the study: (1) basic general values: political, religious, national, etc.; (2) basic professional values: competence, expertise, efficiency, etc.; and (3) basic personal values: the ability to behave in socially accepted ways, etc. Both sets of lawsuits were characterized by a mild response to insults against the basic social values. This could be the result of many factors, among them perhaps a relatively small number of conflicts of this kind, or a belief that on such occasions other means were more efficient than a court suit in which the chances of success could be estimated as rather slim. In the light of such data, the hypothesis that a reaction against a journalist is apt to be the more severe the higher the rank assigned to the values offended by a press publication is not quite valid.

However, the research data seem to confirm our hypothesis number three, to the effect that the higher the social position attacked, the greater the probability of a reaction in the form of a lawsuit. Since this regularity holds at least up to a certain level of position, we can see that the data confirm the hypothesis. Those who sue a journalist for libel are usually those who care very much about their social 'image,' sometimes defined in sociological terms as the 'reflected ego.'[4] An individual tends to evaluate himself with reference to what others think of him. Thus, any public statement about a person (a printed statement in particular) is nothing short of an attempt to change the public image or the reflected ego of the person so cited. Such treatment can be more painful than a civil litigation (which is concealed within the walls of the court building), though the latter may lead to a loss of material property. For a person's public image to be assaulted can sometimes be so frustrating that the attacked person may prefer to seek immediate justice by himself, rather than suffer the inevitable delay of a libel suit.

The fourth hypothesis formulated in the initial phase of the investigations also turned out to be sound. The higher the social position of that which is attacked, the more probable it is that the public interest (an institution, a public office, etc.) will be involved in the suit, which means that in such cases the prosecutor would be expected to act *ex officio*. An analysis of the cases ending with convictions revealed that there were two such verdicts out of the four cases brought in by the public prosecutor. A general conclusion seems to follow that in the course of court proceedings the important thing is not only—as generally in life—what is said but also who says it and from what social position. This conclusion can also be understood as a praxiological principle.

The last supposition to be tested by the research was that the more strictly a newspaper observes the principle of anonymity for informants, the greater the number of lawsuits against its employees. In spite of the high degree of probability of this hypothesis, it is difficult either to accept or to dismiss it on the ground of the research results. In no case was the name of the author of the allegedly libelous press item concealed by the newspaper's editors. The files did not indicate either that the journalists involved in press suits tended to conceal their own names. However, it was found in many cases that the identities of informants, i.e. of those who had passed 'inside' information on to the journalist, were never revealed during the court proceedings. It could be inferred from the analyzed files that their anonymity had not been discussed at all in the court. Either they had been identified from the outset and were sued along with the journalist, or they remained unknown and the case was prosecuted against the journalist only. In any event, the problem of revealing the identity of informants never emerged as a special issue in the cases researched.

The results of our research lead to several reflections concerning legislative problems. For example, the following situation is not regulated by the law. A journalist submits a piece of writing to the editorial board. It is then subjected to modifications and changes, so that a new version arises. In some newspapers the practice is that the original writer is not consulted about the revisions, usually on the ground that there is no time to do so. If the article contains some allegedly libelous material, the question arises as to who should be legally liable for what is to a great extent a collective piece of journalism. A number of solutions can be suggested. The editor-in-chief could be made responsible for the collective changes; the position of co-ordinating manager could be introduced (i.e. an editor responsible for the changes and for discussing them with authors); or the most practical solution might be that the editorial board be obliged to submit the final version of the text to the original author, who would be obliged to accept or reject the modifications.

Another problem posed by the analyzed materials is the need to change the essential concept employed in press suits, viz., the notion of good faith, to a different one: due care in data collecting. If newsmen were expected to investigate more carefully what they intended to write about, and in particular if it was directed that they give up the habit of taking for granted whatever information is offered to them by official agencies, then the methods of data collecting by the newspapers as collective bodies would have to be made more efficient. In this eventuality, of course, it would be necessary that mutual confidence between journalists and readers become enhanced. An essential element of this is knowing that the sources of confidential information offered to a newspaper must remain anonymous. A journalist should be authorized to take responsibility for information supplied by his informant, and similarly, an editor-in-chief should be in a position, on special occasions, to take responsibility for publication of certain materials and to refuse to reveal the author's identity.

It is also worth noting again the distribution of the press suits instigated during the period covered by the study. There were 7 in 1956, 16 in 1957, 11 in 1958, 7 in 1959, and 2 in 1960. The remarkable decrease in the number of cases brought to the courts might be accounted for in several ways, but the most probable seems the assumption that the number of cases filed is proportional to the expected chance of winning the litigation.

184

A general analysis of the investigated court files suggests that the conflicts in which journalists become involved during the course of their work are in part brought about by clashes between various not quite compatible roles performed by them.[5] For one thing, journalists have no way of knowing who will be reading their articles. Indeed, it is difficult even to identify a reading public in socio-demographic terms, as the circulation of some dailies reaches a quarter of a million. However, we do know that information does not spread in a straight-line pattern; at least two levels are involved. The news is assimilated first by the leaders of opinion, whose evaluation of it will determine how it is treated at the 'follower' level. Hence, it is the opinion leaders who must be the focus of attention. As we know, they are usually people with relatively higher education. Consequently, all of the available pro and con aspects should be presented on any issue, since this is more effective as a means of persuasion for educated people.[6] Pieces covering all sides of a question are thus apt to be more effective even though an implicit argument one way or the other may emerge from the information.

As earlier researches have shown, there are two types of legal knowledge that can be the object of popularization: legal *principles* and legal *precepts*. The difference is essential. Knowledge of legal precepts is the concern of professional lawyers. It is they who are expected to know which law is applicable in a given situation, where its sources are to be found, and the scope covered by it. Among the 'average' people this kind of legal knowledge is practically non-existent. On the other hand, knowledge of legal principles is the knowledge of certain basic norms regulating what can and what cannot be done, pointing to the conditions and scope defining the limits of acceptable behavior. Such knowledge can well be detached from the legal precepts on which it is based, and still remain compatible with them. A reasonable legislator approaches such changes in law as are reflected in the precepts but do not modify the principles (such changes have no wide social resonance, since it is mainly professional lawyers who will have to deal with them), differently from the way he would approach changes which encroach upon principles. The latter should not be changed unless there is a clear necessity, since their functioning is based on their being widely known and accepted. Too frequent changes in this area (even though they may be meant to rationalize the legal system in some of its parts) are apt to bring about an effect the reverse of that expected: they can impair the legal order and legal awareness. It follows from this that it is better to focus public attention on legal principles than on legal precepts. A reasonable program for legal writers and reporters ought thus to emphasize the observance of principles.

The results of the investigations of press suits shed light on the

185

instrumental role of legal regulations. On the one hand, the law can provide the ground for solving conflicts between parties whose positions are more or less equal. On the other, it can be used to the advantage of the side which is on somewhat better ground than the opponent. Analysis of the research results reveals that journalists, though they fear becoming the target of lawsuits, are in a relatively favorable position when it actually comes to litigation.

# part three

# Theoretical considerations

# 10 The concept of a legal norm

Analytic and descriptive definitions are particularly important in the social sciences, for they try to grasp the encountered social reality. Synthetic (projective) definitions, arbitrarily stipulating the meaning of a term, are more significant in the deductive disciplines (e.g. mathematics, logic), where the basic requirements are that the propositions and statements entail each other, and that their systems are coherent. Although analytic definitions that attempt to describe basic concepts of social reality are paramount in the social sciences in general and in the legal disciplines in particular, still it is often quite difficult to construct them. The reason is the multiplicity of meanings inherent in a number of terms, especially if they are basic ones. It is often very hard indeed to find a definition that would cover all the intuitions, frequently quite diverse or even mutually incompatible, associated with a term. An author who enjoys a well-established authority in matters of semantic and sociological disquisitions on morals has written:[1]

> I do not regret the effort once spent to outline the concept of morality, for I have learned a lot from these attempts; today I still insist that an effort to build up an analytic definition of morality, i.e. a definition relying on the apparent common-sense intuitions related to this term, is doomed to failure in advance. Any analytic definition ought indeed to be formulated only after public opinion has been polled. But in this particular instance we have very good reason to suppose that opinion polling, even if it were limited to a single social group, would not produce compatible results.

Thus it would appear we might as well give up attempts at analytic definitions and turn toward the building of synthetic ones, taking care to make them methodologically the most useful. Doubtless this would be one way out of a situation which is not only methodologically but also theoretically bewildering. However, such an approach would not be quite smooth either, as it would also be deficient in precise communication, owing, not to ambiguity of terms, but this time to the too great abundance of differently constructed ones. Perhaps if every writer in every discipline of the social sciences were rigorous in sticking to the meanings he had stipulated by his own arbitrary decisions (as they would be if any and all synthetic definitions were to be respected), then the meaning of each isolated publication might well be clear but a multitude of non-translatable meanings would soon pile up, constituting an essentially new kind of barrier against the striving toward intersubjective understanding.

The considerations offered below are meant to suggest a possible way out of this vicious circle, which has led to the intuitions hitherto underlying analytic definitions being drawn from accidental experiences and observations, and being selected unsystematically and by means of illustrations according to idiosyncratic semantic tastes. These experiences and these tastes, in spite of a unifying tendency resulting from such communication as does occur and from the similarity of the stock data available to all academic environments, are still essentially different; in consequence, the systems of concepts and models based on them must also differ widely from each other.

In this situation, and particularly in respect of the concept of a legal norm, the alternative that emerges as a way out is that of attempting to base the analytic definitions not upon private terminological intuitions but rather on an analysis of operational definitions (i.e. those adopted for concrete considerations and researches) and on the results of empirical investigations of public opinion. Even though such investigations are still in their germinal stage, some synthesis of what has been done can be attempted already; we can also begin with generalizing the data already collected on different types of experience (historical, psychological, sociological), drawing both from the output of individual writers and from the store of established knowledge.

Anticipating the most obvious objections, it can be said that such an approach is arbitrary in selecting its starting points. It can be charged that what is proposed is an analysis of only some selected definitions concerning law; that only a few sociological investigations of public opinion on law and morality are proposed for consideration; that the extensive literature concerning various concepts widespread in legal science is apt to be dismissed, etc. Charges of this kind could be multiplied. However, over-riding such objections is the fact that the number of judicial definitions which could be analyzed is enormous and that some selection or other is absolutely necessary;

that sociological investigations relevant to an analytic definition of law are, in contrast, quite few; that since such spurious problems as the so-called levels or layers of legal science have been so piled up, this Gordian knot of misunderstandings can only be cut by leaving them aside. Finally, such objections miss the point of the proposed considerations: it is not to make a full survey of all possible definitions, with due account of their methodological shortcomings and merits, but rather to focus attention upon those data which promise to be particularly useful for constructing a definition of law as a social phenomenon.

Leon Petrażycki wrote the following at the beginning of a book in which he formulated an interesting and fruitful concept of law:[2]

> The genius philosopher Kant ridiculed his contemporary science of law because it could not define what law was. 'Lawyers are still looking for a definition of their concept of law,' he remarked ironically. Kant himself worked to solve this problem, but to no avail. After him many other eminent thinkers, philosophers and lawyers worked towards it, but for all that lawyers today are still looking for a definition of their concept of law.

Formulating his own definition, Petrażycki believed that it was an ultimate one. He was not quite right. This is why the task—which is perhaps not methodologically hopeless—must be undertaken once again and from the beginning. Let us start by considering the most important achievements of others.

According to Petrażycki, by law we should mean that which is experienced as imperative-attributive in its character. In this definition each term has its special meaning. Thus by emotions he meant not feelings or sentiments but the peculiar qualities of psychic life, its central and essential elements marked by a coherent structure of stimulus and reaction. Such elements of psychic life as cognition, feeling or will are—according to this conception—derivatives of the essential phenomenon of emotion. Imperativeness refers to obligation, while attributiveness refers to right or claim. In effect, a law is that which has to do on the one hand with someone's obligation to do (or to desist from doing) something, and on the other with someone else's demand that the action or desisting identified by the obligation be carried out. Thus, a law-related engagement between A and B can be illustrated as follows: if the person A has borrowed a book from another person B, then A experiences the feeling of obligation to return the book to B and he also believes that B has the right to claim it back; for his part, B has the right to have the book returned to him by A under the force of his obligation, thereby ascribed to A by B. This conception makes it quite easy to distinguish

191

THE CONCEPT OF A LEGAL NORM

between moral and legal phenomena: a moral experience is marked only by the feeling of obligation, while a law-related experience is additionally marked by the ascription of a right to someone. Accordingly, a beggar, X, who demands charity from a person, P, has no claim whatsoever upon that person. P can feel an obligation to be charitable toward X, but he does not ascribe to X any claim or right to receive alms. Thus, mass behaviors of the type relevant to the beggar X are regulated by a one-sided sense of moral obligation, while behaviors of the kind illustrated by the contract of borrowing and lending a book are regulated by two-sided experiences of obligation and right to claim.

The merit of this definition has been pointed out,[3] but more often it has been criticized, not always justly. Its main value is not only that it brings together the contents of various legal precepts making clear the often widely scattered and complex elements of a given law-related engagement, but also that it allows one to see law in action, its function and involvement in individual and collective life. But the definition has a certain significant shortcoming. Let us imagine, for example, that a maniac quite seriously enters a lecture room in a Polish university in 1972, saying: 'I am the owner of this university; I do not permit any classes to go on; please get out of this room.' According to the proposed definition, this crazy guy would experience a law-related feeling, since he would believe that he had the right to demand certain behavior (that university classes be dismissed, and that others be obliged to submit to his claim to get out of the lecture room). The character of his experience would be consistent with the structure of a law-related experience according to Petrażycki's definition, namely, it would entail both obligation and right. Obviously, such a situation would be absurd. Although this kind of absurdity would be very rare, and although the situation would be formally classified as law-related, it cannot be accepted if we do not want the whole concept of law to degenerate into a caricature. (Only litigious phenomena, or excessively quarrelsome attitudes in which someone claims disproportionately much in relation to obligations or in which there is an atrophy of the feelings of obligation, are somewhat different, though sometimes structurally similar to the fictitious case described above: they are usually related to abnormal profusion or under-development of a law-related sub-culture.) We may conclude that L. Petrażycki's definition of law, in spite of its significant merits, also has some shortcomings; we should therefore try to save what is valuable and significant in it, and at the same time attempt to find a definition that would be free of the shortcomings.

The classical definition of law which considers coercion by the state (a frequent instrument of class power), also reveals an important fallacy.

Here are a few definitions of law.

By 'law' we thus mean a system of forms, by their origin and functioning related to the activity of the state apparatus of coercion, a system where functions and contents are determined by the pattern of class forces and the level of development of the civilization.[4]

Law is an aggregate of general social norms of conduct, differing from other such aggregates in the following ways: the legal norms express the interests and strivings of the class which controls the society, i.e. the ruling class in all the states with class exploitation, and the working class and its allies in socialist states, in the first phase of their development. In a socialist nation state, law expresses equally the strivings and interests of the whole society. The interests and strivings expressed by law are ultimately objectively determined by the material conditions of the society, and of its ruling class in particular.[5]

Law is a definite aggregate of norms of conduct. Its distinguishing features are said to be the following: (1) these norms are either established or recognized in a proper manner by the 'state,' i.e. by the appropriate agencies of the state administration; (2) the realization of these norms is warranted by the state by the threat of coercion; (3) these norms express the pursuits of the ruling class to establish and maintain social and economic conditions advantageous to that class.[6]

A number of objections can be made against these definitions.
Historical experience reveals, above all if we analyze the development that has taken place in the socialist countries, that in some fields of social life and of economic conduct, state coercion is no longer decisive and is gradually being replaced by social pressure. The range of such pressure is extensive. On one hand, extreme social pressure can coincide with coercion by the state so that the two *add* up; on the other hand, social pressure alone can be at work to support the feeling of legal obligation, without the benefit of legal intervention. The example of the so-called 'voluntary jobs' (social works) may be the best illustration of this point. The label denotes an avowed obligation by a group of individuals (e.g. the staff of a factory or a company) to carry out some collective task without pay; now, if a member of such a group withdraws, he cannot be sued or exposed to criminal investigation, but the consequences of social pressure against him can be even more painful than the burden of a standard legal repression would be. The social courts are instituted by a bill of law, but they do not operate with the classical legal

193

sanctions; they present a middle case between state coercion and pure social pressure. Although in the case of social courts public pressure has been wholly formalized, none of the classical *penal* repressions may be carried out. Studies reveal that sorcery is sometimes substituted for official legal procedure.[7] In so-called primitive societies it is often easier to use sorcery to retaliate against evil, than to resort to litigation. In such societies, however, those who are recognized as sorcerers may well be expelled from the community or even killed. (The relevant studies concern the Chausson Indians in the State of Oregon.) Thus, the fear of being suspected of sorcery can bring about a tendency to conformism. Taking this into account, the following hypothesis has been formulated: wherever there is an authorized power, the scope of practical sorcery is narrow. How is this relationship explained? In the Chausson communities, and in all others, there is a need to exact obedience to accepted norms, and to functioning legal norms in particular. If there is a centralized nation-wide power, it assumes the *duty* to warrant such obedience by force. However, such power is by no means always present, and at any rate, no such power could be observed in the investigated Indian community. But then magic can offer substitute measures. For it is believed that behavior inconsistent with the norms of social interaction, or unlawful conduct, can be eradicated by magical means. In consequence, the fear of being exposed to sorcery deters one from breaking the law. In detailed investigations of thirty clan groups, a significant correlation was found which makes the above hypothesis highly probable. The hypothesis can be applied to different social settings, and developing it further one can say: in societies where there is a strong need of respect for a centralized legal authority, there is also a need for the use of magical and mystical means to reinforce this respect (the recent examples of Nazi and similar political systems with their conspicuous layout are additional illustrations to our hypothesis).

These considerations reveal the shortcomings of the classical definitions of law, which regard coercion by state as an essential element. The empirical studies, however minor, clearly point out the need to look at the notion of law from a new and different viewpoint.

Some results of field studies which might be particularly interesting for a discussion on the meaning of law and morality follow.[8]

As it has already been said, the results of studies on moral and legal attitudes of Polish society (comparative investigations of the Dutch society confirm these results) reveal that legal condemnation is followed by moral condemnation. Prior to the Polish survey it was assumed that various kinds of technical and administratively regulated behavior—remaining in the field of the formal—were morally indifferent, and that breaking such norms would not evoke moral condemnation. But the research results did not confirm this expectation. How can this apparent paradox be accounted for? Is it really true that any regulation, e.g. requiring one to walk along the right side of a street, contains an element of moral pressure? Although such a rule cannot assign moral status, the general principle from which it in some indirect way is derived does have such a status. The principle is that conflicts between people ought to be avoided, that any clashes between them, even unintended 'rubs,' should be prevented. In a way all legal procedures, technicalities or administrative regulations could be treated as morally indifferent in themselves, but since they are elements of a legal system, they are essential to the integrity of the system. Since the legal system formalizes generally accepted social values, or the progressive values advanced by the best forces of the society, all the elements of the system can be morally evaluated even if they do not directly concern moral issues. People tend to approve, morally, the legalistic attitude, because it assumes and supports the maintenance of favorable conditions, the efficient functioning of the legal system. If there was no stipulation that streets should be crossed at places with white stripes, nobody would care if someone crossed the street elsewhere. That people do become indignant is a secondary or derivative phenomenon, implied by the fact that the rule has been included in the body of laws. It is evident that the existence of this norm is of common advantage. But there are norms which, if broken, evoke a primary spontaneous moral indignation independent of the resultant formalization of the norm and whether the relationship between the relevant type of behavior and common advantage is understood or not. The difference between the two kinds of moral reaction seems to be evident: (1) the primary moral indignation occurs when an action evokes moral repulsion because of its content and character, not because of its tactical import or the existence of a formal interdiction. (2) The secondary moral condemnation occurs when an action is considered repulsive not because of its content (and independent of the content of the relevant norm), but because all the norms which contribute to the common welfare or to the social order are approved.[9]

The research results presented here and elsewhere in this book can be generalized even more. The following general propositions can be suggested:

1   A legal condemnation of definite actions always entails their moral condemnation, while the reverse is not always true: a moral condemnation need not entail a demand for a legal sanction against these actions.

2   The stronger the moral condemnation (after a peculiar, qualitatively identifiable barrier has been crossed), the stronger is also the legal condemnation.

3   Minions of the law who are engaged in demanding the strict obedience of the formal and structural requirements of the legal system are apt to condemn less strongly than others the breaking of basic norms in social interaction.

These findings are by no means banal. The first is obviously inconsistent with the previous assumptions. The traditional views on this matter can be represented as shown in Diagram 1:

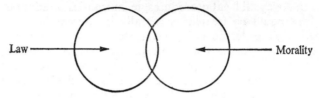

*Diagram 1*

According to this, there are three kinds of human behavior related to legal and moral norms: (a) those that are subject to moral evaluation only; (b) those that are subject to both moral and legal evaluation; and (c) those that are subject to legal evaluation only. The results of empirical investigation of public opinion on the issues reported above have proved that Diagram 1 is misleading. A sound model, according to the research results presented here is illustrated by Diagram 2:

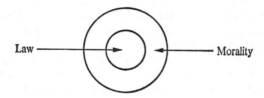

*Diagram 2*

According to that, all behavior which has been backed by a legal sanction evokes a demand for a moral evaluation, while only some behavior that is morally condemned is also regulated by law.

Public opinion tends to express moral reaction toward all the phenomena which 'ought' to be regulated by law, while not all behavior which is generally considered morally condemnable calls forth reactions that demand formal sanction. In other words: in the social sentiment there are certain phenomena of moral character only, and a field of mixed reactions: moral-and-legal; there is no behavior, however, which would be subject to legal evaluation alone.

As we have already said, the first of our propositions is controversial, particularly from the earlier point of view. The second, concerning the relationship between the strength of the moral and legal condemnation, is in agreement with common sense and with traditional theories. The third, pointing out the attitudes of minions of the law, brings knowledge which is not immediately obvious.

The discovery that minions of the law are less severe than the average population when essential norms of interaction are broken, and more severe in the case of trespassing against formal and procedural regulations, is significant. It reveals that minions of the law see efficiency of law as a means of social influence, and are more skeptical of the effects of severe punishment as a rational tool of social engineering; it also reveals a stronger involvement by this group of people in matters of the inner structure of the system of law, its pattern and its coherence.

To what extent are the reported results able to bear suggestions about the meaning of law? We must make the reservation that the discussed studies have concerned only a few essential problems, and that further research is indispensable; however, the existing reflections do provide us with certain important elements for our attempt at a synthetic approach to the definition of a legal norm. Thus, it can be said, in a tentative way, that *law is a psycho-social phenomenon, a socially coherent relationship between obligation and claim, inculcated by internalization.* If an anthropomorphic metaphor is allowed, it can be said that a social system can also attain its aims, whenever it considers it appropriate, by cheaper means requiring less waste of energy—i.e. by moral attitudes, or by inculcating a feeling of duty. On the other hand, whenever more significant values are at stake, the social system produces and welds legal attitudes, making them doubly binding—in terms of obligation and claim. The *do ut des* principle, an expression of a certain pattern of social, economic and other forces, acts as the unifying and motivating social link. To make things simpler, if we compare the social system with a pyramid (with a rather flat top), then the norms of obligation and claim would tie the important elements of the system together by securing a relative balance of forces along the horizontal plane. Obligation and claim are like equal facets of the same phenomenon—of a certain pattern, arrangement, or contact. Along the vertical plane the social system operates with additional constructions—privilege and obedience (held together not by the *do ut des* principle, but by power).

A privilege occurs, when there is no balance between obligation and claim (supported by the *do ut des* principle), or when extensive rights correspond to much narrower duties (although sometimes rather risky). Going back to the anthropomorphic metaphor, we can say that the social system believes that some individuals should be offered premiums (because of qualifications, rarity, role, etc.) at the costs of others. On the other hand, obedience is a symptom of a profusion of duties and a scarcity of claims. The smaller the proportion between the duties and rights of individuals, the less flat is the hierarchy of the social system. Although in various situations the proportions between duty and claim, obedience and privilege may be different, and although in various concrete social systems they can be very remote from the most stable principle *do ut des*, the structure of these relations always remains the same: obligation on one side, right on the other.

If we accepted the above assumptions (and the empirical materials induce us to do so), then many of the institutions we have cherished would be relatively easily explained. Thus, morality would be functioning in areas where the practical account of gains and losses dictated such a strategy: against certain types of negatively evaluated behaviors it is not worth while to engage means other than collective and individual condemnation; to start the institutionalized apparatus of repression would cost more than the possible loss brought about by the inefficiency of the condemnation. On the other hand, law would represent norms protected by sanctions (for a penalty or civil sanction expresses the social interest invested in maintaining the type of social system to which the norm corresponds). When the inertia in identifying the current interest does not permit one to follow the changes which occur, then the system builds up new germinal relations of the type obligation-claim, which begin to function as the new, alternative ways to be opposed against the former patterns which are already dysfunctional. A reform or a revolution then sets in.

J. Skolnick, when summing up his very interesting research concerning riots in various American cities, suggests the following tentative explanation of these phenomena, which can be an illustration of our general thesis formulated above. He says:[10]

We find conventional theories of riots open to challenge on the following grounds:
1. They tend to focus on the destructive behavior of disaffected groups while accepting the behavior of authorities as normal, instrumental, and rational. Yet established, thoroughly institutional behavior may be equally destructive as, or considerably more so than, riots. No riot, for example, matches the destructiveness of military solutions to disputed political issues. Further, available evidence suggests both that (a) armed officials often demonstrate a greater propensity to violence against persons than unarmed civilians; and (b) these actions often escalate the intensity of the disorder and comprise a good part of the 'destructiveness' of riots, especially in terms of human deaths and injuries. Furthermore as the reports of our Chicago,

Cleveland, Miami, and San Francisco study teams well illustrate, riots are not unilaterally provoked by disaffiliated groups. Collective protest involves interaction between the behavior of 'rioters' and the behavior of officials and agents of social control. Each 'side' may on close inspection turn out to be equally 'riotous.' The fact that the behavior of one group is labeled 'riot' and that the other is labeled 'social control' is a matter of social definition.

2. They tend to describe collective behavior as irrational, formless, and immoderate. As we will demonstrate in the next section, less emotional scrutiny of riots indicates that they show a considerable degree of structure, purposiveness, and rationality. Nor is 'established' behavior necessarily guided by rational principle. . . . A measure of irrationality, then, is not a defining characteristic of collective behavior generally or of riots in particular; rather, it is an element of many routine social processes and institutions and forms of collective behavior. The more significant difference may be that established institutions are usually in a more advantageous position from which to define 'rationality.' . . .

3. Finally, it is insufficient to analyze riots in terms of 'tension' and 'frustration.' It is not that this perspective is wrong, but that it tells at once too little and too much. Too little, because the idea of 'tension' or 'strain' does not encompass the subjective meaning or objective impact of subordinate caste position or political domination. Too much, because it may mean almost anything; it is a catch-all phrase, that can easily obscure the specificity of political grievances. It is too broad to explain the specific injustices against which civil disorders may be directed; nor does it help to illuminate the historical patterns of domination and subordination to which the riot is one of the many possible responses.

These results illustrate our thesis formulated above: they reveal the discrepancy between the legal and moral sentiments of certain groups (or segments) of society on one hand, and the legal sentiment tied to the letter of the law, represented by the establishment, on the other. When social groups with legitimate claims cannot find official channels to approach the official and controlling agencies, they are apt to look for ways and means to do so beyond the valid law. These ways and means are, from the viewpoint of a universal feeling of what is right and just, expressions of moral and legal claims. Although they lack the hallmark of belonging to the sphere of the officially legitimate, still they are legally valid though the system of law brutally represses the claims and rights expressed by the rioters.

# 11 Anomie, conformism, legalism

The most interesting subjects in the sociology of law are legal norms and, to some extent, the related moral norms. The legal and moral norms, however, do not subsist in a social void, but are special categories of social norms in general. In a social system there exist not only legal and moral norms, but also various norms of customs, manners, religion, politics, tradition, etc. Among these categories moral and legal norms are distinct, as their role in the social system is particularly significant and important. Legal and moral norms are the basis for order and regulation in a social system.

Considering the diversity of social norms and the role legal and moral norms play, it should be considered what the various social norms have in common, and which specific features distinguish our two basic types from the other ones. In one of the theories that attempt to offer an overall look at the problem, we find the concept of anomie. According to R. Merton[1] who has developed the earlier theories of É. Durkheim, it means a situation where the basic social norms in a given system are considered with less respect than usual, or even considered no longer valid by the people. Thus anomie does not mean a situation where there are no norms at all, or even where they are not clearly understood, but means that people know the norms they are expected to obey but have ambiguous attitudes toward them. There are two important elements in this concept: it introduces a conflict between the norms which should be obeyed by individuals, and it brings in a peculiar view of the means by which the general objectives (goals) can be attained in a social system. Even if the objectives that should be pursued are obvious, the legitimate means to attain them are lacking in case of anomie.

On these assumptions Merton proposes a relatively simple typology of various individual ways of adjustment which can serve as a ground for characterizing deviant behavior.[2]

According to this typology, conformism would mean acceptance of the objectives of the culture as well as of the institutionalized means related to the basic values of the social system.

Innovation would mean the individual's acceptance of the basic values of the social system on one hand but, on the other, his rejection of the means the system traditionally offers to attain the objectives. Innovation consists of the search for and finding of means other than those offered by tradition.

Ritualism should mean a refusal to accept the basic objectives of the given culture (or indifference toward them) together with a positive respect for the means expected to lead to such objectives. Thus the stiff traditional ways of acting have been sanctified by having been applied to society for a long time.

Withdrawal should mean rejection both of the objectives of the

TABLE 11.1  *A typology of individual ways of adjustment*

| Ways of adjustment | Cultural ends | Institution-alized means |
|---|---|---|
| 1 Conformism | 1 | 1 |
| 2 Innovation | 1 | 0 |
| 3 Ritualism | 0 | 1 |
| 4 Withdrawal | 0 | 0 |
| 5 Revolt | 1, 0 | 1, 0 |

1 = acceptance; 0 = rejection.

social system and of the means that traditionally warrant their realization. This phenomenon is sometimes called 'inner emigration.'

Finally, revolt means (1) rejection of the objectives as well as the institutional means leading to them, and (2) acceptance of both the objectives and the institutionalized means of another, imagined social system intended as a substitute for the rejected one. The above definitions are set out in Table 11.1.

P. Sztompka developed these ideas and attempted to classify such concepts as: conformism and real conformism, legalism, opportunism, conformism and contraformism. By real conformism he means a compatibility of a behavior with a norm; the contents of the norm are approved in the non-instrumental way (i.e. the norm is accepted with reference to some supreme or absolute values, like righteousness, justice, goodness and their antonyms). By legalism he means a certain variety of conformism, characterized by the formal acceptance of a norm. Opportunism is another variety of conformism, consisting of disapproval (also uninstrumental) of the contents of a norm. Thus, nonconformism is a 'deviation, with non-instrumental disapproval of contents.'[3] Finally, contraformism is, according to Sztompka, an individual's conduct in opposition to the norm, because this norm belongs to a normative sub-system which the individual disapproves of in general.[4]

Some other definitions of conformism: 'Conformism is an action which takes into consideration some norm (or norms) and which is included into the scope of actions permitted by norms.'[5] 'By conformist behavior is meant a behavior reflecting the effective influence of others.'[6] 'It is a mistake to identify conformism with effects of social interaction. . . . Conformism as such ought to be understood as a specific kind of establishing proper interaction.'[7] 'Conformist or nonconformist behavior can be understood as an index of the degree of constancy or of the extent of change in human interactions within the given social pattern, and it points out, if the constancy or change appears mainly as a consequence of coercion, or of voluntary interpersonal relations.'[8] 'Conformism is a frame of mind, sometimes transient and brought about by some types of social pressures, and at other times more solidly built into the human psyche. It is a closed state of mind, assuming a certain type of relation between a person and authority (individual or group). Due to the influence of an effective reward or punishment inflicted by the authority, a person may act or not act with reference to the information he obtains in directions which are desired by the source of the message.'[9]

All the above definitions have one thing in common: they all compare actual behavior with behavior described by a norm, whether approved or disapproved. This important feature of conformist and similar behavior is often neglected. For it reveals that an adequate classification of conformist and deviant behavior cannot be made, if we do not take into account the values these types of behavior are related to. Definitions of conformist and deviant behavior will, for this reason, always be relative. Only with respect to the basic values can an action be sensibly classified as either conformist or deviant.

In common language people who respect the generally accepted norms of social life are called conformists, whereas people whose behavior is inconsistent with the norms are called non-conformists. Among the generally accepted norms of social life the narrower category of legal norms should be discerned. For not all the generally accepted norms are protected by legal sanctions. Thus, people who respect all the generally accepted social norms are conformists with respect to the legal norms, too. However, the opposite is not true. Not everybody who is a conformist, from a legal point of view, is also conformist in the more general sense. In Polish law, homosexuals, or Lesbians,[10] represent such a case. Although their behavior is consistent with the regulations of law, it is not consistent with the generally accepted norms of social life.

In principle, legal norms protect the supreme social values. However, some of the generally accepted norms of social life, like the norms of politeness or good manners, are not protected by law. The law enters only when inappropriate behavior takes a form which is dangerous for others, or when it clearly disturbs the public peace. The degree of intensity determines whether an impolite, inappropriate or indecent type of behavior is considered legally non-conformistic. A rude and noisy individual will violate the law only when he starts using insulting language or being overtly aggressive. But some types of behavior are inherently legally non-conformistic (independently of their intensity) like theft, fraud, etc.

It is the lawmaker's responsibility to study various norms of behavior and to suggest which types of behavior ought to be forbidden, which should be tolerated and which should be encouraged. The pattern these three categories form changes continuously. At some point certain behavior is considered socially noxious and is included in the forbidden category. Other behavior becomes legalized, because of changes in social judgments and modifications of social values. Social life has various levels and changes occur continuously on each level. Such changes concern values and essential evaluations; some norms cease to be generally recognized; the scope of behavior forbidden by law undergoes modifications; behavior itself also changes in accordance with inherent processes.

What is non-conformist today might have been so once; what is conformist now might not always have been so. In various fields changes have occurred with different intensity. The development of changes in evaluations and behavior, and in legal interference, varies in matters of property (individual, collective), protection of life, and sexual behavior.

The above definitions and considerations show that the notion of conformism involves a certain ambiguity. Taking the accumulated semantical experience into account and covering the available investigations of conformism and deviation, it seems that we have to suggest a different definition of conformism and of related terms. The following criteria are assumed: consistency or inconsistency in behavior with the generally accepted social values; inner motivation, inducing acceptance or rejection of these values; the principal or instrumental attitude; the functioning or lack of personal variables.

If we assume this set of criteria, the classification of the discussed types of behavior will look as set out in Table 11.2.

Legalism differs from conformism, as we have already said, in being respectful of legal norms which need not always be compatible with the prevalent legal sentiment. Opportunism refers to behavior which is positively appreciated, but its underlying motivation is instrumental (contrary to one of the above definitions, characterizing opportunism, among other factors, by the uninstrumental attitude), i.e. ready to accept norms because of the expected advantages, but without an inner belief in the norms that have been chosen as the ground for action. Coercion is also defined as behavior consistent with what is prescribed by the generally accepted values, but what is essential in this case is not personal motivation at work, but rather pressure (quite often physical) from the group sub-culture or the general values and the appropriate system to control their realization. Various types of deviant behavior (innovation, ritualism, revolt, withdrawal) are incompatible with the generally accepted values either because of personal variables or because a negative sub-culture (e.g. the criminal underworld) exerts its influence, or because

TABLE 11.2  *Conformist and deviant behaviors*

| | Behavior: consistent with norm (*1*) or not (*0*) | Values of norm accepted (*1*) or not (*0*) | Principled (*1*) or instrumental attitude (*0*) | Personal variables active (*1*) or not (*0*) |
|---|---|---|---|---|
| Conformism | 1 | 1 | 1 | 1 |
| Legalism | 1 | 1 | 1 | 1 |
| Opportunism | 1 | 0 | 0 | 1 |
| Deviation | 0 | 0 | 1 or 0 | 1 or 0 |
| Coercion | 1 | 1 or 0 | – | 0 |

there is a pressure by a backward culture on the whole social system (Fascism). A person can also be a deviant for reasons of pure principle or because he believes it to be of advantage, i.e. for instrumental reasons.

However, instead of multiplying classifications of abstract concepts, it is more important to trace various investigations and to pick out what might be significant for the problem of deviation and conformism. In the present considerations we shall leave out most detailed findings concerning conformist behavior, and only mention the result of an investigation of a small group. The problems are too remote from what is our main concern here. Although the literature on conformism and deviation in small groups is extensive,[11] we shall quote only a single characteristic study. The study was based on a famous experiment by Asch.[12] From the results of this study we can formulate the following: often an individual cannot withstand a group pressure of opinion, or unity of a group, even if the group as a whole is obviously wrong.

This proposition is based on experiments where eight persons were asked to compare the lengths of three unequal lines. Seven persons were instructed consciously to declare false evaluations of the lengths of the observed lines, but the eighth person, the real subject of the experiment did not know this. It turned out that about a third of the responses of the tested persons (the eighths) were consistent with the untrue opinions of the majority, while only about a quarter were able to oppose the majority and not renounce their judgments. So this experiment shows that by influencing an individual it is relatively easy to change his views on reality, even if he had a direct contact with it by his own senses. When there is a discrepancy of opinions about a state of affairs which can be objectively ascertained or checked, then the opinion of the majority, even if it is inconsistent with reality, might still prevail; the view of the majority can often distort the image of the outer world. Of course, an individual rarely has such a conspicuous choice between the two worlds as in the quoted experiment: the choice between what his own eyes tell him and what the majority says. Usually an isolated individual who knows the views of some majority on a certain matter is not in a position to check the reality with his own senses. A man with ideas about something based on second-hand knowledge is even more vulnerable to the opinion of others. In the discussed experiment it also turned out that if the isolated individual (the eighth person) was backed by someone he could stand the pressure of the majority quite successfully.

It can be said in this context that sometimes people strive more intensely not to be left out than to insist on the reality of the evidence of their senses. This intense striving to agree with evaluations and opinions of others can be an important element in manipulating people, and at any rate it is an essential factor in forming the tight links of conformism.

Since there seems to be a general tendency to respect the opinions of others, and in particular a propensity to obey the directives of authority, the question about the origin and causes of such attitudes arises. An attempt to answer it was made by an ingenious experiment which was designed to investigate the degree of obedience of orders issued by an administrative agency of authority.[13] Before the study was carried out, three basic hypotheses were formulated:

1 If an official holds his position without sufficient training or knowledge, then his subordinates are not inclined to recognize his authority as legitimate.

2 An undermining of the superior's authority negatively influences the performance of the subordinates, as well as their obedience to the technical orders and advice given to them by the superior.

3 Obedience to administrative orders and rules is not dependent

upon the manner in which the subordinates are treated by their superiors (competent or not).

To carry out the experiment, a team of scientific workers established a fictitious organization. Forty-five students were hired as employees of the 'organization'. Their task was to fill in questionnaires usually used in sociological investigations. The employees were assigned to superiors, i.e. scientific workers carrying out the experiment. Their power consisted in issuing technical and administrative orders to the employees. Among the technical orders were instructions concerning the manner of elaborating the questionnaires. The general instruction obtained by the employees contained specially prepared traps (ambiguities), designed to compel the employees to ask their superiors how the job should be done. The employees worked in separate rooms, without being able to contact or consult each other. They were observed by collaborators of the experimenting team who pretended to work on other assignments in the same rooms. Communication with the superiors (in order to ask about details related to the questionnaires or about other matters) was possible by telephone. The intention was to exclude any other means of contact and resultant extra-factual suggestions. The superiors were divided into three categories and gave their answers according to assignment: (a) some who gave sound answers showing solid knowledge, (b) some who betrayed the lack of appropriate knowledge or orientation, and (c) some who pretended to know just as much as those asking the questions. During and after the study, evaluations concerning the superiors and the performance of the employees were collected. At the end the employees were informed about the actual experiment.

The main point of the study was to see how subordinates are influenced by competent and incompetent superiors; the results can be summarized as follows:

*Re 1* It proved to be a very complex task to verify the hypothesis that if an official holds his position without sufficient training or knowledge, then his subordinates are not inclined to recognize his authority as legitimate.

*Re 2* The hypothesis that different approaches to subordinates would influence their obedience in performing technical orders was confirmed by the data of the experiment.

*Re 3* The hypothesis that different approaches to subordinates would not influence their obedience in performing administrative orders was also confirmed.

In general, the authority of an office frequently levels down the perceived lack of competence of the superiors, modifying the inner attitudes of the subordinates and their performance in favor of the institution. (Appreciating the results of the described experiment, it

206

must be kept in mind that it was rather narrow in its scope and thus its results should be handled carefully. For example, it can be supposed that the employed students would work with particular diligence, treating their jobs as a test for later steady employment, so that their level of performance would make up for the influence of the style of management.)

So it seems we have to take it for granted that law enjoys a certain degree of prestige or respect, credited to it simply because of its legitimacy. Perhaps two parallel processes are at work here: respect for the law is induced and it is radiated. It also seems that respect for law is the accumulated net result of judgments of its functioning in various fields. These judgments build up the global phenomenon of respect of law. In turn, a part of the global respect can be transferred, when necessary, to fields that have not acquired it yet or have already lost it.

We can suppose that various institutions and legal regulations evoke different degrees of respect. Accordingly there are different degrees of respect for criminal law in general and in particular for regulations about foreign currency, traffic regulations, inheritance rules, laws on alimony, etc. A multitude of sections of social and economic life is regulated by law, and there is a multitude of legal stipulations, normatively prescribing the relevant behavior; this raises the question: to what extent do the partial respects go together or cancel each other, and how do they cause the accumulation of a global prestige of law? These significant questions are related to other important theoretical and practical ones. There is also a semantic problem, how prestige of law, with its many different shades of meaning, ought to be analyzed. Respect for the law can arise from fear of its coercive apparatus and its sanctions. Respect can be the result of a cool calculus that suggests it is ultimately better to respect the law than to break it. Besides, respect for the law can be a result of inertia, or of lack of will to break it, i.e it can be passive subjugation to law rather than its inherent acceptance. Respect for the law can also be an expression of the acceptance of the whole institution of law, in spite of criticism towards some part of it, or it can be acceptance of constituent elements of the legal system. Finally, respect for the law need not have its source in the material acceptance of it (as one can be opposed to the given normative system, but still respect it), but in the formal and normative directive, the Kantian imperative saying that whatever happens to the world, the norms of law must be obeyed.

Our reports on various empirical investigations presented earlier in this book (on parental authority, on the prestige of law, on legal and moral views) pointed out that the original of respect for the law and the degrees of its internalization can be quite diversified. However, in the study on the prestige of law, concerning the problem of respect for the law directly, three basic and separate versions of legalism emerged. The first version consists of accepting law as a matter of principle (the Kantian notion of law); this type of legalistic attitude is usually represented by people with strongly developed super-egos, remarkable self-control and emotional stability, who are dependable, practical-minded, married and over thirty. The second version of legalism is essentially instrumental, conceived as a means to curb others; it admits respect for the law even if it is unjust, and is related to such personality traits as dominance, aggressiveness, unconventional behavior, extra-punitiveness (i.e. a tendency to inflict very severe punishments), and lack of respect for the property of others. The third version of legalism consists of obedience to superiors even when their orders are considered wrong. It should be noticed that the three types of legalism emerged as a result of two types of inquiries: a public opinion poll of a nation-wide representative sample, and control research by personality inventories. The two series of results were in agreement with the first and second version of legalism, but not with the third one. According to the nation-wide opinion poll, the third attitude tends to be assumed by persons fifty or more years old, psychically inhibited but without insecurity feelings; according to the personality tests, such an attitude is related to the following characteristics: suspicion, timidity, poor adjustment, low resistance to threat, low self-evaluation, propensity to depression and pessimism.

Rationalizations underlying the above three versions of legalism can be formulated in the following way: if law is accepted as a matter of principle the view is that it has an autonomous value; if law is generally accepted by well-adjusted people the idea is that law can be an effective means of controlling others, as well as oneself; obedience to law expressed by respect for superiors is the attitude of people with authoritarian propensities, who are apt to be afraid of power or, to release anxiety, are likely to identify themselves with power.

A number of conclusions can be drawn from what has been said. There is reason to believe that purely theoretical terms are not adequate for defining such concepts as anomie, conformism or legalism, as they depend on evaluations referring to behavior included under the headings of anomie, conformism or legalism. The available definitions of these concepts either fail to embrace all the related problems or they fail to correspond with the empirical investigations which have been carried on in this field. Legalism is by no means a variety of conformism since there is room for legalistic types of behavior or attitudes that are not conformist. The distinction between fundamentalist and instrumentalist attitudes allows one to distinguish conformism from opportunism more precisely than was formerly possible. The introduction of personality variables permits one to ascertain which motivations were actually engaged in supporting the various conformist or legalistic attitudes. There is a general or global prestige of law with various partial results for its different ramifications. Finally, there are various versions of legalism and their respective underlying psycho-social determinants.

The problems we have been dealing with here are far from being neatly arranged, and in the present stage of considerations and inquiries, particular effect ought to be made toward a systematical confrontation of the empirical research results with semantic discussions about their essential concepts. In this field, more than in any other, further investigations, as well as attempts at general theories, seem to be indispensable.

A Chinese fable warns against neglecting theory:

Kiu-sey asked Si-tien vehemently: 'My lord! Please explain to me why nobody pays attention to the new system of recording and handling of numbers, which has been desired for centuries and which I have invented?' Si-tien answered: 'Seek for new, unusual devices. Burn your body, lighting with it the description of your method. Write it down on the buttocks of a beautiful woman. Offer it to a powerful lord so that he avows it as his own. You can also use the most effective trick!' Kiu-sey continued to inquire: 'What trick, sir?' whereupon Si-tien answered, 'Show them how to count money by your method.'

# 12 Theories of the functioning of law

Physicists ignore the nature of the atom, electron or neutron, but know exactly which laws govern their motions and interactions. In contrast, lawyers 'know' exactly what law, the validity of law, or a legal norm are, but they have rather vague ideas about the functional properties of these elements. How can we explain this paradox? Physicists are aware that it is possible to gain insight into the elementary particles only by the careful and systematic collecting of data concerning their interactions. They also know well that by discovering minor or partial regularities they are eventually able to gain a general understanding of the nature of atoms, electrons or neutrons. Lawyers on the contrary believe that direct insight into the meaning of such terms as law, validity or norm will reveal the essence of the entities denoted by these terms. They also tend to ignore the important consideration that basic legal terms actually influence social life by their various usages in legal enactments and their interpretations. But knowledge about the regularities that control the exercising of such influence is rather scarce among lawyers. We should then ask if this is an appropriate road towards understanding law. Perhaps it is more reasonable to try to arrive at the general propositions concerning the functioning of law by observing its partial expressions, in order to come finally to the essential problem—to the explanation of the riddle of law.

Leaving to the formalist lawyers the verbal disputes on what law can possibly mean, we shall devote some thought to such tentative generalizations that refer to the descriptions of the functioning of law as a part of social reality. We will discuss two hypotheses of the functioning of law along these lines.

## The ideas of Leon Petrażycki

When a delineation of some historical trend or the development of a given scientific discipline is wanted, especially in the area of social sciences, an arbitrary decision has to be made. Keeping this in mind it is possible to say, probably without essential errors, that the empirical sociology of law was born in 1962 in Washington, DC, when a research committee of sociology of law was established by the International Sociological Association. The founding of this committee can be regarded as a symptomatic event which reveals a specific stage of systematic development of empirical studies in the field of social inquiry about law and can be considered a sign of maturity.

The task is probably more difficult when we attempt to pinpoint the approximate time of the appearance of the sociology of law as a loose but independent branch of sociology, a sub-discipline aware of its own problems and, although lacking empirical content, nevertheless potentially ready for empirical testing of hypotheses already generated. According to N. Timasheff, the work of E. Ehrlich, *Fundamental Principles of Sociology of Law* (published in Germany, 1913; translated into English, 1936) might be considered the landmark showing the beginning of sociology of law as an independent science. He writes, 'E. Ehrlich is commonly regarded as the founder of the sociology of law, a disciple, standing somewhere between jurisprudence and pure sociology.' Other scholars would rather denote M. Weber's work, *On Law in Economy and Society* (published in Germany, 1922; translated into English, 1954) as the creation of a systematic sociological approach to law. Still others would say that this field of inquiry was generated collectively by those mentioned above plus scholars like T. Geiger in his work *Vorstudien zu einer Soziologie des Rechts* (1947); N. Timasheff, *An Introduction to the Sociology of Law* (1939); and G. Gurvich, *Sociology of Law* (1942). Some American scholars (although the sociology of law, according to the prevailing opinion, has its origin in Europe) might consider (with some justification) R. Pound's work, *Sociology of Law and Sociological Jurisprudence* (1943) and his earlier writings (published around 1907), and claim him as the father of the independent branch of sociology—its legal ramification.

Although questions about the origin of a given science are almost always disputable (as a by-product they generate some sort of unnecessary excitement) it is nevertheless usually convenient to find a starting point, a historic (sometimes a heraldic) point of reference. This state of confusion seems to create a convenient situation in which to draw out of oblivion a thinker who was the teacher of G. Gurvich, N. Timasheff, and P. Sorokin; a person who apparently influenced Pavlov, a lawyer, psychologist, philosopher, methodologist and sociologist, who had the misfortune to write and publish only in German, Russian and Polish—Leon Petrażycki. Sometimes the state of 'social visibility' (or rather 'academic visibility') does not correspond to the scope, depth, and creativity of a given area. The Petrażycki case is, without any doubt, a perfect example of 'social invisibility' which hinders his work from being generally used and recognized.

It is still an open question in which way (direct or indirect) Petrażycki's ideas were able to influence the current development of the sociology of law. There are some indications that his impact has been quite powerful. According to N. Timasheff:[1]

It is noteworthy that, during the past two decades, there has arisen, in the Scandinavian countries, a new school of the sociology of law, the so-called Uppsala school whose members have posed the same problem as Petrażycki, the problem of a realistic interpretation of law on a psychological basis. They try to replace the objective 'ought to be' (belonging to the realm of ideas) with the subjective experience of right and duty. This is very close to Petrażycki's theory; but, contrary to Petrażycki, the Scandinavians are not inclined to expand the concept of law to cover what the latter called intuitive law and unofficial law. The partial coincidence of views is an example of the familiar phenomenon of converging development in science; in any case, the members of the Uppsala school did not have direct access to Petrażycki's work. This did not prevent one of them, Karl Olivercrona, from writing a lengthy criticism of the theories of the Russo-Polish master.

## Law and morals as products of social processes

Leon Petrażycki's conception of the sociology of law is one of the theories that try to describe the influence of social processes upon law—and the influence of law upon social processes. His sociology of law, although he never used the term is based on his general sociological ideas.[2] L. Petrażycki's sociology is a theory of social development. Even more can be said. It is a theory of social progress. He was not only interested in finding the regulations of social development, but also believed that social changes were directed towards a definite end. According to him, this end was the sovereignty of universal, rational and active love among people.

Sociology as a theory of social development deals, according to Petrażycki, with collective behavior. It is controlled by certain regulations. What are they? The process of social change is governed by

the principle of 'unconsciously congenial' (or unconsciously ingenious) adjustment. There are three archetypes of adjustment:
philocentric, i.e. related to the biological species, sociocentric, and
egocentric.

Philocentric adjustment is the adaptation of a species to its physical
and collective conditions that allows it to survive in the Darwinian
struggle for existence. If a mother risks her life to save her child, she
acts under the urge of her emotions[3] which are products of philocentric adjustment. She risks her life to save the next generation of the
same species. If mothers, or parents in general, preferred their own
lives to those of their offspring, the species would (considering the
harsh conditions of the biological environment) be doomed to perish.
Defensive mechanisms of the species inculcate motivations into the
psychical patterns of behavior of individuals to defend the existence
of their species, not only of the individual. Philocentric adjustment
provides a link between man and the animal world. In these terms we
cannot speak of sociology as a science dealing exclusively with human
behavior. The scope of sociological inquiries is thereby extended. In
some cases interpretation of human behavior can help understand
animals, but the reverse is also true.

We can explain egocentric adjustment by giving the example of the
pet dog which J. Lande[4] was fond of mentioning in his lectures.[5]

A pet dog learns quickly to be tidy at home. The fact that he is
beaten for untidy behavior is not enough to explain it, for the
dog does not understand the causal relation between his trespass
and the flogging, nor the instrumental link between his pleading
to be let out and the avoidance of punishment. After the first
beating, the repulsive emotion of the dog will be associated
with the images of all the elements, both 'rational' (trespass,
beating) and 'irrational'—if there was a piece of golden paper
within sight, he would be afraid of golden paper and run away
from it; if he was beaten with a blotting pad, he would be
afraid of blotting pads. But each consecutive experience will
make the association of emotion with accidental and changeable
elements weaker, while the association with the significant
elements will be reinforced. This process is similar to logical
induction, although there is no reasoning in it.

Petrażycki formulated his theory of emotional (impulsional)
adjustment before I. Pavlov's ideas became known. It might be
interesting to investigate more carefully to what extent Petrażycki
possibly influenced Pavlov, or, maybe, to what extent Pavlov's discoveries reinforced Petrażycki's ideas. It is also possible that both of
them expressed, in some way, the emerging climate or 'mood' of a
scientific community trying then as now to grasp possible links

between attitudes and behavior. In his interesting introduction to L. Petrażycki's book, *Law and Morality*, N. Timasheff writes, 'At this point, Petrażycki made another discovery, resembling the almost simultaneous discovery of conditioned reflexes by the Russian physiologist, Ivan Pavlov.'

Egocentric adjustment is adaptation to the external conditions favorable for the individual. In this case, the end of the adjustment process is the establishing of behavior that allows the individual to function in his environment with a minimum of punishments and a maximum of rewards. However, such modes of behavior are not shaped by insight into various factors and elements recognized as meaningful with definite results, but by way of trials and errors. Besides, and this is a vital point, they are shaped by associating repulsive emotions with noxious behavior (fear—a snake; aversion—a swindler; repulsion—an informer, etc.) and positive emotions with advantageous behavior (pleasure—a pineapple; enjoyment—rest, etc.). Intellectual understanding is often too slow to follow the pace and complexity of events.

When G. C. Homans half a century later says, 'this is a book that will try to explain behavior and not just describe it . . . the behavior must be social, which means that when a person acts in a certain way he is at least rewarded or punished by the behavior of another person . . .'[6] he just repeats the basic idea which already was expressed by Petrażycki in his theory of social behavior and which was applied to explanations of human behavior governed by legal and moral norms.

However, from the point of view of social life, the sociocentric adjustment is the most important. J. Lande quotes the following example from Petrażycki's lectures:[7]

> In a primitive group, when a man committed some deed for the first time, e.g. he killed one of his tribesmen, slaughtered a sheep and invited friends for a feast, various members of the group would pass different and incompatible judgments, negative or positive (the latter, e.g., among the killer's family and his guests who disliked the victim). But if assassinations were repeated, judgments unadjusted to the group's welfare would be eliminated, a strongly negative evaluation would take place, and killing a tribesman would eventually come to be treated as a crime. Killing a member of an alien group would equally soon come to be judged positively and be regarded as a merit. Individual judgments are constantly shaped, and factors like the struggle for survival and natural selection are taken into account; judgments that do not contribute to the group's welfare are eliminated, and the 'net results of collective experience,' i.e.,

well-adjusted judgments, relevant to the assessed behaviors of the group, are retained. Such social adjustment is, according to Petrażycki, more 'congenial' than individual adjustment; it is 'supracongenial.' It is 'addressed' to the welfare of the group within which the intellectual and emotional exchange occurs.

Every social group is a laboratory where judgments are shaped, the whole process being directed toward the welfare of the group. However, not all groups are alike. When they get in contact, an exchange of experiences occurs; priorities are then modified; values are reassessed and new evaluations arise which are more general and adjusted to the interests of larger groups. But then new solidarities and values do not arise by way of intellectual arguing or understanding of the import or soundness of the arguments, groups only exchange experiences by 'contagion' of emotions in the process of judging, evaluating, and declaring of opinions, condemnations, approvals and individual or collective verdicts. Condemnations are apt to be proportionately more severe as a group defends its basic values by surrounding them with an emotional aura, high emotional prestige, and, often, sacral elements. Small groups sometimes risk their own destruction by defending their values when threatened with annihilation (altruistic suicides).

The three types of adjustment—sociocentric, egocentric and philocentric—complement each other, but on the other hand they also collide. The processes of adjustment can be unsynchronic, forming emotional residue. The emotional excitement of hunting (stronger when the game is 'bigger,' though the hunter-murderer with his automatic rifle is absolutely safe) is not justified in our eyes, because the hunter is superior to the game. Another example is gathering mushrooms or fishing. Fish can be killed by other methods—for example by throwing a grenade into the water or by electric current. But a fisherman (if he is not a poacher) would be most indignant at such a suggestion although it sounds 'reasonable' (many fish would be killed quickly) and sensible. These and other phenomena, according to Petrażycki, should be explained as relics from our remote ancestors' conditions of life when hunting, gathering and fishing were vital. Although that is no longer the case, the emotional aura has remained. In this respect there is no essential difference between human beings and domesticated geese.[8]

Uninterrupted gaggling, or a verse of at least seven syllables, something like 'gen, gen, gen, gen, gen, gen, gen,' means: 'It's fine here, plenty of food, let's stay.' Six gaggles means: 'Food is scanty on this meadow, let us nibble a little more, and then on, in first gear.' Five syllables signal shift to second gear. There is a clear mood of marching. Four syllables: 'Third gear, necks forward.' Only three gaggles: 'Maximum speed. Attention, we fly off.' To inform that the speed of marching can be increased to the maximum, but no flight is possible, the three-syllabled gaggle: 'gen, gen, gen' is replaced by a high-toned middle 'gen, gyn, gen.' For those who understand the language of geese, it sounds rather comical, when domesticated geese which cannot fly, still eagerly emphasize by their 'gen, gyn, gen' that they are not going to start up. In some peculiar way the 'dialect' inherited from the wild geese has been so deeply established in their genetic substrate that it has survived the ability to fly.

Thus, sociology deals with the collective types of behavior that are subject to the processes of 'unconsciously congenial' adjustment. Two of the results of these processes are particularly vital to the organization of collective life, namely law and morality. They have a special character. From the point of view of those to whom they are addressed, they are mystically authoritative, as if voiced by a superior being. They are understood as categorical imperatives and as obligations imposed from outside, without any reasons or purposes being offered. Consequently the legal and moral norms (together forming the category of ethical norms), have crystallized the welfare of the given social group. These norms are imposed upon its members by social 'inculcating' or possibly persuasion. The norms, as a net result of various individual interests, represent the welfare of the group, and thus impose certain modes of conduct on the group as a whole, without considering the individual ends or objectives. According to Petrażycki, law and morality are inculcated by a particularly intensive socialization. However, in spite of the similar general processes of socialization or inculcating, both types of norms—law and morality—perform different social functions. Morality aims at creating an attitude of obligation in people, molding human personality toward the passive role of fulfilling duties. Law, on the other hand, aims at building up the feelings of rights or claims. Law creates a type of 'man-citizen,' aware of his own dignity. Considering this, Petrażycki says that law is socially more valuable and more important for mass behavior (he compares it with water—'the wine of geese'), while morality appears less often (and so is compared with champagne—it is more valuable because it is rare, but water, though easily available, is indeed more vital).

It is possible to assume (as a comment) that the trial-and-error procedure embodied in a given social system (the mechanism Petrażycki called 'unconsciously congenial adjustment' or unconsciously ingenious adjustment) in the long run selects some violations of the conformity norms as more dangerous to society and consequently attacks them with more vigor; the same procedure considers some violations relatively less important and consequently assigns for them more flexible and appropriate means of social control. The reverse would be also true: the more important certain acts are to the group or community, the more rewarding the sanctions selected by the methodism of unconsciously congenial adjustment.

Morality is sometimes an auxiliary of law. It demands some deeds performed that otherwise only after some time (processes of socialization having done their job) would be encompassed by the field of legal behavior; morality also sometimes supports legal motivation when the pressure of law alone would not be sufficient to make individuals perform socially valuable behavior. Morality, like duties imposed by honor, imposes certain kinds of behavior (including desistence) on some definite, selected individuals. Not only 'what' is done, but also 'who' does it is important. However, the legal mind mainly cares about the effect or result of an action, for its being carried out (or not carried out), while it is often indifferent as to who carries it out—whether the person under obligation or someone else. The sanction of morality is condemnation, but there is no tendency to force moral obligations physically. The legal mind, on the other hand, has evolved the whole apparatus of compulsion and of securing recompense. Moral evaluations are diversified and flexible—while legal regulations are stiff and strictly observed, as the quantity of cases and the possibility of various interpretations and conflicts make it impossible for law not to be uniform. Hence the tendency to unify law, to set forth uniform patterns of behavior or established schemes, to define strictly the rights and obligations (their place and timing, and the exact amount of punishment to be inflicted, etc.), ultimately embodied in the institution of court. In morality there are no unifying processes of a similar scale, and no profession would have such a unification as its task.

Law influences social life, internalizes its values in patterns of behavior, and embodies them into roles and types of human interaction. It intrudes systematically into various types of interrelations, and in consequence, what used to be a novel obligation or right becomes a habit after some time.

## Social functions of the law

According to Petrażycki, there are three particularly remarkable tendencies in the historical processes of legal change. The first of these is a tendency toward increasing demands. As time passes, law and the legal constitution require increasingly more from individuals, quantitatively as well as qualitatively. Both the number of obligations and the quality of what is required of citizens increases. It is particularly interesting to trace the development of legal institutions of criminal law along epochs and social systems. Slaves and even children could once be killed. Only assassination of superior or equal persons was punished. Eventually these differences disappeared, and the interdiction against killing strangers was introduced. Now the prohibition covers even the cases defined as euthanasia.

It should be noted here that Petrażycki omits a quite important problem. Just as several types of crime have a tendency to die out (or just cease to be crimes due to changes in the law itself), a considerable number of new types of crime emerge all the time. New social, economic, political and especially technical and organizational conditions create new opportunities not easily overlooked by professional criminals.

The second tendency is to change the motivational stimuli. In various systems, as they are more and more developed from the organizational and technological standpoint, law offers increasingly more sublime motives to warrant the same kind of behavior. Once upon a time, people had to be compelled to labor (on a mass scale) by the cruel mechanisms of coercion and fear. Eventually, the same effect—work—could be secured by creating favorable conditions and by suggesting the motives of gain and advantage. Although in the latter kind of social system the few attain huge profits, various motivations such as greed, hope, or desire to share the profits are still sufficient to induce strained efforts. The exorbitant success of the few stimulate those who would be apt to fall into laziness, fatigue or indifference. In turn, the motives of social service and of work for the welfare of the community ought to replace the motive of individual profit. This is the socialist ideal, according to which the model of a socialistic person is a human individual motivated mainly by unselfish, task-oriented aims which transcend the boundaries of his own existence and are oriented toward the general good.

The third tendency is to diminish the motivational pressure toward legal behavior. The burden of pressure exerted on a debtor by the Law of the Twelve Tables used to be enormous. A debtor could be cut into pieces, and even Dickens's heroes were imprisoned for debts. Nowadays, an insolvent debtor can, formally speaking, deride the creditor who is sitting at the next table in a restaurant.

These three tendencies overlap in two basic functions of the law: organizational and educational. N. Timasheff summarizes them in the following way:[9]

> The organizational function of law, according to Petrażycki, molds the motives conducive to human actions, coordinates the very actions and thus creates social order. The educational

function modifies the behavior tendencies of human beings, eradicating the anti-social and fostering the social elements. Thus, for instance, the civil law of liberal society has greatly developed thrift, the spirit of enterprise, and love of work, whereas the different types of constitutional law have differently molded the political mentality of the corresponding nations, inducing the members of some to independence, consciousness of rights and the tendency to fight for them, while the members of other nations have been taught to display obedience and acceptance of oppression and egocentrism on the part of those in power.

Laymen and even lawyers believe that law is above everything which appears in the files of courts, prosecutors, solicitors, offices, agencies, etc. L. Petrażycki says that such a belief is charged with dogmatic notions and normative, peculiar points of view and therefore is professionally biased. Cases which reach judges, solicitors or administrative officials are peculiar, ambiguous, and pathological—they are instances of the abnormal functioning of law. They reflect behavior in which the normal (usually unperceived, automatic, smooth) legal routines have failed. Clashes, challenges, and competitive violations of norms occur, bearing the need to resort to specialized agencies for solutions.

This is a very significant observation. It changes the classical outlook on the functioning of law and drives us to the following declaration: the main social agent is the law which acts at any moment and in various social contexts in the most numerous human interrelations occurring all the time everywhere (like unconflicting contracts, transactions, offers, determinations of terms, conditions of payments, agreements, loans, etc.). Thus, it is not only the law in courts, offices and bureaus of solicitors, though the most conspicuous, which is charged with everyday but significant social tasks.

### Different types of law

L. Petrażycki makes a distinction between positive and intuitive law. The law containing ideas of normative facts (regulations, official agencies, authorities, etc.) is the positive law, while the intuitive law is what obliges without reference to any outer authority. In turn, official law is used and supported by the power of the state, while unofficial law is not. Although the two classifications are not quite coextensive (there are differences in the images of normative facts or in the objective data pointing to the valid norms), the positive law is virtually correlated with the official law, and the intuitive law is correlated with the unofficial. The relationship between these types of

219

law is interesting. For example, legal experiences can be stimulated in individuals by normative facts of the positive law and, when repeated frequently and emotionally approved, they can gradually attain an independent character eventually appearing without normative ideas or facts, as intuitive-legal experiences. On the other hand, the cumulating claims can be a powerful set of intuitive-legal images, and their impact upon the positive law can result in its change; when the positive law is not vulnerable to such changes, it can be violently assaulted as a whole or in part. N. Timasheff presents a concentrated summary of Petrażycki's views on these matters.[10]

He divided law and morals into two types, positive and intuitive. The *differentia specifica* was the presence in positive law or morals of reference to 'normative facts' from which the individuals derive their judgments on rights and duties, while in intuitive law such reference is conspicuous by its absence. Among the normative facts one could find not only statutes, customs, and judicial practices, but also *communis opinio doctorum*, contract, and so on. Petrażycki, further, divided law into official and unofficial. Official law was that used by courts and other state institutions, while law not used by such institutions he termed unofficial law.

The two classifications are independent of one another so that, according to Petrażycki, law may be (1) positive and official; (2) positive and unofficial; (3) intuitive and official; and (4) intuitive and unofficial. He conceded that official positive law, as defined by him, was very similar to law in the conventional meaning (not covering, however, international law).

The meaning of the classifications above may be best demonstrated by the following examples: (1) When a court renders a decision and refers to Article X of the Civil Code, or to a precedent, this is positive law (because of the reference to a normative fact) and simultaneously official law (because of the character of the agency). (2) When a freely chosen arbitrator solves an industrial conflict by reference to a well-established practice, this is positive law (because of the reference to a normative fact) and simultaneously unofficial law (because of the character of the agency). (3) When an English court decides a case on the foundation of equity, or a Swiss judge decides a case on the basis of a norm which he would have enacted if he were the legislator, this is intuitive law (because of the lack of reference to a normative fact), but official law (because of the character of the agency). (4) When, in a frontier situation, men take the law in their hands and hang a 'bad man' because 'he deserves it,' this is intuitive law (because of a lack of reference to a normative fact) and unofficial law (because of the absence of an official agency).

Thus use of law has two trends: positive and intuitive. In some situations the two support each other, in others, they are partly in conflict. (As when, for example, positive law struggles against the social relics of the past system, or when intuitive law attacks petrified and dysfunctional positive law.) Sometimes, such as during revolutions, the two currents of law are in open conflict. A reasonable legal policy cannot neglect the implications of intuitive law if legislative activity is to be effective. If problems raised by intuitive law are neglected, new enactments are apt to come into conflict with legal beliefs and opinions which, unless they are deftly released, can change the best of intentions into evil and unexpected effects.

### General remarks

We cannot discuss all the possible consequences implied by Petra-życki's conception of law. It would be particularly interesting to trace various instances of the reception of law, i.e. the case of borrowing an existing but foreign law from another legal system. In cases where the positive law of one social system is transferred into another system, it meets the intuitive law already existing there, and from a certain moment on the two have to co-operate. For example, Roman law was widely borrowed in Europe during the Middle Ages. In Polish law,[11] the reception of the so-called Magdeburg law played an important role. Acceptance of a law can be voluntary, when it is believed that it is worth while to adopt some products of development from an alien system which is in some respect superior. At other times such reception is compulsory, such as during the occupation of a country by a foreign army. Yet another possibility is a multiplied reception of law, such as for example, in Japan after the Second World War, where many modified institutions of the American legal system were superimposed on the elements of German and French law adopted earlier and voluntarily. In terms of the functioning of positive and intuitive law we can try to explain the international spreading of certain ways of solving judicial problems.[12]

If elements belonging to various economic levels come in contact, such an economic selection and such an adjustment occur (which is but natural and unavoidable) that the representatives of the higher virtue and economic culture perform the appropriately higher economic functions, requiring most qualifications and being the most valuable, demanding more of industrious intelligence and of virtue in general. If we divide the economically useful deeds and the expressions of economic activity into

221

two classes: physical-technological (agriculture, husbandry, crafts, etc.) and psycho-judicial (legal contracts, buying and selling, provision of credit, etc., and their respective activities), then it is *a priori* obvious and it can be foreseen that the activity of the representatives of the higher economic culture must be directed towards, and be focused upon, mainly the latter psycho-judicial fields of trade, credit, etc. If, as a further step, we divide the deeds and functions of the former kind, i.e. the physical-technological, into two classes: (1) the repeated and routine, such as the perpetuation of the existing, inherited types of the explorative industries, husbandry, agriculture, etc., or of the processing industries, the traditional crafts, etc., with the application of the inherited habits, patterns and routines, and (2) the innovative, such as the introduction of new kinds and varieties of industry, or of new types of enterprises in general, or of enterprises which carry out the old functions, but by means of the new, progressive organization or technology— then, if it is at all possible for the representatives of the higher economic culture to participate in the physical-technological section (permitted, e.g. by their continuous residence in appropriate sites, etc.), their activity in this field ought to be focused in the sphere of innovation, within the functions of economic progress.

Although Petrażycki's conception—his sociology in general and his ideas of sociology of law in particular—is potentially extremely promising as a source of explanation of phenomena which occur in various narrower fields, and though it attempts a general synthesis of various observations concerning the functioning of law, important objections can still be raised against it; we shall mention at least two of them. First, Petrażycki neglected the significance and the rank order of particular factors in the process of the shaping of law. Second, Petrażycki's thesis that law is an expression of the crystallization of values and judgments of a social group, and that such crystalization remains in a certain proportion in the interests of such a group, requires discussion.

Some Marxist and Weberian analyses have stressed the significance of the economic factor in the modeling of a definite legal system in a given society and at a given time. Indeed, there are various factors that affect law and in many ways determine its contents and scope of influence, like the climatic, geographical, demographical, religious, political, and economic ones; still they cannot all be placed on the same level. What is necessary is some 'formula' expounding a model of the import and influence of those factors and explaining in what historical situations each of them is significant. Without offering at least a tentative model describing the relationships of such complex determinants, a sociology of law, like Petrażycki's theory, fails to give an insight as to which of the considered factors are crucial or strategic and which of them are negligible ornaments.

In Petrażycki's sociology of law it is assumed that a social group is a sort of laboratory of judgments, and the ultimate evaluations resulting from various clashes within a group emerge as a net product or a synthesis of the interests of that group. It is assumed that a social group has, as it were, a definite hierarchy of values; in the course of social interaction with its multitudes of contracts, conflicts, co-operations, agreements, crossings of links and relationships, a moral and legal system gets 'melted' representing and expressing the hierarchy of values which is the optimal embodiment of the interests of the whole group.

However, we cannot fail to notice the rather arbitrary optimism of such an ideal. Within social groups there are factions, coteries which are apt to gain such preponderance inside the group that they can eventually shape its moral and legal system at their pleasure. Such shaping can foster the interests of a minority and be incompatible with the welfare of the larger social whole. This objection holds not only with respect to situations within groups, but also with respect to broader and more constant patterns, connecting various social groups. The fact that there are 'pressure groups,' with complex reciprocal balance (or imbalance) of power and influence upon the collective life, undermines, if it does not cancel, the optimistic ideal. As we know, pressure groups can form morbid tumors or even lethal cancerous growths in an otherwise wholesome social substrate. The optimistic image of a social group as a laboratory of synthesis of group interests and judgments strongly reminds us of situations typical of small groups. It can be suspected that Petrażycki transferred his observations of small groups, like family, neighborhood, peer group, and academic community, to larger and more complex processes, without accounting for the essential differences. Our former distinction between individualistic and public-minded ethics encompasses this peculiar element of the narrow social vision of the small group perspective, since small groups are the natural site of individual involvements.

In spite of any objections, however, it can be said that Petrażycki's conception is perhaps the most developed theory on the social influence and functioning of law, although perhaps not of its social origin.

Among several problems which can be raised in this context, one seems to be of special interest. Petrażycki ascribes a rather broad field of activity to law; he tries to explain the instrumental results of its manifold uses; but besides, his theory expresses a faith in the powerful and socially beneficial role of law. Is this faith justified, and what is its source? Let us suggest a hypothesis which might shed some light upon Petrażycki's position.

As we have already said, the bulk of matters appearing in various social groups is settled without resort to institutions or precepts of official law but still in accordance with their directives. Members of groups behave conformistically because of various pressures, such as public opinion, multilateral expectations, a feeling of reciprocity, the *do ut des* principle, fear of vengeance, and moral pressure, so that resort to law is not necessary. The authority and the complex machinery of law is summoned only when the normal means of social control fail to perform their role (it can be observed, by the way, that their strength and effectiveness is proportional to the integrity of the group); the necessity to apply the law increases only when such means become inefficient.

Petrażycki's belief in the social mission of law can be explained in terms of our investigations of the prestige of law. It was discovered that individuals who are generally well adjusted to life and to social interaction tend to be more legalistically oriented. Petrażycki seems to have transferred his intuition on individual behavior to that of a group. It is perhaps one of his assumptions that a well-organized and well-adjusted group, with proper mechanisms of interaction, tends to approve of the law created within it. This assumption can hardly be taken for granted since, as we know, there are social groups which respect the general human values, while others cherish values that may well be called pathological from a human point of view.

So it should be taken into account that Petrażycki's conception of the functioning of law, although it is based on sharp insight, is not founded upon systematically collected empirical data.

The continuous increase in the amount of data concerning the functioning of law demands that we deal with the problem differently, i.e. by taking into account the whole range of collected partial observations.

As an attempt at a synthesis of this kind we shall now present a hypothesis of the three levels of the functioning of law, an outline of a summary of various investigations shedding light on this problem.

### Three levels of the functioning of law: a hypothesis

There is a view, tacitly accepted by almost all theorists and practitioners, that a legal enactment, legitimately issued and marked by valid authority, functions automatically. Is it really so?

The paradox is that a lawmaker always devotes very much effort to prepare his normative act, but—as a matter of principle—is not interested in its efficiency; he can be compared with a person who sends a letter by registered mail but fails to put down his own address, assuming naïvely that the post office will find the addressee even if he has moved out, or has become ill and has been sent to hospital. Similarly, the science of law is interested mainly in the origin of law, its sources and its interpretation, but not in the actual functions performed by it. The only legal reality for lawyers is the world of legal enactments. Often they fail to see the real world behind it, although that is what the enactments are meant to refer to.

The hypothesis of the three levels of the functioning of law states the following: an abstract legal precept enacted by the legislature influences social behavior through a threefold connection. The first independent variable in the process is the content or meaning of the letter of the law in the given social and economic system where it is an element of the valid legal pattern. The second independent variable is the type of sub-culture functioning within the larger social and economic system as a link between the directives of the law-makers and the actual behavior of people to whom the law is addressed. The third independent variable can modify, in various directions, the actual functioning of an abstract legal precept within a given social and economic system and within a given legal sub-culture. It represents the personality types of those who are the ultimate agents carrying out the legal directives. An abstract legal precept begins to function (and to be expressed in social behavior) when it reaches its interpreter in the form of a complex conjunction. The constituent parts of such a conjunction are: the precept in itself and three meta-norms: the first derives from the character of the social and economic system, the second takes its contents from the definite legal sub-culture, and the third follows from the personality of the individual who makes the decision to behave lawfully.

This scheme might appear to be another abstract model, built of synthetic definitions. However, we shall present considerations and data from empirical studies, aiming to prove that this model is an attempt at a synthesis of empirical observations.

Article 93, paragraph 2 of the penal code of July 15, 1932, valid until January 1, 1970, stated: 'Whoever attempts to change by force the constitution of the Polish state is liable to a term of imprisonment of not less than ten years, or until the end of his life.' In a somewhat modified version (article 79 of the Polish Army penal code) this regulation has been valid for many years in the People's Poland. Thus, the same precept has been functioning within a social and economic system quite different from the one that existed when it was issued. Its functioning, however, has been quite different. Before the war (1939) it protected the system of private property, the means of production and large land estates, a political system within which the communist party was illegal; the main task of this precept was to prevent the realization of the conditions which prevail now. After 1945, until 1970, the same precept has had a quite different meaning. It was aimed against the system in which it had been issued, since the repression provided by it threatened those who wanted to restore the capitalist system.

The proposition that a legal precept can be regarded as a vessel with contents poured into it by the actual conditions of its functioning is also confirmed when we analyze the detailed data concerning several institutions of a legal system.

In the commentary to the Polish Family Code we read:[13]

The most essential element of the principle of contradictoriness, conceived in a new way, is the complete abandoning of the passive attitude of the court, more or less typical of the bourgeois legislative regulations. In the People's Poland the lawmakers demand from the court an active attitude, expressed by the stimulation of the initiative and activeness of the parties in the litigation, as well as by undertaking officially the necessary activities toward a complete elucidation of any legal issue. By way of illustration we can point to articles 116; 213, 214; 218, Para. 1 of the Code of Civil Procedure. These regulations, though they were enacted by a bourgeois legislature, have only now acquired their full application as the result of changes in the essential assumption of the civil procedure introduced by the amendments of July 20, 1950 and April 23, 1953. We must particularly emphasize the role of Article 118, para. 1 of the Code of Civil Procedure, which should now be so interpreted that a court can by no means remain passive. On the contrary, it is the duty of the court—and the presiding judge in particular —to behave actively during the whole course of litigation so as to have the actual state of affairs elucidated thoroughly in all its aspects.

The general statement that the action of an abstract legal precept depends on various extraneous elements which, while the law remains unchanged, modify its contents, adapt and fit it into the changing social and economic situations, could be further justified by other similar examples. However, it is not necessary to multiply examples. The significant point is that in general the same legal norm can act in various ways under different systemic conditions. It can function as it used to; the direction of its impact can shift totally; it can cease to have any effect at all (although it has remained valid and legitimate); or its influence can in part be modified.

Our former distinction between legal principles and legal prescriptions finds a particular application in the present context if we take into account that the social system is a variable factor. Let us remember that a legal principle is a piece of law based on social acceptance and inculcated into the common legal sentiment of a group, or several groups, or of the whole society. Although every legal principle is written down in the form of a legal precept, it is additionally supported by several norms of custom, ethics, social interaction, etc. On the other hand, legal prescriptions deal above all with the formal, procedural aspects of behavior, and they are addressed to professionals who are versatile in handling them. Legal prescriptions form the base of the legal constructions. Sometimes the constructions are also supported by elements of principles giving them social meaning. Now, if we take this distinction into account, it can easily be seen that a change of a social system would have a different influence upon the legal principles and the legal prescriptions. When the social, economic and political structure undergoes some changes, and when the new administrative machinery has already been established, it is easier to introduce new prescriptions than to modify the principles. Since legal principles are not susceptible to rapid changes—if only because of their deep social rooting—it is much easier to change the conditions of their application, the categories of persons to whom they apply, the procedures of their realization, etc.

Sometimes revolutionary changes (which cause social and economic changes without parallel changes in the major parts of the legal system) offer what can be considered experimental situations clearly revealing the role of the independent variable denoted as the social and economic system. However, if the changes are introduced gradually and inconspicuously, an illusion can arise that the new system contributes nothing to the independently functioning legal norms. Thus, we may conclude that the first prism through which the legal precept is refracted on its way from lawmakers to those whom it concerns, is the set of social and economic conditions in the given type of social system.

In every society there is a set of general social values such as ideas, knowledge, art, institutions, patterns of behavior, material products, etc., which together constitute the culture of the society. On the other hand, various narrower social environments and circles within a society cherish their different, specific sub-cultures. Their peculiarities are that the values cherished by the particular sub-cultures are typical for them only and they frequently contribute little to the general cultural store. But in cases when the sub-cultures are socially negative, their influence upon the encompassing culture of the whole society can be more or less noxious or destructive. Very often, if we observe behavior occurring in some specific environments, e.g. among artists, soldiers, hippies, or students, we cannot understand what is going on without considering the peculiarity of the observed social group.

There are also legal sub-cultures. Besides the valid legal system, in every society (if we leave aside the primitive societies which usually do not have valid legal systems) there is something else, described as legal sentiment, legal feeling, intuitive law, etc. Without going into semantic niceties here let us say that in every society there is some degree of obedience to law and it has a certain prestige; there are always moral attitudes, customs and social patterns which support or impede the functioning of the whole legal system. The total set of habits and values related to acceptance, evaluation, criticism and realization of the valid legal system can be called the general legal culture of the society. The legal culture can be more or less developed, and its particular parts can disclose various degrees of harmonization with the rest. As we have already mentioned, deviations from the principles of the general legal culture occur, for in various environments law is administered and realized in various ways. The types of the czarist Russian 'chinovniki' (officials of minor rank) as sketched by Chekhov or by Dostoyevski represent a quite peculiar legal culture. There are also negative legal sub-cultures of criminals, e.g. thieves with their complex set of habits and rituals, their rules about distribution of loot, their moral and honor codes, their 'dintoira' (Polish slang for a tribunal of thieves; the lynch law of criminals settling their disputes), old age security measures, etc.; all such institutions involve elements of the *sui generis* 'law' of the group, although this law is at odds with the general legal order. As we know from the study by Z. Bożyczko,[14] there is a principle forbidding a thief to take away his partner's wife or mistress, in particular when he is in prison. It is forbidden to hamper another pickpocket at work; on the contrary, if one notices that another works without sufficient protection, one should provide a 'curtain' ('wall'), without the right to claim part of the profit for such service. The military sub-culture, highly formalized, is based less on the respect of attractive legal principles and more on the habit of obedience to the actual directives and orders of superiors. One of the most remarkable observations on the negative hooligan sub-culture—particularly strongly opposed to existing legal principles—reports that a person who passes from this sub-culture to one of people seeking a more stable status as a result of marriage, almost overnight begins to accept a legal sub-culture which is incompatible with that of his former group.[15] In business circles where the turnover of goods and money is so rapid that if all the formalities were respected the intensity of trade would be impeded, a specific legal sub-culture evolves, legalizing most of the illegitimate procedures in negotiating and promulgating the otherwise bureaucratic contracts. In an interesting study on businessmen and lawyers, S. Macaulay remarks that although the business world tends to formalize its activities to a high degree, some types of very important trade contracts are made neglecting all formalities. 'The businessmen very often appreciate more "a word spoken out," a short memo, even a shake of hands or the "general honesty and decency"—even if their contracts involve serious economic risks.'[16] Of course, such informal habits can be explained by common solidarity of people in their pursuit of profits, but—independent of the appreciation of the general social role of the world of business—what is important is the finding that a great number of trade contracts are concluded to the neglect of any formal requirements.

Studies on legal sub-cultures are new in sociology as well as in the sociology of law. Synthetic surveys are still lacking. There are no general theoretical synthetic discussions about this problem yet. But there are several investigations directly or indirectly related to it. With reference to these investigations, several types of legal sub-culture can be discerned. We can speak about negative, positive, or neutral legal sub-cultures. We can also speak about the legal sub-culture of people who are ultimately affected by law (to whom legal norms are addressed), about the legal sub-culture of people shaping the law (deputies, members of councils, administrators), and about the legal sub-culture of people administering or realizing law (the so-called minions of the law, professionally inducing others to lawful behavior).

The most puzzling problem for traditional formalist lawyers is the existence of negative legal sub-cultures. They ask, how on earth can a negative legal sub-culture exist if valid law is in principle positive? In spite of such naïve (or based on pretended ignorance) statements, there are data pointing to the existence of broader or narrower negative legal sub-cultures. Studies of recidivism show that imprisonment is not very effective in discouraging repetitious crime. Recidivists have their own outlook and legal awareness, their own peculiar evaluation of law consisting of negative judgments about legal precepts as well as legal institutions. Here are some typical attitudes: 'Only some people are afraid of punishment.' 'Punishment (in prison) is no obstacle to anyone.' 'People who are not afraid of stealing are not afraid of punishment either.' 'If someone is out to steal, he'll do it, punishment or not.' 'If someone is about to do something, he will do it anyway, even if a dozen cops were on guard.' 'It can happen to anyone—that he gets caught and nobody minds.' 'As to myself, no prison would stop me from stealing.' Another recidivist, thirty years old 'laughs out of the courts and prisons.' 'Only a sucker is afraid of prison, or if he falls under recidivism for the first time' (i.e. if he is put in a cell with recidivists). 'Prison won't help or scare those who steal; they don't while they're in, and as soon as they get out, they'd do it again even before they get home.' 'No punishment will stop him; he must make a break and stop by himself.'[17] These declarations clearly illustrate the atmosphere of the recidivist sub-culture from which the re-socializing function of punishment is returned as a table-tennis ball.

Another study revealed that the percentage of juvenile delinquents having collaborated with adults in criminal actions did not exceed 9 per cent of all the juveniles sentenced for offenses;[18] this proves that it is not adults who push the juveniles toward delinquency. Other investigations suggest that there is a specific intervening factor involved. With reference to his research data Cz. Czapów has pointed out that the three basic features of the negative juvenile delinquent sub-culture mentioned in literature have been found empirically in Polish investigations also. The features are: malevolence, negation of all values, and the non-pragmatic character of damage or injury.[19] Of course, not all offenses committed by juveniles are direct effects of the negative influence of the legal sub-culture, and not all offenses by juvenile delinquents are committed in groups. But, what has been committed by team work (and the percentage is as high as 34–39 per cent) bears the imprint of criminal collusion—and thus of the criminal sub-culture.

From the above data we can conclude that a negative legal sub-culture (or, rather, anti-culture) influences the behavior of those to whom the legal norms are addressed. In turn, different investigations indicate that legal behavior and, in particular, legal decisions taken by the so-called minions of the law also depend on specific legal sub-cultures typical of their professional circles. For example, studies show that the practice of prosecutors in similar cases—prosecuting juvenile delinquents co-operating with adult criminals—can be quite different. A thorough statistical analysis of this problem supports 'a suspicion that what determines the percentage of this category of cases sent to regular courts are not actual differences between situations in various parts of the country, but rather the *local practices of prosecutors*'[20] (emphasis by the present author). Thus, a definite judicial *usus*, or a specific clerical sub-culture, may cause deeds which are identical from the point of view of their normative qualification to be handled differently in practice.

Another study of the practical activities of courts concerned Norwegians who refused to be drafted into the army (conscientious objectors). It showed that there were essential differences in the practice of decision-making by various courts. Namely, courts in southern and northern Norway clearly displayed different styles in handling such cases. The differences could be explained, on one hand, by the specific features of the accused (e.g. the accused was an emotional atheist, a Nordlander, and an unskilled worker, who refused to be drafted from the outset) and, on the other hand, by the peculiar styles of verdict-making prevailing in the different circles of judges.[21]

The investigations carried out, point to a regularity which concerns all the law-breakers: what is usually defined as an offense—its discovery and hearing in court—is a result of two processes. The first of them involves the trespassers, the other is related to the court authorities. This principle, revealed by our investigations, has obviously great and important consequences, as I believe, for various important fields of criminology.

This study also pointed to the fact that an institution—in this case, the courts—can evolve practical stereotypes of decision-making which are locally observed and transmitted and which differ from the patterns of settling similar cases elsewhere.

A similar situation was found in a study, already discussed in this book, about assessors. At least four distinct styles of presiding over the conference for verdict by a judge collaborating with assessors were discerned.

Type I: a conference with absolute dominance by the judge who not only neglects the opinions of the assessors, but also ignores their presence, and makes arbitrary decisions which he communicates to the assessors. The decisions are not subject to any discussion and the assessors approve them without visible signs of opposition (20·6 per cent of all conferences).

Type II: a conference with a clear dominance by the judge, presided over by him but with the observance of some formal elements of exchange of opinions, or even with some signs of activity on the part of the assessors—although the judge clearly imposes his position and from the outset proposes a definite solution which either is approved by the assessors without discussion, or is persistently maintained by the judge in spite of attempts by the assessors to modify it (31·1 per cent of all conferences).

Type III: conferences in which the judge leaves the initiative to formulate propositions of verdict to the assessors, but they fail to do so, and thus the judge has to express his view. The judge must make arbitrary decisions because the assessors remain passive (8·0 per cent of conferences).

Type IV: conferences during which there is a real discussion—the assessors express their personal opinions before they hear the judge's suggestions, which might be different. All views are discussed before decision is made (40·3 per cent of all conferences).[22]

In another investigation, also quoted above, extensive differences among local styles of settling affairs were discovered, e.g.[23]

The factor which had an obvious influence upon the univocal observance was the *local custom* (emphasis by the present author), typical either of the whole institution, or of a definite jury. During the study many cases were disclosed in which given regulations had always been obeyed by certain colleges, while not respected at all by other ones.

Summing up what we have said about legal sub-cultures and using the quoted results of various empirical studies as illustrations, we can say that the second prism, through which a legal message is refracted on its way from the law-makers to those for whom it is aimed, is the specific content of a legal sub-culture influencing the attitudes of those who create the law or who control its creation. Thus, within the same social and economic system, various types of legal sub-cultures cause or determine various types of legal behavior.

However, even within the same socio-economic system and the same legal sub-culture, legal and illegal actions of particular subjects will be different because of the personality differences among people to whom the law is addressed. As has been said, different types of psycho-social determination generally bring out various attitudes toward law. For example, the following categories of people tend to obey the law more strictly than others: people in the age brackets from 35–49 and above 60 years; people with proportionately higher education; white-collar workers; individuals whose parents belong to the intelligentsia; people without feelings of insecurity; people with few personal contacts; and rationalistically minded people engaged in social activities (although the latter also reveal some law-related cunning).

On the other hand, the following categories more often than others admit a wish to by-pass or to disobey (break) the regulations of law: those in the 25–34 age bracket; people uneducated or with elementary education; unskilled workers (breaking the law); persons with symptoms of insecurity; dogmatically minded persons (by-passing law); psychically inhibited persons (breaking the law); frustrated persons; those without a clear hierarchy of values; and those who are not engaged in social activity.

The above results derive from the questionnaire method and have thus raised some doubts. As we have already mentioned, they have been further verified by supplementary control research using other methods and tools. One study was parallel to the research on the prestige of law; it was based on L. B. Cattell's personality inventory (translated and elaborated for Polish respondents by M. Chynowski and M. Nowakowska).

The verdict of the death penalty was a most provocative problem from the point of view of the eventual influence of personality factors due to the lack of socio-demographic determinants. In the national survey it turned out that only personality factors such as symptoms of insecurity, social maladjustment, and severe rearing in childhood were of significant relation to positive attitudes toward a death penalty. These intricate results were then subject to additional test investigations. It turned out that there was no correlation concerning the death penalty with views on being an only child, coherence of rearing patterns, preferences toward peer groups in childhood, authoritarianism (as measured by the shortened F scale) and various other factors discerned by L. B. Cattell. The only exception was the resistance to threat. The test study revealed that low threat resistance correlated highly with a readiness to approve the death penalty.

As we remember, another problem analyzed in the national survey on the prestige of law was the scale of legal rigorism and tolerance. The general hypothesis suggested by the data can be summarized by saying that stronger rigorism (a propensity to select more severe punishment) is related to poorer adjustment in social life, while tolerance is correlated with better adjustment. The test investigations allow us to declare that there is a synthesis of opinion determining relative severity of punishment for individuals. Such a punitive attitude is favored by severe rearing in childhood, low resistance to threat, insecure feelings, and low self-application. Thus, the test study confirmed the results of the national survey.

Although the questionnaire and the test study gave corresponding results, the temptation persists to use the same type of utterances (declarations) in both analyses. To refute any such trend, an attempt was made to investigate if there existed a consistency between verbal declarations and actual behavior. Here are some of the results.[24]

In the pursuit of an at least partial retort to this charge, the files of the penal-administrative college at N were analyzed. The college of judges worked in teams, the members appointed by rotation, but each team had its steady president (in our case there were twelve of them). For ten team presidents, who responded to questionnaires and were interviewed . . . the averages of fines they imposed from November 1964 to June 1965 were established. The other two presidents were not active during this period. We attempted to analyze similar numbers of verdicts for each of them, but this was not quite possible, as most cases in the college were judged by a small group of the college members. Verdicts in 82 cases against so-called hooligans were analyzed. The Spearman rank correlation (Q) between the scores attained by the judging team presidents on the scale (S) (severity) and the average amount fined by each of them was positively and statistically significant ($Q = 654$; $N = 9$; $p \leq 0.05$).

This result was rather surprising, especially since the investigated

233

judges had been subject to much pressure towards more uniform and severe verdicts, in particular with respect to hooligans and offenders of traffic regulations. (The penal-administrative college at N has been a target of charges of the voivodship [district in Poland] authorities for many years, because of its too-lenient verdicts (below the average for that voivodship).) The local inspector for penal-administrative matters in the district national council also played an important role; he acted as a secretary of the college and he often brought about more severe verdicts by threatening that he would otherwise make formal motions against them to the higher-level council. It was also discovered, by the way, that although the judging teams announced their verdicts to be majority decisions (there are three members to a team), in reality only their presidents have any say.

These results provided a stimulus to further, more detailed verification of the influence of personality factors in legal behavior. Eighty-five executors of law—i.e. judges—were investigated through a questionnaire asking moral and legal questions, plus questions about items that had been found significant in the former study. The supplementary questions were taken from Cattell's personality inventory and from Gough's scale of severity.[25] The general conclusion for the project can be formulated in the following terms:

Judges are more tolerant than the average population with respect to deeds which are not forbidden by law (suicide, adultery, alcoholism) and more rigoristic with respect to unlawful conduct (bigamy, incest, euthanasia). When there are differences of opinion on legal or moral issues, the views of judges are similar to the views of socially better situated people. The judges rank highest in rigorism with respect to judicial offenses (the breaking of administrative regulations). However, they are a little less rigoristic than socially well-situated people with respect to deeds which are not punished by law.

These results, and the earlier ones concerning the legal and moral attitudes of judges, have led the cited author to the following conclusions:[26]

Some more general hypotheses on the role of a professional judge can be formulated with reference to the above results. The differences in the patterns of severity between laymen and judges (frustration versus rigorism) suggest that even the personal biases of a judge are determined by his role. His partiality for the legal system also modifies the relation between his social affiliation and his moral views. However, a judge is not a 'legal machine,' producing verdicts as a result of applying the legal regulations to the objective circumstances of a given case. Even if it is difficult for us to determine the genetic relationship, the very fact that there is a correlation between certain deeper personality traits, e.g. rigorism, and verdict-making, supports the belief that the role of a professional judge, though he is intensely expected to be objective, is not unexposed to the influence of social and individual psychology.

A Chinese fable expresses these matters in a simple way:

The judge Sie asked Si-tien: 'My lord. How should I judge the cases which are submitted to me? Should I follow what is written in the books, or take into account what I see in the eyes of the accused, or else perhaps listen to those who know better?' Si-tien answered: 'You'll do the best if you listen to what your own guts whisper to you.'

The above summary of various cross-controlling investigations (carried out by different intentionally selected techniques and based on analyses of data concerning two distinct populations—average people and judges) confirms that personality traits are factors which significantly modify views and opinions on law. Furthermore the research results, though incomplete, show that the stated views on severity of punishments (the degree of severity) are significantly related to the actual decisions, authoritatively and legitimately taken and avowed. Thus, the third prism through which legal regulations are refracted on their way from the legislator to those to whom they are addressed are various personality types.

In our considerations on the hypothesis of the three levels of functioning of law we have intentionally left out, as factors of minor importance in this context, the extensive category of formal, semantic and procedural framework which can influence the transmission of information about legal norms. Thus, we have ignored the contents intended by the lawmakers as well as the actual contents of the legal enactments; the valid interpretations (authentic—done by the legislator himself) of such contents; the sources of information about laws (official publications, mass media, the experiences of the legal profession, individual and other informal experiences, etc.); the ways the normative acts are brought to life by the minions of the law; the changing directives of those ways; opinions about them, etc. All this has been set aside, because our main focus was an attempt to grasp the most significant or strategic variables determining the functioning of law.

The multi-level conception of the working of law proposes, as we have said, three basic variables: the type of social and economic system, the type of legal sub-culture, and the personality type. We can develop this hypothesis further referring to the familiar proposition of social engineering that the degree of acceptance of received information depends on the degree of acceptance of the authorities giving this information; this proposition is relevant if we admit that a legal norm is a special (protected by its sanction) kind of information. We can expect any given normative act to work efficiently in proportion to the degree of acceptance of the discerned three variables. Thus, optimal effectiveness can be expected from a normative act functioning within an accepted social and economic system, supported by a pro-legal sub-culture and realized by legalistically-minded individuals. In turn, the least efficient would be a regulation functioning within an unaccepted system which is subject to an antagonistic influence of an anti-legal sub-culture, and which is received by anti-legalistically oriented individuals. An example illustrating this is the attitude of the Polish population toward the enactments of the occupant's authorities during the Second World War. In real life the three factors interact in various ways and ideal types can rarely be found. The intensity of influence in a concrete social system is an important prerequisite of effective action since it shows where to look for the social environments and individuals who are apt to fulfill the directives of law and, also, where resistance may arise. This shows that the three-level hypothesis of the functioning of law is important for social engineering, too.

The theory of law can be pursued in four different ways. It can be seen as instruction or counseling, i.e. not as a scientific discourse but as the source of general suggestions about the right and wrong directions of legal reflection. The second notion of theory of law can be developed as a speculative enterprise by suggesting several more or less comprehensive analytical propositions which fail to remain in any definite relationship with reality (or at least, we do not know the techniques and methods to determine if the general and abstract views can be related to reality and tested) so that any relationship between them and reality might be regarded as possible. Considering the results of the research reported above about the individualist and social moral orientations, it is worth while asking: what social advantage besides the gain for the authors of such speculative disquisitions is there in various versions of the abstract legal-theoretical conceptions? How is this happy-go-lucky style of learning seen by the hard-working people—workers, white-collars, editors, physicians, teachers, policemen? How long shall we suffer the optimistic and apologetic lingo as directives for practical activity instead of recommendations based on a thorough study of social reality which thus warrants practical success? There remain, however, the third and fourth approaches to the theory of law. Within the third approach, the main task of the discipline is considered to be genetic and historical inquiries aiming to reveal which social and economic factors influence the changing shapes of various legal constitutions and enactments. The social reality is treated as an independent variable, and the legal system and its elements as dependent ones. The fourth approach, finally, regards the legal system and various normative acts as the independent variables modified by the controlled variables, like human actions having various consequences—social, economic and other. The present author believes that only the latter two approaches are scientifically fruitful and that they are the only ones able to provide a sound basis for formulating which regularities govern the working of law in society—and which regulations can be used by a rational legal policy.

The historical-genetic standpoint, although it has proved to be worth while, is the domain of historians rather than lawyers and sociologists; the task for us is to concentrate our efforts on analyses concerning the influence of the human and social factor on law. Consequently, our hypothesis of the three levels of the functioning of law has been an attempt at a general synthesis of various empirical contributions, or at a construction of the model-mechanism of the impact of legal norms on the living social process.

# part four

# Legal policy

# 13 The concept of legal policy as a science

The concept of legal policy was created between 1893 and 1895 in L. Petrażycki's work, *Die Lehre vom Einkommen*,[1] and it has been developed in many of his later works. He saw its tasks in the following terms: 'The essence of the problem of the policy of law consists in scientifically justified prediction of the effects if certain legal enactments are introduced, and in elaborating principles which will bring about some desirable effects.'[2]

Though Petrażycki returned to the idea of legal policy many times, he failed to elaborate its basic assumptions, propositions and methodological background. He believed that a proper elaboration of the foundations of this science was dependent on a revision of the methodological assumptions of various disciplines which he considered logically preceded legal policy. He wanted a radical change of the methodological approach to the social sciences, as well as a change of their contents. In the attempt to carry out this plan, he undertook the task of a new elaboration of the foundations of such disciplines as psychology, sociology, logic, social sciences, jurisprudence, moral theory, etc. However much we appreciate his efforts and their results now, it must be emphasized that Petrażycki's contribution, as well as later developments (especially empirical ones) of sociology, psychology and the methods of social sciences, has provided the ground to take up the task of elaborating the foundations of legal policy again. J. Lande expresses it as follows:[3]

Indeed, the policy of law can prove in teleological terms that a given legal precept is the proper means toward a definite social end, thereby classifying the precept as desirable—or it can prove that some other precept leads to undesirable effects, thereby classifying it as undesirable. Legal policy classifies law not as 'just' or 'right,' but as purposeful, desirable because of its

241

effects. As technology recommends the use of certain natural forces as means to its ends, . . . as medicine recommends the use of drugs, so legal policy recommends the introduction of certain legal enactments, or the maintenance of existing ones, to attain definite social effects.

Legal policy as a science belongs to the practical social sciences. It is supposed eventually to constitute the section of social engineering dealing with rational influence upon social life, applying law as the basic means of such influence. However, an elaboration of sufficiently precise assumptions in this discipline is continually hampered by the unsatisfactory state of reflection in the field, as well as by resistance and inhibitions on the part of the legal profession.

Even if we set aside the widespread ignorance of the methods of social research among lawyers, the development of a legal policy is hampered by two basic and fairly common attitudes. The first of them can be labeled retrospective: the tendency to look for novel solutions within the existing legal system. The other attitude, randomly prospective, approaches new problems by the trial and error method, looking for solutions suggested by common sense or professional experience.

Both these attitudes raise serious objections. As to the retrospective attitude, it can be said that the available solutions usually fail in novel situations, and the cumulated experience is not necessarily always useful beyond the limits of the familiar. Thus the retrospective attitude ought to be transformed into a rationally prospective, rather than a randomly prospective, one. Such an approach would induce the prediction of the consequences of various alternative legislative motions supported by systematical investigations, and the choice of the alternative promising the most positive effects and the least negative ones.

During the last twenty-five years there has been a particularly opportune social and legal situation in Poland, allowing us to observe how revolutionary political and social changes have modified law, and how law has influenced these changes. This period has been a laboratory where legal regulations have been one variable (usually the independent one) and social changes another. We are now in a position to make use of the errors and achievements of legislation, by connecting the empirical data with theoretical and methodological considerations, so achieving a higher level of collaboration between theory and practice. The newly accumulated experiences allow us to abandon traditional, insufficient ways of thinking and to assume new and more scientific means.

Legal policy as a science of rational social change, obtained by means of law, based on generally accepted social values and on the store of knowledge about social behavior, is concerned with formulating directives for the planning and realization of social change. A reasonable lawmaker who intends to use legal policy as his guide ought to take into consideration three basic principles of effective legislation: (1) the legislative principles (legal-political principles in the proper sense); (2) the principles of codification; and (3) the principles of codificatory technique.

The first types of principle and the directives based on them are supported by the regularities disclosed by analyses of social interaction. They supply general evidence, relevant to an elaborated normative act, or a coherent set of legal regulations, from the standpoint of effectiveness. The legislative directives are the guide for all considerations and activities which lead to an explanation of the normative act, and their purpose is to secure the efficiency of its future working. To fulfill such a task, we must first know the situation which is to be legally regulated (i.e. have an exact diagnostic image of how things are), second we must know and consider the values accepted by the lawmaker, since he elaborates the new normative act or changes the old one. We must consider data concerning the actual state of affairs, the suggested means, the intermediate effects and the predicted final results; we must know the general propositions referring to the causal relationships, upon which the proposed normative act might base its functioning; and finally, the effects of the already enacted legal regulations should be studied. Formulation and application of legislative directives ought to be based—besides methodological assumptions and diagnostic studies on the given situation that requires intervention of the lawmaker—on data supplied by social sciences, and mainly by the sociology of law.

The directives of the second type are derived from the principles of codification. Their scope of application is much narrower than that of the legislative principles. They determine how legal precepts ought to be edited to make them clear, compact and coherent with others. These directives can be applied when the basic assumptions of the intended normative act have been accepted, and since it is necessary to translate these assumptions into the language of jurisprudence, those directives deal with the syntax of the legal idiom.

Finally, the third types of directive are derived from the technique of codification. They deal with the arrangement of various regulations within a single normative act, and the reconciliation of precepts or sets of precepts in normative acts. Such rules might seem to be of minor importance, if not simply ornamental, but in fact they are rather important in practical legislative activity.

The reflections beginning the development of legal policy are related to exactly codificatory problems. Although the principles of codification are directly useful in the work of editing and justifying normative acts, we need not emphasize that the legislative directives influencing the contents and effectiveness are much more significant. So our forthcoming discussion will be limited to the legislative directives only.

We can look at the enacted law as the first cause in a chain of consequences: legal enactments—behavior described by them—actual situations resulting from such behavior. According to this pattern, wanting to use enacted law as a means of attaining the intended states of affairs, we must have enactments based on verified hypotheses that establish the links between law and behavior affected by law (the motivational functioning of law), and also based on the hypotheses that establish the relationship between such behavior and the actual states of affairs resulting from it. With such an image of law, it is obvious that any legislative motion calling forth a new law, or modifying or cancelling an old one, causes several social effects, some maybe unexpected, some undesirable. To grasp the more important issues involved here, we must make use of the relevant theoretical concepts for their analysis. In particular, we must refer to such concepts as description of the actual situation, legislative diagnosis, partial evaluation or global evaluation, side effects, unexpected negative effects, etc.

The first step in analyzing such complex problems is to consider the following basic directives: (1) sufficient description; (2) analysis of the basic evaluations; (3) verification of hypotheses; and (4) analysis of the effects of the functioning of the legal precepts.

*Re* 1 The directive of sufficient description proposes that it is indispensable to describe the existing situation before any decision to change. If a legislator intends to regulate normatively some field of social life without having acquired sufficient insight he takes the risk of not achieving what was intended, which might lead to unintended negative effects. A sociological, economic, demographic and statistical description of the actual situation ought to be made, or at any rate a description giving full understanding. Various empirical methods and techniques of research ought to be applied at this stage.

*Re* 2 A legislator wanting to regulate some behavior ought to consider whether the effect of his decisions would offend one or more evaluations he himself accepts, as the effect would, by definition, be to some extent negative. There are three fields where such a situation can arise. First, to change the existing situation may be more expensive than to tolerate it. Second, the means suggested to change the existing situation may lead to offering values otherwise approved by the legislator. Third, the effect (and in particular the side effects) can offend certain values respected by the legislator (or values he is obliged to respect by society). In connection with the directive of respect for the acknowledged values, the methods and techniques of social research should be applied to analyze public sentiment, and in particular to compare the values of the legislator with those cherished by wider communities. However, besides the methods of social research, the principles of effective teleological performance should not be neglected either in this context.[4]

*Re* 3 The directive of verification of hypotheses suggests that the causal links upon which the intended normative act might be based should be realized. To find the relevant empirical regularities serving as such a basis, we should either rely upon the available knowledge, or try to determine experimentally which of the considered propositions would be the proper one. As we have said, a traditional lawmaker uses the random prospective method, i.e. he acts by trial and error, trying to find the causal link on which to base his normative act. Verification of hypotheses offers a possibility for conscious prediction (or at least an opportunity to attempt that) of the probable effects and the eventual negative side effects, as well as an indication of the efficiency of the proposed law.

Thus, according to this directive, it is necessary to formulate hypotheses or sets of hypotheses, and to employ the appropriate methods, e.g. sociological, economic, statistical, etc. to determine the scope and degree of the validity of the hypotheses and under which conditions they can be at all valid.

*Re* 4 The three directives discussed above refer to the phase of legislative activity preceding the enactment of an intended normative act. These directives serve to give information about how the intended social objectives can be attained, and how unintended side effects can be avoided. The fourth and last of the essential directives refers to the phase of legislative activity after the normative act has become valid. To study the effects of the normative acts (and of any legal enactment) one must employ the appropriate methods (sociological, economic, demographical, statistical, etc.) in order to learn what the effects of legal regulations are, and to assess them as negative or positive with reference to the accepted values. Only after this has been determined can it be said whether the objectives intended by the lawmaker have been attained—fully, in part, or not at all.

The traditional methods applied in lawmaking, and even more the effects of such applications, call for our efforts to their modification or improvement. The social life of our epoch, with its rationalism, industrial growth, and complex technology, requires the rejection of random, home-spun, unsystematic methods, and instead demands rational, systematic and effective knowledge. The science of legal policy is a field which may contribute some of the means towards the socially desirable ends.

For these reasons there is a need for a systematic development of theoretical reflection on the methods of legal policy as a field of social engineering and on the sociology of law as a theoretical ground for legal policy.[5]

# 14 Effectiveness of the law in operation

In general, it can be said that the science of legal policy is composed of three essential sections. First, the set of information concerning the social regularities where law is a significant element. Within such regularities legal precepts function either as the dependent variable (they are conceived as effects of social processes), or as the independent variable (they are the causes bringing about social processes). The second section of legal policy is the universe of general social values accepted in a society and binding for the lawmaker, who in some cases can envisage efficient means of bringing about social changes, but cannot use them because they are incompatible with the essential collective values. The third field of legal policy consists of the directives or suggestions that can be derived from the two former types of element. Their objective is to provide solutions for the basic problem of legal policy—the effective functioning of law. This includes the attainment of the expected ends, but also the avoidance of negative effects likely to injure the essential and binding social values. It is worth while to emphasize once more what we have already said several times: theoretical investigations satisfy cognitive needs and they can be of high value here, but their main ultimate objective is practical—it is social welfare and justice.

Traditionally there are two extremely opposed approaches to the problem of the efficiency of law.

According to the first approach, defined as belief in the omnipotence of legal means, all fields of social life can be fully regulated by law. According to the second approach, defined as the position of skeptical pessimism, all that law can do, contrary to what might seem, is to sanction the existing state of affairs.

We can hardly accept either of these extremes. The first position, assumed, indeed, more often by those who order that legal means be used than by those who execute such orders or who are concerned with theoretical reflection on legal phenomena, is essentially fallacious. For legal means can influence social life only when certain definite types of social changes are involved, and then only in some phases of the changing process, as their efficiency is limited by the general social regularities by no means always vulnerable to legal manipulations.

According to the second position, legal means are essentially unable to influence the course of social life, and their effectiveness is wholly dependent upon the degree of their informal acceptance. This view is obviously false, for we cannot fail to notice that in many cases legal means appear as independent causes of various extra-legal social phenomena.

These extreme attitudes can be maintained only because we still lack sufficiently precise considerations on legal policy. The sound approach is intermediate between these two—the realization that law is an important means of social engineering, but that its effectiveness depends on several conditions.

In this book we have reported a number of studies showing that the efficiency of legal means is limited. Now it is worth while to attempt a synthesis of various conditions which intensify, hinder, neutralize, or exclude the influence of law.

Before we present such a list, we have to make a number of general reservations.

The problems of the effectiveness of law, however, are not the same for the various fields of law. The underlying conditions are different for criminal, civil, administrative, or international law.

The general problem of the efficiency of law is rather a detailed version of a more basic issue, i.e. the universal problem of effective action. As this problem is the concern of praxiology,[1] its notions, propositions and directives must also hold when dealing with the problem of the efficient functioning of legal precepts. However, not only praxiology, as the most general science of efficient action, applies to legal policy. Another discourse more general than legal policy, and more detailed than praxiology, is social engineering; its findings are also methodologically binding for legal policy. Social engineering deals with the problem of effective legislation, and thus co-operates with the two other disciplines: it draws general assumptions and theories from them, and in return provides them with detailed data and directives.

But what exactly is meant by efficient influence of legal regulations? Many issues may be involved, and it is not very easy to offer an exhaustive and systematical list. If we leave out the issue of information about legal precepts and their interpretation, the following issues seem to emerge: threatening sanctions for breaking the law, the apparatus warranting the realization of legal precepts, methods of determining their degree of effectiveness, the index of (motivational) and educative functions of law, compatibility of binding (official) law and of legal sentiment, and the prestige or authority of the legal system.

The term 'effectiveness of the functioning of law' may require initial elucidation. What is usually meant by it is only the compatibility of the intended and realized effects of legal regulations, and the means of ascertaining such compatibility. As we have already said, this is the traditional point of view of the problem of legal efficiency. In legal policy, the problem of the effectiveness of the functioning of law is seen in a broader view: legal policy is interested not only in the intended effects, but also in the whole gamut of unintended, indirect side effects. Legal policy as a scientific discipline is concerned with some methodological aspects of the realization of accepted objectives, and it aims to determine to what extent the postulated ends have been realized. Legal policy can be defined as applied sociology of law. The latter deals mainly with determining the causal relationships involved in the functioning of law; the former applies these relationships in practice to attain the intended ends.

It has been assumed here that the science of legal policy does not evaluate the ends it can serve. Such ends depend on the accepted ethics and ideologies. Discussions on whether the ends are right or justified are a matter of different emotive attitudes, or of different ultimate outlooks beyond the field of legal policy (applied sociology of law) as a practical discipline. Because of the many disagreements and misunderstandings, we want to stress a significant point. Science should not be seen in anthropomorphic terms. Legal policy is a product of culture; it can function autonomously and it can have its own inherent principles and methods; on the other hand, there are the people who deal with it. Individual scientists cannot possibly remain neutral, because they also have various other involvements: moral, political, ideological, etc. However, what is true about men or groups of men should not automatically be transferred to scientific disciplines as cultural creations—for example, it would be absurd to require logic or mathematics to cease being morally indifferent, and the same can be said about legal policy.

A bill may be considered a good job from the legal-political standpoint, at the same time being condemnable because of the ends it serves (e.g. 'well done' in the Nazi legal system meant efficient for Nazi purposes). Such a bill should be condemned, and the object of the condemnation would be the use made of legal policy, but not the science itself. Legal policy as a practical science can be applied to right as well as wrong ends. The indispensable condition for lucid reflection on the effectiveness of law is the reduction of the evaluating approach, which persistently blurs the scientific character of

I

legal policy (the resistance evoked by the term 'legal policy' in some theorists should be accounted for by emotional connotations of the term 'policy,' as well as by their neglect for neutral definitions).

To consider the conditions for the effectiveness of the functioning of legal precepts we must set forth a series of synthetic definitions on several essential concepts.

By a legislative authority or power we mean any agency authorized to issue legal enactments. By a normative act we mean a set of legal precepts forming a consistent whole. An objective of a legislative authority is a state of affairs positively evaluated by that authority, and which it intends to bring about. The effects of normative acts are any or all their empirically discernible consequences. The intended effects are those expected and accepted by the legislative authorities. The unintended effects are those not foreseen by the legislative authority, whether positive or negative. The unintended negative effects are a particular type of consequence. The secondary effects are expected by the legislative authority but not accepted in some of their aspects, but are nevertheless allowed or suffered by it as they constitute some of the indispensable conditions of the realization of the essential intended objectives. The negative unintended effects and the secondary effects can be labeled as losses, since they impede the efficiency of the functioning of a normative act. The degree of effectiveness of a normative act is thus the proportion of losses to intended effects.

It follows from these stipulations that a legislative power is in the most opportune situation if it can distribute the intended positive effects at will, without having to suffer the losses, as the intended effects are the objectives of the legislators. It is also obvious that the unintended negative effects are the most detrimental for the legislative authorities, since they are plainly incompatible with their desired ends.

A normative act (for example a set of regulations, a bill, a decree) attaining its intended effects is an effective act. One of the hallmarks of effective work—of any kind—is efficiency. As we know, one of the meanings of efficiency is the amount of product at the given cost. To measure the effectiveness of the functioning of normative acts is an important, though often neglected, problem.[2]

The notion of the efficiency of a normative act is important in the diagnoses of the particular sections of social life. It points to certain significant relationships in the ways of introducing social changes. Usually a normative act is brought to actual functioning by the administrative apparatus which also controls its effectiveness. The apparatus as such is not socially productive; its existence is justified by its bringing about the effects of normative acts and controlling them. In consequence, the more efficient the norms of a working normative act are, the more justified is the maintenance of the administrative apparatus. The reverse is also true. Hence, an administrative apparatus must be evaluated by its productivity, related to the normative acts introduced by it. If we know the productivity or efficiency of the administration, we can determine how profitable the effects of a normative act are apt to be at the given level of expense for the development and maintenance of the administrative apparatus. For it can often happen that a low degree of efficiency of a normative act (even if it is carried out in an orderly way) does not justify the existence of its executive machinery.[3]

Besides, we must distinguish between direct and indirect effects of the functioning of legal regulations. This distinction is important, because the end intended by a lawmaker can often be attained only through a chain of practical effects, where the consecutive partial results seem only remotely linked with the initial moves, and it is impossible to assess the effectiveness of the normative act as a whole without investigating the distribution of its indirect results. The direct results can be defined as the state of affairs following from the legal enactments without any additional (especially procedural) activities. The indirect effects can be defined as the state of affairs resulting from legal actions being intended results of some additional activities.

The general, abstract considerations presented above find their justification if we apply them to the problem of determining the degree of effectiveness of law, and the conditions for its effectiveness. Two types of conditions influencing the effectiveness of the functioning of law should be pointed out: the conditions which completely exclude or cancel the influence of law; and those that modify the degree of effectiveness of legal regulations.

Law can be ineffective for matter-of-fact reasons, or for formal ones. The former type of limitation occurs when a legal regulation is made impossible by the character of the object involved. The formal type of limitation appears when information about law cannot be transmitted, or when law itself stipulates that it should not interfere.

Absolute material limitations concern not only the physical conditions of definite conducts, but also some psychological domains excluded from the scope of possible penetration by the law. There is a restricted area of privacy (differently drawn in various societies) inaccessible to legal interference. Eventual legal interdiction, e.g. to have dreams of specified content, to create intrigues, to gossip, or to reveal family secrets, would be completely ineffective, since nobody would consider such legal regulations just or permissible, and, most important, nobody would believe it possible to uncover such forbidden behavior, at least not on an extensive scale. Of course, the domains of privacy can be drawn more or less generously. In Poland, for example, the law does not interfere in the sphere of conjugal sexual life, however perverse it may be; while the law in parts of the USA forbids so-called unnatural sexual behavior between husband and wife.

Time is not vulnerable to the power of law. What has been once, cannot be restored; the flow of time cannot be made faster. This is not a fictitious problem. One cannot attain maturity at the age of twelve, and one cannot make up for moral injury by restoring years spent in prison.

There are some mistaken beliefs as to the impossibility of legal regulation in certain fields of social life. Among them is the view that the action of law is ineffective when confronted with fixed social or folk ways. Empirical investigations persuade us to reject the classical proposition by W. G. Sumner to the effect that 'administrative measures cannot change social customs.' In particular, it has been proved by the studies of M. Deutsch and M. Collins[4] that administrative measures, if undertaken without ambiguity as to their objectives, can well cause extensive changes in behavior and attitudes, regardless of previous resistance toward those measures.

Apart from material limitations bringing about complete ineffectiveness of law, there are formal limitations. One of them is defective transmission of information about law. Unknown precepts are ineffective, though some legislators do not recognize ignorance as an excuse, partly to prevent trespassers from resorting to their ignorance of the law, and partly—even more significantly—to exert pressure towards learning the law. However, in spite of such motivational pressure it must be said that legal precepts cannot be effective if they remain socially unknown.

Extensive disruption in the transmission of legal information, sometimes so gross that the information cannot be understood at all, impedes the effectiveness of legal precepts. But not only that: legal regulations distorted by faulty information can produce the intended effects together with the unintended. A legislator may sometimes make use of ignorance as to certain significant changes in law to make it even more effective. If we set aside moral or political evaluation of this type of conduct, we can say that it attains, besides the intended results, many unintended results, among them negative, ones. Of course, it is absolutely necessary that new legal regulations, different from earlier ones, be made public if the legislator's intentions are to be at all attainable. Legal regulations, and the required behavior of people to whom the law is addressed, must be known. One thing is certain: a completely unknown legal system would crush the basic foundations of social order.

Sometimes law itself excludes the possibility of its own interference. This is true, in particular, about some fields of private life.

For example, the Constitution of the Polish People's Republic of July 22, 1955, declares in article 70 paragraph 1: 'Nobody can be compelled to abstain from religious activities or rites. Nobody can be compelled to participate in religious activities or rites either,' and in article 74, paragraph 2: 'Immunity of abodes and secrecy of correspondence is protected by the present bill. An abode can be searched only in cases provided by law.' And sometimes law compels itself to substantial changes: the criminal code of Greenland was based on sociological investigation. But the criminal code itself contained the following provision: 'The criminal code shall be revised during the parliamentary session of 1959–1960. The revision bill shall be accompanied by a report based on regular examination of the manner in which the code has worked during the period elapsed.'[5]

There are several factors which change the effectiveness of law. These can also be defined as either material or formal. Among the formal factors, we must mention the scope of knowledge of the law, the degree of understanding, the margin for multiple interpretations of valid laws with respect to other (earlier) laws, related ones, or with respect to their inherent vagueness, incoherence, ambiguity, lack of stability, inflation, multiple legal authorities, multiple sources of interpretation, etc. However, from the point of view of the sociology of law the more important factors are those with origin not in the faulty formal patterns of law, but in social determinants. We propose to call such factors the material ones and shall consider them in more detail.

Many of the studies reported in this book show that the degree of respect for legal norms is determined by the degree of socialization, i.e. of internalization of the generally accepted norms. If a group or an individual accepts the norms of the given legal system to a high degree, then no supplementary motivations, such as promise of profit, or fear of punishment, are necessary to secure the behavior defined by the norms. In such a situation norms are obeyed on their own behalf and the law is respected because it is the law. The degree of socialization of criminal law is expressed by avoiding unlawful behavior; of civil law by keeping contracts; of labor laws by carrying out the required activities.

It might appear that sanctions, both lenient and severe, like compulsory situations—loss of freedom, loss of the opportunity to dispose of things, loss of rights, etc.—are specific for criminal law. Social experience assumes a definite relationship between punishment and the effectiveness of the functioning of the relevant norm. However, this regularity is in many ways limited. It does not hold in extraordinary situations, e.g. during wars, revolution or pestilence; it does not work either if the sanction is obviously too severe and legal sentiment suggests that it is unreasonable or unjust. The factor of a sanction and its severity takes various forms in different fields of law. In criminal law it has the form of punishment; in civil law it has the form of compensation; in labor law it acts as fear of losing the job or an advancement, etc. Sanctions, or compulsory situations of some kind or another, are instruments of legal pressure.

The functioning of law cannot be separated from the institutions which execute it. Their efficient working leads to the effects intended by the lawmaker. Their inefficient working—e.g. delay, deficient and over-complex procedures, vagueness as to competence, inappropriate facilities, lack of experts, a tendency towards biased decisions (or even bribery, in extreme cases)—has the result that the legislative objectives can hardly, if at all, be realized. A work style contrary to that described above would bring about a more efficient realization of the normative ends.

There are legal precepts which can only function if there is a properly developed institutional support for them. Legal institutions are the junctions in the network of a legal system. The stream of legal activities and enactments flows through them, and their proper passage depends on the efficient functioning of the institutions. A lack of appropriate control, merely fault-finding control, or control without advice, too indulgent or incompetent, too narrow or partial, schematic or corrupt, makes it impossible to evaluate the work of the institutions and to correct it. The reverse is also true. A correct evaluation can provide the basis for improvements in the functioning of institutions. Thus faulty or corrupt control may hinder the effectiveness of legal precepts. The controlling agencies can be oriented to investigate only some kinds of institutional activity (not necessarily the most important ones). Besides, they can fail to improve their own work systematically, especially when their bureaucratic endeavors become ends in themselves, absorbing all their energy. Such bureaucratic alienation or withdrawal also causes weakness in the efficiency of the functioning of law.

Legal precepts determine certain types of behavior: performance or desistence. If such performances or acts of desistence correspond with the values approved by social groups or individuals, they can be carried out without legal sanctions. However, the need for a sanction increases in proportion with the degree of disapproval. Some types of behavior are ambiguous in this respect. They could be profitable, but fear of sanction lessens the temptation. These are situations of labile balance. Very often they create rationalizations of anti-legal behavior.

A sentiment of illegal behavior is an important factor impeding the effectiveness of the functioning of law. For example, investigation of crime is made difficult by unorganized but spontaneous resistance in criminal environments. But not only there. When there is a divergence between the lawmaker and the actual legal sentiment of society, and when the prevailing sentiment is opposed to the legitimate authority, an emotional social support emerges for those who break the law. If the divergence concerns political matters, society will sympathize with those who are subject to political repressions—and besides, by a peculiar association, also with those who break the law in other fields. Of course, such sentiments are by no means disinterested. There are definite interests behind them. In some situations they may be the interests of minorities, or of the majority. In many cases sentiments of this kind are suppressed by various means, including penal repression. However, in the present context we are not concerned with identifying the relationships between the anti-legal sentiments and their underlying interests (though it is a significant problem, particularly interesting for the sociology of law); we only wish to point out that such sentiments are social facts which must be taken into account when the effects of intended legal regulations are studied, to avoid unexpected negative consequences.

The effectiveness of law is further impaired or limited by the delegitimization of valid norms and the legitimization of illegal behavior. If valid precepts are often revoked, some skepticism toward other norms in the given field of law arises. A legitimization of illegal behavior almost always means impairing the effectiveness of law and diminishing the authority of the agency which recognizes the precepts as binding, but is unable to warrant obedience to them. Consequently, other precepts enacted by the same agency are depreciated and evaluated negatively. It should be added that if illegal behavior is made legitimate (i.e. is accepted by way of some rationalization), the interested parties are thereby encouraged to expand into fields not yet touched by legal corrosion. The process of corruption, also of law, is not static—sometimes it is explosive.

There are paradoxical situations where the effects desired by law are brought about, not by applying legal precepts, but by behavior incompatible with, or opposed to, the law. In such cases observance of the valid precepts would cause several negative effects; to avoid them, a negative double of the given set of legal precepts arises through adjustments and approximations—an informal rule, advising disobedience of the legal demands, while it apparently leads to breaking the 'formal structure' of the law, in reality acts in favor of the legal system.

It should be said again that lack of knowledge of some legal precepts adds to the limitations of the effectiveness of their functioning. Indeed, if some law is violated (and thus fails to cause the expected effects), and the facts of such violation remain unknown, no action can then be taken against the trespassers.

However, there are at least two possible ways of seeing this problem. The regulations in a certain field may be broken but the agen-

255

cies of justice fail to learn about it (sometimes segments of the public may remain ignorant as well) and no action is taken against the offenders. However, it can also happen (and it does happen more often) that a law is broken, action is taken against the anti-legal elements and some of the offenders are caught and punished, while others simply improve their methods. In the next phase of the process, the violation of the law is more sophisticated and the offenders enjoy the profits until a new action against them turns out to be successful. Here follows a brief description of such an escalation of methods. The story begins in the USA in the 1930s.[6] At the beginning it was easier to steal cars parked with the ignition key left in, or to steal open cars. So people avoided parking their cars with the keys left in, and tried to protect their convertibles better; the police kept a keener eye on such cars. Car thieves answered by improving their methods of opening car locks. In turn, this led to better locks. In Chicago there was an eighteen-year-old boy who was so clever that he could open any car lock in no time at all. He was hired by gangs as an instructor for training others in his craft. The president of a company boasting the invention of a 'thief-proof' lock went to Chicago to test his device, avowed by experts to be absolutely invulnerable. The boy was found and he opened the lock with simple tools in three minutes. The president insisted that this was pure luck, but the boy opened the lock the second time in just two minutes. The gangsters then started working with garage workers, who co-operated in fake burglaries. The next step was to repaint cars and to dismantle them into spare parts. The police increased their observation of garages, and stolen cars were taken to other states. When the police became 'sensitive' to those methods too, cars were taken abroad. So lawbreakers perfect their methods to make them more profitable until they are discovered—while lawmakers improve their laws and their execution (or at least they ought to do so). Of course, carrying out a rational legal policy, rather than 'keeping pace' with the criminal 'progress,' requires consideration of criminal calculations in advance.

We have said that ignorance can limit the effectiveness of law. Now, we must not miss another, related point. Knowledge of how to break legal regulations constitutes a peculiar pattern of behavior. This pattern, like any other, can be imitated. Thus, knowledge of how to break the law can either be a motive to act in favor of those who defend the law, or it can encourage others, nonconformists (in particular when the defense of law is not efficient enough), to take up activities according to anti-legal patterns.

It is clear that respect for the lawmaker, or lack of it, influences the effectiveness of the functioning of legal precepts. The more respect and authority the legislation enjoys, the more eagerly are the norms obeyed, and on the contrary, the less respect and authority, the less effectively are norms carried out. As we have said earlier, there are various sorts of respect. For example can religious support and absolute acceptance of law lead to fanaticism? On the other hand, rational respect for law (a concern for what the objectives of law are and how they are pursued) systematically leads to relativism.

We have mentioned some of the social conditions for the effectiveness of legal norms. It seems that these conditions refer, with due modifications, to all the fields of judicial activity, with the sole exception of international law.

We have attempted to present some of the factors which make the functioning of law impossible, as well as those which make it more or less efficient. Our intention has been to point out that the science of legal policy deals with problems of crucial and strategic importance. The neglect of such problems by the traditional legal discipline is a paradox difficult to account for.

Summing up what has been said about the effectiveness of the functioning of law, we wish to suggest the following generalization. There are two alternatives which must be faced by anyone who realizes that some legal norms apply to him. He can either act on the ground of the social obligation inculcated in him (corresponding with the rights he has), or on his own teleological consideration.

In the former case, the effectiveness of the functioning of legal precepts is secured, since law evokes an appropriate resonance in the form of lawful behavior. The latter situation is more complex. A subject of a legal norm tends to make a peculiar calculation (cognitive or affectional) of means and ends. He will consider, on one hand, his own interests, those of his family and group, the profits and the positive expectations, or the import of the matter; all these considerations can be compatible with the legal order or not; on the other hand he will consider the claims of the law as such. If he finds out that his interests and the demands of the legal system are compatible, it will be easy for him to take conformistic decisions. If, however, he discovers a gap between these two sets of factors, his behavior will depend on the outcome of his calculation of the expected gains and its pressure on one side, and the following factors on the other: the probable punishment, the efficiency with which the apparatus discovers unlawful behavior, the efficiency of the functioning of the apparatus of prosecution and repression, the degree of discomfort or pain related to the eventual repression and the fear of social condemnation.[7]

# part five

# A synthesis

# 15 Towards a general theory in the sociology of law

Both stupid and wise will, alike, try to acquire the power of
eloquence, and if scholars study with those eloquent speakers,
the people will lose touch with reality and will recite empty
phrases (Shang, who held high office in the state Ch'iu between
359 and 338 B.C.)

## Problem

The sociology of law has, in its recent development, passed through
several consecutive stages: problematic, empirical and engaged in
policy formation. It was hoped that, as a by-product of the studies
which took place at each stage and level of progress, a new comprehensive theory of the sociology of law would emerge. At present
these expectations are still no more than a hope. Thus, an attempt to
present a general theory of the sociology of law is now more than
ever urgent.

There are at least three possibilities for building a theory of the
sociology of law: (a) to apply general notions and propositions which
have been produced (and tested) by general sociology; (b) to generate
a theory of the sociology of law on the basis of existing empirical
and comparative studies; and (c) to follow a middle, Aristotelian,
course. Let us investigate which type of approach might be regarded
as the most comprehensive.

## Application of general sociological concepts

Several concepts exist which might be transplanted and applied
from general sociology into the area of legal studies. They are for
example: reference group, cognitive dissonance, and status incon-
sistency-notions. Let us try to find under which conditions these (and

possibly other) concepts can be used in the field of the sociology of law. One general remark, *a priori*, should be made: applications of general concepts should not be introduced in a mechanical way; rather should they take into consideration those specific elements which exist in the area of study.

The concept of sub-culture is quite well elaborated in criminology, studies on deviance, and the sociology of law. Nevertheless only a limited attempt (if any) has been made to discuss the usefulness of the sub-culture concept in relation to the reference group notion. Let us summarize briefly the basic ideas of the so-called reference group theory. Several types of reference groups might be distinguished. *Positive reference groups* are those to which an individual aspires or strives to belong; they largely determine the behavior of the individual, being the main source of the rules and values accepted by him. *Negative reference groups* are those which an individual actively or passively avoids. He dislikes being identified with such groups in his own mind and even more he avoids others associating him with them. *Comparative reference groups* are those to which an individual does not aspire, but whose standards provide him with a convenient criterion for the evaluation of his own and other status. It was suggested by J. Kubin[1] that the concept of *fictitious reference groups* can be constructed by introducing the criterion of the actual and empirical existence or non-existence of an imaginary group. According to this idea, a social group which is able to satisfy certain obvious social needs is sometimes lacking. Then an attempt is made to create fictitious groups allowing the comparison of their standards with actual behavior. (This concept of fictitious reference groups was generated on the basis of several studies in the area of the sociology of mass media.)

These notions, although theoretically quite useful, have been neglected in the sociology of law. Nevertheless, different types of 'negative' reference groups such as the conflict-prone, drug, thief, semi-thief, criminal middle-class oriented sub-cultures might be spelled out.[2] From the point of view of an observer, the above-mentioned sub-cultures could be regarded as negative reference groups. This would not, however, necessarily be the case from the point of view of the participant or an insider. For him the criminal sub-culture could have the value of positive identification or, where he is on the edge of the criminal world, it could have an ambivalent (positive or negative) character. Legal clerks and officers usually, although not necessarily, represent the positive legal sub-culture and, at the same time, 'positive' reference groups. In some social systems which are characterized by a substantial gap between the legal system and its social and political acceptance, the legal profession might be regarded by the average citizen as a negative reference group.

Again support for the legal system and a lack of support for the political establishment (these two types of legitimacy are not necessarily the same) could create a state of social ambivalence toward the law in general. The legal profession would then be regarded as a comparative reference group (as far as knowledge of the law is concerned).

According to an interesting study on conscientious objectors in Norway,[3] courts in southern and northern Norway clearly displayed different styles of handling the accused. These differences, according to the conclusions of the study, could only be explained, on the one hand, by the specific characteristics of the case and, on the other, and this is more interesting here, by the peculiar styles ('micro-climates') of sentence-making prevailing in the judges' different circles. So, this study has pointed to the fact that an institution—in this case the courts—can evolve practical stereotypes of decision-making which are locally observed and transmitted (neutral but differentiated subcultures) and which are different from the patterns of settlement which may prevail elsewhere in similar cases.

So, the notions taken from reference group theory appear to be (with some additional specifications which should take into consideration the unique features of legal relations) useful in the area concerning the functioning of law. But the relations between general sociology and the sociology of law are somewhat dialectical. Inquiries in the area of the sociology of law (as was the case with the contribution taken from the sociology of mass media by J. Kubin) might enrich the spectrum of concepts in general sociology. The Polish study on lay assessor judges furnished some hints for the coming of the concept of the *control reference group*. By the control reference group one might mean a group whose (or in which) evaluations of the principles of behavior are taken into consideration, though this group is neither an object of aspiration nor of avoidance. The fact that the presence of this group is acknowledged or taken for granted modifies behavior towards an adjustment of the appropriate criteria of the subject's behavior to the norms which are known to be reinforced by the control group.[4]

General sociological concepts might be applied and used not only in the field of research and reflections on the sociology of law, but also in relation to more complex matters. The dynamic interplay between reference groups can be used as an explanatory factor in processes which generate deviant or criminal behavior. Under certain conditions the final rejection of the family (as a negative reference group) might result in a decisive affiliation with a delinquent subculture of peers. Although they were earlier evaluated in a negative way, now they become attractive, providing a sanctuary away from family tensions. Double revolt—first against the negative images of

263

the family, second against the negative image of the peer-group—could, paradoxically enough, result in an affiliation to the general law-obedient patterns of life.

The basic proposition of the theory of *cognitive dissonance* can be spelled out in the following way: inconsistency of opinion functions as a punishment, while consistency of opinion works as a reward.[5]

Although this general statement seems to be quite simple it has a number of theoretically interesting ramifications.[6] And again: although the concept of cognitive dissonance is used primarily as a theoretical tool for explaining the individual psychological processes it might also be used for broader applications in the area of social psychology. And finally, the concept of cognitive dissonance could also be used in a quite illuminating way for socio-legal reflections. Let us take an example from Polish socio-legal studies.[7] A nation-wide sample shows that divorce as a new socio-legal institution is widely accepted. Indeed: there were 30 per cent negative answers to the general question concerning the acceptance of the institution of divorce. However, when the general question of whether the divorce should be permitted at all was reduced to a series of more detailed cases the percentage of negative answers was diminished to 7 per cent. This ought to be considered as the general proportion of those whose attitude toward divorce was really negative. Anyway, the study of divorce confirms the general conclusion that if there is a discrepancy between a social need and the relevant legal institution, then, if the intensity of such a need increases (as was the case in Poland after the Second World War), there is inclined to be a comparable increase in the range and intensity of views and behaviour opposing or breaking the norms in force, in favor of a functional solution. This acceptance of divorce is especially interesting because, at the same time, at least 80 per cent of the whole population would accept religious beliefs which strongly contradict a positive evaluation of divorce. Nevertheless the institution of divorce, when it is given formal validity, is accepted even if it is inconsistent with traditional attitudes as well as with the religious beliefs concerning the given issue.

These findings point out a sharp contradiction in beliefs and opinions. So the question arises: in which way will this contradiction (which according to the theory of cognitive dissonance constitutes a constant source of punishment) be resolved or frozen? Apparently through rationalizations. To what extent is this explanation satisfactory? Only partially.

Another Polish study encounters a very similar paradox. According to this study[8] the average Polish population has quite a good knowledge of basic legal rules and accepts the law (on the whole) as basically satisfactory. Nevertheless, an increase in deviant and criminal behavior in the areas of juvenile delinquency and economic crimes (theft and white-collar crimes) is visible, when—taking into consideration comparative and supplementary data—the general rate of crime is low and stable. Socioeconomic factors (i.e. those connected with the socialistic social system) are not sufficient to explain this contradiction; neither are the features connected with different types of negative sub-cultures operating inside the system. Neither do personality factors (maladjustment, frustration, etc.) present the possibility of a full explanation. Rather, interrelations between these elements offer a useful and more approximate explanation; negative social conditions and the situation of an 'underdog' might push one towards crime. But still the influence of the positive sub-culture could contradict this pressure. So, is this explanation completely adequate? The *notion of 'invisible factors'* might be useful at this stage of analysis. It seems that the gnostic and explanatory use of the concept of these factors enables us to take an additional explanatory step forward. These 'invisible factors' might be described as certain personality traits which are internalized through the processes of (positive or negative) socialization and which constitute a link between moral and legal beliefs and relevant behavior. Indeed the picture which is usually tacitly accepted is a simplified one: it seems to be reasonable to distinguish at least three levels of acceptance of the law and basic moral norms: (a) lip-service and declaration (a purely external manifestation of certain values often displayed to accommodate clearly perceived social expectations), (b) internal acceptance (commitment to internalized values which sometimes are not externally expressed); and (c) acceptance that is consistent with the behavior guided by accepted values.[9]

Taking these considerations into account it might be said that the explanation (if any) given by the theory of cognitive dissonance for the coexistence of contradictory beliefs through rationalization is superficial because rationalizations themselves could be regarded as the product of additional, interplaying forces or invisible factors.

General sociology has created another concept: *status inconsistency*, a convenient notion which has been neglected as far as its usefulness in the sociology of law is concerned. It could be said that modern societies are quite successful at disseminating widely-held notions of legal equality. Citizens (with exceptions provided by law) seem to be equal when they face the legal system. Citizens are supposed to have equal access to the legal system and also equal protection under it. Is this really the case?

An Italian study introduces some interesting data for further discussion.[10]

The average citizen's feelings regarding recourse to the judicial apparatus are on the balance unfavorable, at least to the extent

265

of surpassing, on the evidence available, a simple wish for reforms to be effected. In synthesis the average citizen looks upon the judicial apparatus as fairly inaccessible. The high cost of legal proceedings (partly, not solely, on account of the venality of lawyers) creates an objective selection among those who need legal redress. Justice at law is a luxury beyond the reach of many, even though all are entitled to employ it for defending wrongs. This explains why each social group considers the prevalence of social injustices to be related to the way in which the legal apparatus actually functions. The man-in-the-street obviously has no faith in the objectivity of the legal process because, in the last analysis, financial factors prevail. The litigant with the greatest means has the best chance for a favorable outcome. In this light, the cost of legal proceedings appears as an insurmountable barrier, preventing the law-in-action from living up to its lofty ideals of equality and impartiality for all. Therefore, the judicial apparatus seems to betray its basic duty by legalizing the perpetuation of wrongs: the cost of law dis-courages recourse to it; and the time taken over legal actions outlives any interest in the outcome and the usefulness even of the right decisions.

Similar results, quite consistent with those of the Italian studies, have been found by R. Blom.[11] These findings disclose a unique type of status inconsistency. In modern societies, from the point of view of the citizen's status, a normative provision is designated which attributes to everybody the same right to legal protection, and from another point of view (due to the influence of economical, social, and political factors) this status is systematically biased or denied. This particular type of status inconsistency (not an individual but a social one) might create several consequences: (a) it could further unify those social groups which are affected by it; (b) it could encourage the types of illegal solutions which exist outside the legal order to erode the legal system; (c) it could support attitudes which are prone to anti-legal behavior; (d) it could create an atmosphere of mistrust toward the legal system as a whole; and (e) it could stimulate political beliefs which reject the existing type of legal and social establishment. There is some similarity between this category of status inconsistency and those types which are usually analyzed by general sociology: both types of status inconsistency lead, under certain conditions, to radicalization of beliefs. A basic difference still exists. In general, people in cases of status inconsistency perceive their own situation as a source of punishment and consequently have a tendency to change this situation (thought to be a change in status, change of its percep-tion, its denial, avoidance, etc.). In the case of legal systems these techniques are useless; it is not easy to change legal systems according to individual wishes, or to deny or avoid the content of such a system. Thus the frustrations which might be accumulated by the impact of a legal system, although quite often invisible, are intense. Still, the inadequacy of legal systems as a possible cause of revolution is neither sufficiently linked with status inconsistency nor theoretically elaborated as it should be.

The examples of reference group theory, the concept of cognitive dissonance and the status inconsistency notion have been employed to show that they can be quite useful in the area of the sociology of law. It was quite easy to observe that this type of application should not only take into consideration the peculiar characteristics of the field of inquiry but also, for this reason, open up new avenues for further study and induce the modification of concepts already elaborated.

## Specific concepts generated by socio-legal studies

Socio-legal studies may, as a by-product of their diagnostic goals, generate concepts which have a validity which transcends the area of original inquiry. Therefore these studies contribute something not only to the world in which they are carried on but also to general sociological theory. Nevertheless this type of observation seems to be proper: quite often notions generated by research in a given, restricted area of sociology are used only in this limited area without any attempt to confer on these notions a more general sense of validity.

The concept of a *control reference group* has been mentioned already. This concept was generated in connection with the diagnostic study on lay assessor judges (in the area of the criminal law). The study was conducted in Poland in 1964.[12] The lay assessor judges enjoy all the rights and obligations of professional judges, except the title to preside over trials and trial sessions. There are two assessors and a single judge in the jury, so that the social factor represented by them is in the majority, except in those cases when only a single professional judge is admitted. Both the judge and the assessors are entitled to an opinion differing from that of the majority, in the form of the so-called *votum separatum*. The intention of the legislature, when the institution of the assessors was first established, was to introduce an element of everyday experience into the court procedure, an element represented by the assessors. Another function of the assessors was to graft the legal awareness gained and shaped by them in the court (there were about 50,000 assessor judges in the country during the period of the study) into their original social and professional settings. According to the

267

findings of the study, the role of assessor judges was found to be a passive one (in opposition to their own image of the role they play in the penal process). However, various other indices (like the fact that they are rarely absent from the court, that they are interested in what is going on, ask matter-of-fact questions, tend systematically to make the verdicts more lenient, and get involved in controversies with judges) tend to suggest that the study's conclusion is not accurate. So are they passive or active? To give a full answer to this question the concept of a control reference group was created. The real sense of this concept boils down to the notion of a watchdog. Lay assessor judges, seen on cursory inspection to be passive, in fact play an active role in safeguarding against routine, formalization, haste, prejudices, anti-legal practices, etc. Used in these terms this concept of a control reference group might be extended beyond its original legal context in order to explain sexual behavior, fashions, and the behavior of the snobs of political control institutions. Without going into a more extended elaboration of these possibilities (though such an endeavor might prove promising) let us comment only that concepts which are generated from socio-legal studies may have wider potentiality in the realm of social engineering. This is because socio-legal studies usually deal with legal norms and institutions which are designed to change the social reality.

In connection with the notion of cognitive dissonance the *concept of 'invisible factors'* was mentioned earlier. Invisible factors were defined as certain personality traits which were internalized through the processes of (positive or negative) socialization and which constitute a link between moral and legal beliefs and relevant behavior. During the Polish study[13] the following invisible factors were recognized, operationalized and preliminarily tested: principled and instrumental attitudes, individually and socially oriented ethics, and affiliation attitudes. To clarify, let us make an assumption that the invisible factors as personality traits do not deal directly with this or an other area of human behavior. They do not have direct links with legal, moral, sexual, economic, political, etc., behavior. Invisible factors might be regarded as meta-attitudes. They structure, or put together different types of attitudes according to a certain, more general pattern and paradigm. A 'principled attitude' was defined as a direct, spontaneous acceptance or negation of some rule relative to an imaginary or actual mode of behavior. The 'instrumental attitude' was described as one where the acceptance or negation of imaginary or actual behavior is dependent upon weighing the possible alternatives of behavior against an evaluation of their effects.

Social and individualistic attitudes encompass different dimensions of posture toward social reality. 'Socially oriented ethics' refer to the roles and positions which are occupied by an individual, whereas individually oriented ethics regulate the social behavior of people according to patterns which are prevalent in small, more or less informal groups. According to 'individually oriented ethics' an individual is evaluated on the basis of his personal performance; socially oriented ethics, however, also take into consideration the long-range social effects of behavior which seem to be, at first glance, morally neutral. This notion of depth of 'attachment to' the group, subculture, or social system constitutes an additional dimension for regulating morally and legally relevant behavior.

The studies devoted to the problem of the functioning of the law introduced a great deal of evidence indicating that the space between legal and moral attitudes and the behavior relevant to these attitudes is not quite empty. What were described as 'invisible factors' seem to fill in this space and influence this behavior in an essential way. Hence, if such factors as instrumental attitudes, individualistically oriented ethics and lack of affiliation to the social structure enter into the picture, then in spite of healthy moral and legal attitudes on the lip-service or even acceptance level, it would be possible that behavior eroded by the cumulative influence of invisible factors would visibly contradict manifested and viable moral and legal values. Again: why do some people remain morally intact although they are surrounded by the same negative sub-cultures and lack of religious restraints (in the state of prevalent social and political anomie)? The intervention of invisible factors could be considered as, at least, an essential part of the explanation. Thus invisible factors could be regarded as independent variables which produce, among others, dependent variables—rationalizations.

Several studies on the 'second life'[14] clearly indicate that a strange type of social life has a tendency to develop in certain conditions of seclusion. A study of several closed institutions revealed that the life of the inmates of these institutions is divided into two basic areas: official life which could be characterized as the law-obedient and conformist (one related to school and controlled activities) and, on the other hand, a hidden second life (negative toward conformity, rejecting the law) governed by its own rules. The essence of the second life consists in a peculiar stratification which can be reduced to the division of the inmates into 'people' and 'suckers.' The 'people' are equal; they differ little in the degree of acceptance of the patterns of behavior which constitute the second-life rituals. Every day of the second life is strongly ritualized and the most severe offense in the inmate community is the denunciation of other men. This offense and also that of being the passive object of homosexual practices pushes someone to the bottom of the social ladder. This type of 'dirty sucker' becomes the target and object of different kinds of manipulations lacking any human emotion except one: the exercise of power.

In consequence, the 'second life' consists of an artificial, but rigorously observed, social stratification. Being pushed to a lower position in the rank order is a punishment, while an advancement is considered a reward. Thus in a world in which there is a scarcity of real things and the rewards connected with them, a man is reduced to the status of *a thing* as punishment and is pushed to the lowest position in the rank order functioning within a system, for there are no extra-personal achievements by which to judge relationships.

The analysis of the second life which creates an unknown (when it is widely active) but strong obstacle to resocialization and which efficiently counteracts many arrangements designed to reintegrate law and order into correctional institutions has furnished much data towards the development of a *concept of autotelic use of power*. The autotelic attitude towards power cannot be reduced to values; instead values are reduced to power. Such an autotelic attitude towards power finds pleasure in the pure exercise of power, whereas heterotelic attitudes towards power gain rewards from the realization or implementation of values. Paradoxically enough, the autotelic character of some treatments of power reveals that power, once gained, might be used in a peculiar type of heterotelic way. Indeed, if power is treated as an end in itself, then it becomes a substitute for goals which are out of reach. The notion of the autotelic use of power can be applied in explaining the puzzling features of the second life. So, when desired goals and values are blocked (as happens in reformatories, correction houses, prisons, closed institutions, total societies, etc.) or when they are so far removed as to preclude their achievement, then the climate of social emptiness generates conditions for the emergence of power as an ultimate value, as the goal itself. And then an additional artificial social stratification—which is dysfunctional from the point of view of the normative social system but functional from the inmates' perspective—is created in order to establish conditions for the exercise of that power as a distribution of rewards derived from its own use.

The concept of the autotelic use of power is significant in the sociology of law, for at least three reasons: (1) autotelic power inside closed systems might be regarded as legitimized even when it is not functional for values transcending the pure maintenance of the system (then legitimized autotelic power does not govern due to sheer compulsion but because of a certain type of acceptance); (2) autotelic power presents this face of power which is not functional despite the fact that law (on which the power is supposed to be based) ought to play only a functional role within the social system; and (3) autotelic power emphasizes the importance of the study of living law (not only its formal façade) and its links with the other essential elements of social life.

## Towards a synthesis

Previous considerations, when treated in a meta-way, substantiated a great deal of evidence which shows that concepts borrowed from the general theory of sociology and those generated from studies on socio-legal problems are strongly interrelated. This mutual interdependence of both categories of notions is so close that the distinction which separates them seems to be artificial and only of didactic value. It is incorrect to understand the law in its functioning only through static or normative analysis. The law is a dynamic element of social life which is constantly generated by the interplay of different social factors. It also influences social life in an instrumental way. The existing concepts in the philosophy of law are not sufficient for comprehensive analysis of this type and therefore the present condition of jurisprudence shall be regarded as unsatisfactory. Let us take as an example a concept which is not as complicated as the notion of the law itself and which is supposed to deal directly with empirical data—punishment.[15]

Recent philosophical discussion has produced a definition of punishment that will serve as a starting point for our inquiry. This definition presents the standard case of punishment as exhibiting five characteristics: (1) It must involve pain or other consequences normally considered unpleasant. (2) It must be for an offense against legal rules. (3) It must be imposed on an actual or supposed offender. (4) It must be intentionally administered by human beings other than the offender. (5) It must be imposed and administered by an authority constituted by a legal system against which the offense is committed.

This definition raises at least the following questions: (a) why must it (is it a logical requirement or an ethical one)? (b) what is unpleasant? (c) what is 'normally'? (d) who is supposed to be the offender (even imaginary)? (e) what does 'intentionally administered' mean (who is supposed to psychoanalyze the administrative agency)? (f) what is a 'legal system'? (g) what is 'authority constituted by' a legal system? (h) what does 'constituted' mean?[16] Of course in order to defend this definition a lot of additional analytical definitions might be produced: undoubtedly a vicious circle of them. But despite semantic shortcomings, the definition cited above deals with two separate and different dimensions of reality: the normative and the factual. The normative deals with 'legal system,' 'authority,' 'constituted,' 'administered,' etc. while the factual points out 'pain,' and 'other consequences' (what sort of consequences?), 'unpleasant,' etc. But conceptual equipment does not create the only problem.

Jurisprudence (or the philosophy of law) is not prepared in a methodologically sufficient way for a comprehensive synthesis. An excellent work in its own field accepts these types of methodological premises as the basic theoretical guide lines ('Towards a Theory of Accident Law').[17]

> I shall try to maintain the following definitions: *goals* will mean particular categories of the broad goals (e.g. reduction of administrative costs); *methods* or *approaches* will mean theoretical devices for achieving the goals or sub-goals (e.g. spreading of costs, general deterrence); *systems* of accident law will mean actual ways of allocating costs of accidents (e.g. the fault system, social insurance, or enterprise liability).

There are at least three essential shortcomings to this type of approach: (1) it does not provide a sufficient basis for theoretical generalizations; (2) it accepts accident law as a category which is proper for the creation of a theory (in fact accident law gives too narrow a basis; it is not a representative class for the formulation of propositions which explain the functioning of the law); and (3) it confuses the social engineering approach (locutions quoted above constitute an excellent conceptual frame-work for a socio-technical way of thinking) with the theoretical one. There is a sort of intrinsic contradiction behind these statements. Jurisprudence which generates these types of confused notions was created as a superstructure combining different types of binding laws: criminal, labor, civil, administrative, family, etc. In any case these notions were designated for the explanation of law in action. It seems rational therefore to distinguish between two incompatible delineations of the law: the practical and the theoretical. The practical (fixed for clearly utilitarian reasons, to give a judge or a lawyer a guide-line between law and non-law) would say that the law is a norm generated by proper authority and supplied with compulsory sanctions. This type of definition, useful as it is, originated different branches of the law and was polished by the analytical work of jurisprudence. The task of the theoretical definition is not a practical one: it aims to say what law is and how it functions in social reality.

The theoretical answer to the question 'What is law?' would be this: *law is a social norm which is based on four reciprocal elements belonging to the parallel parties and containing two corresponding pairs of rights and duties.*

Neither state, nor subject, is able to tell which social norms belong to the category of legal ones. Some norms which are not legal from the point of view of the state (they don't have the compulsory sanctions) are legal nevertheless because they operate as such. Being recognized as such by subjects they act in the same way in which they would function having the full support of the state control apparatus. Some norms are legal even if subjects are unable to perceive the links between reciprocal elements, even if they have a feeling of duty and right without the recognition of the corresponding dyad of duty and right. When a 35-year-old teacher from a highly industrialized country is deeply convinced that he is the only owner of Mount Everest and that all people have a duty to respect his rights to this mountain, his conviction (contrary to L. Petrażycki's view) is not a legal one: it does not correspond to the reciprocal attitudes of duties and rights of any real party. But if a Mafia leader demands obedience and gives dangerous orders, then he behaves according to the law: his rights to do so are recognized, several of his comrades accept the duty to obey and—this is quite important—he has a corresponding *duty* to protect his subordinates, while they have a legitimate claim to his protection. Only this tetrad of duties and rights constitutes the law. Usually the reciprocal dyads correspond—according to the principle of '*do ut des*'—to each other. But how does one determine the law when they don't? The very fact that the complementary interplay of dyads might be disrupted (or not recognized at all) creates a need for a judge or, better, an agency which (after a search for power-related elements: rights and duties) declares its existence (or lack of it).

The tetrad conception of the law is based on the principle of accepted reciprocity. Should an Indian chief give a mountain to a lawyer as a gift, his action would have several consequences. According to this act he would have a duty to surrender the land which he is giving and also by the act of donation he would be obliged to accept the right on the part of the lawyer to possess the land in question. It is obvious (from the point of view of living, intuitive law) that the chief, according to his act, also acquires some right to certain services from the recipient of his gift. The recipient has, even if this is not recognized by the official law, the duty to discharge these services. If the case were a sale of the mountain the four bonds which tie together duties and rights would be even more visible—and more digestible for legal dogmatists. Then the chief would be bound by duty to turn over the land, and the lawyer bound to pay the price; on the other hand the chief would have the right to demand the payment and the lawyer the right to possess the mountain. Unilateral perception of duty and right and insistence on them might, in special circumstances, change social reality. But in such a case the change of social reality is a condition triggered by deviance: results in no response, reciprocity—social resonance. Bilateral perception of duties and rights constitutes several regularities which match attitudes and behavior. Social life allocates duties and rights in patterns which are designated by accumulated experience collected by many repetitions or careful analysis of exceptional cases. Thus, the grand-father has (under certain conditions) a duty to leave the property to his grandson, having also a right to insist on proper conduct. The grandson on his side has a right to expect the transfer of the property at the proper time and a duty to respect his grandfather. The rights and duties cemented by the rule appear especially clear when the links between them are sharply broken (grandson killed his grand-father). The court of the USA said in the case of *Riggs* v. *Palmer* 'no one shall be permitted to profit by his own fraud, or to take advantage of his own wrong, or to found any claim on his ingenuity, or to acquire property by his own crime' (*Riggs* v. *Palmer*, 115 N.Y. 506, N.E. 188 (1889)). It would be a mistake to assume that this case creates an entirely new rule. But it does serve a special function, and is spelled out in order to prevent the improper allocation of obliga-tions and claims (as L. Nader would say: 'it makes the balance').

If the law is understood as such a tetrad, then it is easy to explain why it fulfills its five basic functions: (1) integration, (2) petrification, (3) reduction, (4) motivation, and (5) education.

Indeed, the law integrates the mutual expectations of behavior of two parties (through the reciprocally-structured duties and rights) in a way that is consistent with the general values existing in a given social system.

The *integrative* function of the law could be summarized in the following way:[18]

Law may, according to this conception, fulfill an integrative function by stimulating the processes of integration successively on various levels of social organization with the following objectives: system integration (integration of social sub-systems); institutional integration (integration of social roles and institutions); and social (personal) integration (integration of individuals and groups): objectively and subjectively.

Another description of this function of the law is given by Shang:[19]

Of old, the one who would regulate the empire was he who regarded as his first task the regulating of his own people; the one who could conquer a strong enemy was he who regarded as his first task the conquering of his own people. For the way in which the conquering of the people is based upon the regulating of the people is the effect of smelting in regard to metal or the work of the potter in regard to clay; if the basis is not solid, then people are like flying birds or like animals. Who can regulate these? The basis of the people is the law.

The law—through trial and error—selects those interpersonal relations which, in the forms of tetrads, satisfy changing social needs. In this way the law *petrifies* those schemes of behavior which are recognized as successful and functional. It may be said that law labels as positive only felicitous manifestations of human relations which are generated in the changing laboratory of society. The unsuccessful forms, after several trials, are rejected and abandoned, very seldom undergoing petrification. They may, however, be perpetuated in obscure institutions, disrupted by cognitive dissonance.

Both the processes of integration and those of petrification lead to a *reduction* in the number of acceptable types of interhuman behavior. The number of possible types of interrelations between people among themselves or between themselves and social institutions is vast and complex. Order and predictability are unattainable within such a complicated social fabric. Because each case in its specificity differs from all others, the rules which are generated in connection with a particular case are not applicable generally. This variety of social situation leads to a need for simplification, a reduction of factual possibilities: the law, through its abstract categorization, gives such a possibility. Experimentally established tetrads reduce the endless possibilities for social interrelations to manageable schemes of behavior, the ramifications of which have already been recognized and tested as socially essential and strategic.

Another function of the law is: behavior's *motivation* (the regulation of individual attitudes and performances). The legal norm contains a normative appeal and is, at the same time, informative: this type of behavior is prohibited and that is supported by the legal system. Knowledge of this sort gives individuals the opportunity to select behavior which will enable them to operate successfully inside the parameters of the legal system. Thus, knowledge of legal norms does condition the actor to behave in the manner prescribed by the basic values of the legal system. But even more: the actor is not only motivated to avoid those actions not included in the pre-demanded pattern but is also educated (through the repeated process of reinforcement) to act in a mode fixed by this pattern. Educational function of the law—from this point of view—could be regarded as an extension of the motivational one.

It is observed that from an enormous number of options, the law enforces that which has already been tested and found useful and just as an acceptable relationship between two parties. The final function is the *educational* one. But rewards and punishments not only motivate behavior, but also, in the long run, socialize and educate. Rewards reinforce desirable performances, thus creating positive habits. Punishments can be used to reduce or eliminate situations which generate undesirable behavior or can be used, as B. Skinner says, to break contingencies under which punished behavior is reinforced through this type of training. According to L. Petrażycki the law alters originally difficult patterns of behavior into patterns molded by habit.

The above-mentioned theoretical considerations try to present a new, more comprehensive notion of law. Nevertheless, the question remains: to what extent are these considerations based on empirical findings taken from the area of socio-legal studies and to what extent can they be justifiably generalized? Yes, they may indeed overstep the boundaries, but this transgression seems to be consistent with the major trends of empirical findings.

The living law (being quite often contradictory to official law) is rooted in morals because it distributes duties (morals) and rights according to the informally and plastically established interests which link constantly bargaining parties. It is difficult to introduce into social life a law which contradicts living law; behind it are hidden moral sentiments which are crystalized in principled attitudes —as vested interests. The theories, then, which try to explain the functioning of law using the concept of a law created by lawyers (norms generated by legitimized authority and supported by sanctions) are not adequate: they are too narrow, too limited. They do not take into consideration the impact exercised by the living law based not on the coercive apparatus but on a consensus rooted in a structurally distributed morality and interest. They are also unable to introduce the paradigm, the three-step hypothesis, which explains the operation of the law.[20]

The tetrad conception of the law should not be interpreted in a narrow way. If the given social system is structured by the legal system into equilibrium (by interrelated sets of tetrads) it does not mean necessarily that the law resembles the just distribution of rewards and punishments. W. J. Chambliss and R. B. Seidman seem to be right when they introduce here the Marxist perspective:[21]

> that society is composed of groups that are in conflict with one another and that the law represents an institutionalized tool of those in power which functions to provide them with superior moral as well as coercive power in the conflict. As we have seen, however, this general proposition is not sufficient to account for all aspects of the legal order. We have supplemented this premise with a number of complementary propositions about the nature of the conflict in stratified societies and the relationship of the law to this conflict. We have also added to this perspective the critically important element of the bureaucratic character of the legal system—an element which in and of itself guarantees that the legal order will take on a shape and character at variance with what it might have been if the law reflected the 'public interest.'

If this is the case the concept of power should be taken into consideration. T. Parsons's dilemma connected with the concept of power is well known. '*Power* anchored in the goal-attainment system, is the generalized capacity to make specific *binding* decisions, that is, to activate general political obligations, where these decisions are presumptively in the interest of collective goal-attainment.'[22] H. M. Johnson makes the additional comments: 'Some critics of Parsons are unhappy about his restricting "power" to contexts in which effective action depends upon legitimization and consensus.' And also: 'the effectiveness of criminal gangs, however, or of any other collectivity, including total society, depends upon "power" in Parsons's sense.'[23] The riddle and contradiction seems to be solved when categories are not mixed. When the formal concept of legitimation taken from jurisprudence (the consistency with rules of higher order) is applied to the gang situation, the contradiction is obvious: a gang does not have constitutional support! But when the tetrad conception of the law is introduced the situation is different: the gang leader (being also a symbol of the positive reference group for his followers) has a power to give orders because he also has a duty, corresponding to his authority, to protect and defend his subjects. This concept of legitimization is different from a formal and normative one but is based on real distribution of attitudes, structured by mutual interests.

In realms where many essential values are at stake, a social system produces legal foundations, cementing them reciprocally by means of duties and claims together in a parallel manner. The principle of '*do ut des*,' so skillfully described by B. Malinowski on the basis of anthropological material, being an expression of certain social, economic and other forces, acts as a cementing and motivating social bond. If, to simplify the question, we were to compare the social system to a more or less flattened pyramid, then the duty and claim norms will bind the essential elements of that system on the principle of the relative equilibrium of the forces on the horizontal plane. Then the tetrad of two corresponding duties and claims constitutes some sort of model of two mutually balanced equivalent forces of the same phenomenon. On the vertical plane on the other hand, the social system appears to operate with additional definitions which, after all, boil down to the same things: pure privilege (when only rights are visible and corresponding duties are hidden, consumed by power, tactically suppressed, etc.) and pure obedience (when corresponding claims are discouraged, denied, forgotten, etc.). The 'invisible factors' might cement the pyramid or might change it into a heap of sand. Consequently two notions: the official notion of the law and the notion based on the living functioning of the law might be useful for the avoidance of mistakes. The official notion of the law tends to grasp everything in the dichotomic categories: 'white' and 'black.' Behavior is either legal or criminal. These distinctions, which can be useful as far as normative problems are concerned, are misleading when applied to reality. B. Kutchinsky's extensive study on sociological aspects of deviance and criminality leads to such conclusions.[24]

> First, while it is still possible to uphold a distinction between 'criminals' and 'non-criminals,' the difference between these two groups will have to be redefined. What makes a person 'criminal' is not the fact that he has committed a crime (because also non-criminals have done that), but the fact that he was caught, tried, convicted and punished.

## Conclusions

The application of theoretical concepts elaborated by general sociology to socio-legal problems and the generation of theoretical concepts based on empirical studies in the area of the sociology of law constitute two sides of the same coin.

The difficulty in grasping the specifics of the operation of law is due to the stigma which legal systems have placed on the phenomenon regarded as law: the normative label. The normative and descriptive elements of law should be divorced. Two definitions of the law could be proposed: the normative and the theoretical-descriptive. Normative definition has a pragmatic value—it is useful for the legal profession. The theoretical definition of law explains functioning through the concept of the tetrad notion of law and through the paradigm of the three-step hypothesis.

# Notes

## Chapter 1: Background

1 A. Peretiatkowicz, *Wstęp do nauk prawnych*, Poznań, 1946, p. 26.
2 K. Opałek, J. Wróblewski, *Zagadnienia teorii prawa*, Warsaw, 1969, pp. 10–11.
3 Z. Ziembiński, *Teoria państwa i prawa*, Poznań, 1969, pp. 7–8.
4 A. Łopatka, *Wstęp do prawoznawstwa*, Warsaw, 1968, p. 11.
5 V. N. Kudryavsev, 'Sociology, law and criminology,' *Sovetskoe Gosudarstvo i Pravo*, no. 2, p. 64 (in Russian).
6 *Norms and Actions*. National Reports on Sociology of Law, R. Treves and J. F. Glastra Van Loon (eds), The Hague, 1968. Another encyclopaedic survey of the development of sociology of law is *Sociology of Law*, V. Aubert, ed., London, 1969.
7 T. Eckhoff, 'Sociology of law in Scandinavia', in R. Treves and J. Glastra Van Loon (eds), *Norms and Actions*, The Hague, 1968, p. 30.
8 K. Mäkelä, 'Public sense of justice and judicial practice,' *Acta Sociologica*, 1966, no. 10.
9 B. Kutchinsky, 'Regarding legal phenomena in Denmark,' *Scandinavian Studies in Criminology*, 1968.
10 Franco Leonardi, *Il cittadino e la giustizia*, Milan, 1968.
11 Jerome H. Skolnick, 'The sociology of law in America: overview and trends,' in *Law and Society*, a supplement to the summer issue of *Social Problems*, 1965.
12 H. Zeisel, H. Kalven and B. Buckholz, *Delay in the Court*, Boston, 1959.
13 E. O. Smigel, *The Wall Street Lawyer*, New York, 1964.
14. J. E. Carlin, *Lawyers on Their Own*, New Brunswick, 1962.
15 W. Kaupen, 'Studies on the sociology of the German lawyer,' Cologne, 1969 (unpublished).
16 V. O. Miller and V. O. Steinberg, *Sociology of Law in the USSR Today*, Latvian State University, Riga, 1964.
17 J. Skupiński, 'Postępowanie przed kolegium karno-administracyjnym (w świetle badań empirycznych),' *Studia Prawnicze*, 1969, no. 23.

18 *Ibid.*
19 J. Kwaśniewski, 'Z badań nad motywacją przestrzegania prawa,' in *Prawnicy, socjologowie i psychologowie*, Warsaw, 1970.
20 St. Mika, *Skuteczność kar w wychowaniu*, Warsaw, 1968.
21 A. Siciński, 'Postawy wobec pracy i własności oraz ich społeczne uwarunkowania,' *Studia socjologiczne*, 1961, no. 2.

## Chapter 2: Defining the sociology of law

1 P. Selznick, 'The sociology of law,' in *Law and the Behavioral Sciences*, eds L. Friedman and S. Macaulay, Indianapolis, 1969, pp. 2–3.
2 *Ibid.*, p. 3.
3 J. Skolnick, 'The sociology of law in America: overview and trends,' in *Law and Society*, a supplement to summer issue of *Social Problems* 4 (1965).
4 V. Aubert, 'Sociology of law' (mimeographed material), Oslo.
5 A. Podgórecki, *Sociologia Prawa*, Warsaw, 1962, p. 15.
6 R. Treves, 'The administration of justice in Italy (a sociological survey),' Varese, 1971 (mimeographed).
7 H. W. Babb (trans.), *Law and Morality: Leon Petrażycki*, Cambridge, Mass., 1955.
8 E. Ehrlich, *Fundamental Principles of the Sociology of Law* (English translation), Cambridge, Mass., 1936.
9 P. Bohannan, *Justice and Judgment among the Tiv*, London, 1957.
10 V. Goldschmidt, 'Social tolerance and frustration' (mimeographed paper), Nordvijk, Holland, 1972.
11 M. Gluckman, 'Concepts in the comparative study of tribal law,' in *Law in Culture and Society*, ed. Laura Nader, Chicago, 1969.
12 Pyong-Choon Hahm, 'The decision process in Korea,' in *Comparative Judicial Behavior*, ed. by G. Schubert, D. Danelski, London, 1969.
13 S. Macaulay, 'Non-contractual relations in business: a preliminary study,' in *Law and the Behavioral Sciences*, eds L. Friedman, S. Macaulay, Indianapolis, 1969, pp. 145–68.
14 J. Górecki, 'Divorce in Poland—a socio-legal study,' *Acta Sociologica*, no. 10, 1966.
15 Conversation with a deputy director of the legislative division of the Chinese parliament in 1963.
16 A. Podgórecki, 'Worker courts,' in *Sociology of Law*, ed. V. Aubert, London, 1969.
17 Z. Sufin, *Kultura Pracy*, Warsaw, 1968, p. 172.

## Chapter 3: The historical method

1 W. Voisé, *Frycza Modrzewskiego nauka o państwie i prawie*, Warsaw, 1956, p. 297.
2 Andrzej Frycz Modrzewski, *O poprawie Rzeczypospolitej*, Warsaw, 1953, p. 233. Further quotations from Andrzej Frycz Modrzewski are translated from this Polish edition to which all the page numbers refer.
3 *Ibid.*, p. 97.

4 *Ibid.*, p. 86.
5 *Ibid.*, p. 236.
6 *Ibid.*, p. 593. It can be repeated after W. Voisé that this quotation has become the motto for a very interesting book on the political history of Europe in the sixteenth century: P. Mesnard, *L'Essor de la philosophie politique au XVI siècle*, Paris, 1952.
7 *Ibid.*, p. 607.
8 *Ibid.*, p. 300.
9 *Ibid.*, p. 130.
10 *Ibid.*, p. 329.
11 *Ibid.*, p. 210.
12 *Ibid.*, p. 595.
13 *Ibid.*, 'Mowa o karze za mężobójstwo'/Oration on the punishment for homicide.
14 *Ibid.*, p. 224.
15 Quoted after Ł.-Kurdybacha, Wstęp/Introduction/to *O poprawie Rzeczypospolitej Andrzeja Modrzewskiego*, Warsaw, 1953, p. 20.
16 *Ibid.*, p. 109.
17 *Ibid.*, p. 292.
18 *Ibid.*, p. 241.
19 *Ibid.*, pp. 146-7.
20 *Ibid.*, p. 240.
21 *Ibid.*, pp. 195, 215, 216, 217, 219, 232.
22 *Ibid.*, p. 167.
23 *Ibid.*, p. 262.
24 *Ibid.*, pp. 274 and 275.

**Chapter 4: The ethnographic approach**

1 S. Czarnowski, *Kultura* (Culture), Warsaw, 1948, p. 7.
2 B. Malinowski, *Crime and Custom in Savage Society*, London, 9th imp. 1970.
3 Karl Llewellyn and E. A. Hoebel, *The Cheyenne Way*, Norman Oklahoma, 1953.
4 E. A. Hoebel, *The Law of Primitive Man*, Cambridge, Mass., 1954, p. 28.
5 Introduction to M. Fortes and E. E. Evans-Pritchard (eds), *African Political Systems*, London, 1961, p. 5 (1st ed. 1940).
6 E. E. Evans-Pritchard, 'The Nuer of the southern Sudan,' in *African Political Systems*, p. 293.
7 R. Karsten, 'Blood revenge, war and victory feasts among the Jibaro Indians of eastern Ecuador,' *Bureau of American Ethnology Bulletin* 79, Smithsonian Institution, Washington, 1923.
8 See C. von Fuehrer-Haimendorf, *Morals and Merit*, London, 1967.
9 *Ibid.*, p. 62.
10 L. Pospisil, 'Structural changes in primitive law,' in *Law in Culture and Society*, L. Nader (ed.), Chicago, 1969, p. 225.
11 See K. Busia, 'The Ashanti' in D. Forde (ed.), *African Worlds*, London, 1963.

281

12 See R. Verdier, 'Ontology of judicial thought . . .', in L. Nader (ed.), *Law in Culture and Society*, Chicago, 1969.

13 Llewellyn and Hoebel, *op. cit.*

14 L. Pospisil, *op. cit.*

15 Reconstructed by Hoebel in *The Law of Primitive Man*.

16 For further reading it will be useful to the reader to consult L. Nader, K. F. Koch and B. Cox, 'The ethnography of law: a bibliographical survey,' *Current Anthropology*, vol. 7, no. 3, 1966, pp. 267–94 and S. Falk Moore, 'Law and anthropology, biennial review of anthropology, 1969,' Stanford, 1970, pp. 252–300.

## Chapter 5: Questionnaire and interview methods

1 A. Turska, 'Poczucie prawne a świadomośí prawa,' *Państwo i prawo*, 1961, no. 2, p. 243.

2 A. Podgórecki, *Zjawiska prawne w opinii publicznej*, Warsaw, 1964; *Prestiż prawa*, Warsaw, 1966; and A. Podgórecki, *et al.*, *The Views of Polish Society on Morality and Law* (*Poglady społeczeństwa polskiego na moralność i prawo*), Warsaw, 1971.

3 W. Kaupen and W. Werle, 'Knowledge and opinion of law and legal institutions in the Federal Republic of Germany. Preliminary results.' Unpublished paper presented at the World Congress of Sociology, Research Committee of Sociology of Law, Evian, France, 1965.

4 Sweden, 1947; Denmark, 1954 and 1962; and Norway, 1961 and 1962, summarized by B. Kutchinsky, 'Law and education,' *Acta Sociologica*, 1966, vol. 10.

5 Summed up by K. Mäkelä, 'Public sense of justice and judicial practice,' *Acta Sociologica*, 1966, vol. 10.

6 Initial results of these investigations have been reported in an unpublished paper by P. Vinke (Netherlands), 'Internal acceptance of the legal rules: a law-sociological research.'

7 The design has been undertaken by Prof. A. de Miranda Rosa of the Gama Filho University, Rio de Janeiro, Brazil.

8 W. W. Evan, 'Toward a data archive of legal system: an exploratory cross-national analysis' (unpublished data presented during the World Congress of Sociology, Evian, France, 1966).

9 Z. Sufin, *Kultura pracy*, Warsaw, 1968, p. 172.

10 For example, see research by J. Kurczewski, 'Struktura poglądów na prawo i ich powiązania wewnętrzne' (unpublished B. A. dissertation), Social Sciences Faculty, Warsaw University, 1966.

11 This proposition was additionally verified by data from the research by A. Kojder, 'Prawne i moralne postawy więźniów-redydywistów' (an unpublished M.A. dissertation), Social Sciences Faculty, Warsaw University, 1968.

12 J. Cohen, R. A. Robson and A. Bates, *Parental Authority*, New Brunswick, N.J., 1958.

13 As we know, American law is largely based on precedents and thus it is often difficult to predict the verdict in a given case.

14 It is interesting that a similar problem appears in Polish law. In a paper by St. Batawia and St. Szelhaus, 'Stu nieletnich i młodocianych sprawców wykroczeń chuligańskich,' *Państwo i Prawo*, 1958, no. 2, it is proposed that adolescent delinquents be handled differently from adults (pp. 263–5); see also *Młodociani recydywiści* by St. Szelhaus, Warsaw, 1968, pp. 204–5. The new penal code of 1970 took a small step in this direction.

15 E.g. indirect conclusions drawn from the work by S. A. Stauffer, *Communism, Conformity and Civil Liberties*, New York, 1955, pp. 131–40.

16 Authoritarian: rigoristic, eager to condemn, likely to oversimplify reality and see it as 'black and white,' intolerant, anti-rational. The concept of the authoritarian personality is best developed in *The Authoritarian Personality*, T. Adorno *et al.*, New York, 1950.

17 F. C. Newman and S. S. Surrey, *Legislation-Cases and Materials*, New York, 1950; S. Ehrlich, *Grupy nacisku*, Warsaw, 1962.

18 Bertrand Russell, *Power*, London, 1948, quoted by J. Cohen, R. A. Robson and A. Bates, *op. cit.*, p. 198.

19 A. Podgórecki, *Zjawiska prawne w opini publicznej*, Warszawa, 1964, the chapter on parental authority ('Władza rodzicielska').

20 A. Iwańska-Wagner, *Good Fortune*, Washington, 1956.

Chapter 6: The monographic method

1 P. Blau, *The Dynamics of Bureaucracy*, Chicago, 1955.

2 K. Doktor, 'O stosowalności obserwacji uczestniczącej jako metody badań socjologicznych,' *Studia Socjologiczne*, 1961, no. 2, p. 88.

3 A. Malewski, *O zastosowaniach teorii zachowania*, Warsaw, 1964, p. 93.

4 The team published a number of papers, without A. Podgórecki, 'Udział ławników w postępowaniu karnym,' *Opinie i rzeczywistość*, S. Zawadzki and L. Kubicki, eds, Warsaw, 1970.

5 *Ibid.*, p. 6.

6 The author of the questionnaire addressed to lay judges was L. Kubicki.

7 A. Podgórecki, *Zjawiska prawne w opinii publicznej* (*Legal Phenomena in Public Opinion*), Warsaw, 1964, p. 15.

8 One methodological detail should be noted. Two lay judges for each trial were conventionally labeled as A and B and these labels were applied throughout the whole study. It turned out that the biases on various dimensions were similar throughout, thereby pointing to the reliability of the study in revealing not individual biases but systematic tendencies.

9 The relatively small proportion of answers undermines, in this instance as well as in others, the reliability of the responses.

10 Cf. A. Podgórecki, 'Utajona obserwacja rzeczywistego działania instytucji,' in *Moralność i Społeczeństwo*, Warsaw, 1969, p. 297.

11 Similarly in 'Model ustrojowy prawnika ludowego w świetle przeprowadzonych badań prawno-empirycznych,' by S. Zawadzki, in *Udział ławników w postępowaniu karnym*, Warszawa, 1970, p. 224.

12 *Ibid.*, pp. 238–9.

13 S. Jedlewski, *Analiza pedagogiczna systemu dyscyplinarno-izolacyjnego w resocjalizacji nieletnich*, Warsaw, 1966, p. 55.

14 The research was carried out by the Team for Studying Social Norms and the Pathology of Social Life of the Institute of Sociology, Warsaw University, with the author as manager of the team.

15 Małkowski made skillful use of the monographic method and all its advantages: he investigated in detail the reformatories selected for study; he carried out intensive interviews with all the inmates and most of the tutors; he investigated the histories and the economic situations of these institutions; he analyzed the documents describing the functioning of the institutions and those referring to their inmates; he made sociometric analyses of interactions among the inmates; in a number of cases he carried out catamnestic studies (i.e. he repeated the interviews after some time). In doing all this he revealed exceptional talent, reaching beyond the normal standards of the scientific craft.

16 The results noted here should not be extended to all educational or reformatory institutions, for they derive from institutions suspected prior to the study of having a relatively intensively developed 'second life.'

17 S. Małkowski, 'Drugie życie w zakładzie wychowawczym' (unpublished), 1970.

18 Anna Pilinow and Jacek Wasilewski, 'Nieformalna stratyfikacja wychowanków zakładu poprawczego', *Etyka*, no. 8, Warsaw, 1971, p. 149.

19 It is remarkable that such a risky enterprise—a woman student of sociology, writing her graduate thesis, venturing an analysis of the inner life of a penitentiary for male recidivist criminals—turned out to be so successful. What contributed to this success, along with the knowledge gained from the earlier researches, was the peculiar circumstance that the recidivists strove to make an impression upon the student and offered her information which was not only reliable (consistent with what we had known), but went far beyond our prior knowledge.

20 B. Zielińska, 'Strategia resocjalizacji recydywistów (Wybrane zagadnienia diagnozy i akcji resocjalizacyjnej w środowisku dorosłych recydywistów)' (unpublished graduate thesis), Warsaw University, Social Sciences Department, 1970, pp. 64, 83.

21 The investigations were carried out by Ms M. Rydz over a period of two months; they consisted of intensive interviews, some of them lasting for as long as six hours. The results were presented in a graduate thesis: 'Pierwszy kontakt z wiezieniem młodocianych przestępców,' Warsaw University, Social Sciences Department, 1970 (unpublished).

22 *Ibid.*, p. 35.

23 J. Kurczewski, 'Bluzg, grypserka, drugie życie—próba hipotezy interpretacyjnej,' an address before the conference organized by the Team for Studying Social Norms and the Pathology of Social Life, April 25, 1970.

24 A. Krukowski, 'Socjologiczne aspekty procesu resocjalizacji,' in *Socjotechnika*, vol. 3, Warsaw ed. A. Podgórecki.

## Chapter 7: The experimental method

1 T. Kotarbiński, *Kurs logiki dla prawników*, Warsaw, 1955, p. 162.
2 A 'social court' is a jury composed of a number of the employees of a company, summoned to judge minor offences committed by their colleagues but having vague penalty competence (not able to use fines or jail terms as punishments).
3 The study was carried out by the Methodology Section of the Central Institute of Protection of Labor, managed by E. Modliński. Responsible for the study (elaboration of the research plan, questionnaires, initial results) was the present author. The general assumptions were discussed with the director of the legal office of the Central Council of Trade Unions, Mr H. Borkowski. The initial phase of the research was aided by the Chair of Theory of State and Law of Warsaw University, with S. Ehrlich and A. Turska, as well as the Chair of Sociology of Wrocław University, with C. Buczek. The members of the research team were: R. Chorąży, J. Górski, H. Leszczyna, A. Matejko and A. Pilinow. The final report was elaborated by E. Modliński and A. Podgórecki; cf. A. Podgórecki, *Socjologia prawa* (*The Sociology of Law*), Warsaw, 1962.
4 The quota method consists in a sampling that is random within each of the predetermined categories of respondents.
5 E. G. A. Kaftanovskaya, 'Novyi etap v deiatelnosti tovarishcheskikh sudov na predpriiatiakh,' *Sotsialisticheskii trud*, 1960, no.8; F. Linenturg, H. Leonova, *Tovarishcheskii sud na predpriiatiakh*, 1961 (both in Russian).
6 The study was carried out in 1963 by the Central Institute for Protection of Labor.
7 J. Górski, *Doświadczenia i perspektywy sądów robotniczych w Polsce* (1960–1965), Warsaw, 1967.
8 J. Wasilewski, 'Wpływ wyników badań socjologicznych na podejmowanie decyzji ustawodawczych (analiza oparta na przykładzie sądów robotniczych),' unpublished graduate thesis, Warsaw University, Social Sciences Department, 1970.

## Chapter 8: The statistical method

1 K. J. Newman, 'Punishment and the breakdown of the legal order: the experience in East Pakistan,' in C. J. Friedrich, (ed.) *Responsibility*, New York, 1960, p. 128.
2 The above data, as well as several other in this chapter, have been drawn from T. Sellin, *The Death Penalty*, Philadelphia, 1959.
3 Cited in C. Selltiz, M. Jahoda, M. Deutsch and S. W. Cook, *Research Methods in Social Relations*, New York, 1954, p. 324. The explanation which follows is taken (not verbatim) from the edition published in 1959.
4 M. Ossowska, *Normy moralne. Próba systematyzacji*, Warsaw, 1970, pp. 35–41.
5 In the Polish literature, the fullest presentation of the arguments on the death penalty, with due consideration of data concerning laws in

various countries and philosophical problems, is an article by M. Cieślak, 'Problem kary śmierci (artykuł dyskusyjny),' *Państwo i prawo*, 1966, no. 12.

6 F. Exner, 'Mord und Todesstrafe in Sachsen, 1855-1927,' *Monatschrift für Kriminalpsychologie under Strafrechtsreform*, 1929, Heft 20, pp. 1-17.

7 See note 2.

8 See note 2.

9 Committee on Philanthropic Labor of Philadelphia, Yearly Meeting of Friends. Friends' Social Service Series, Bulletin no. 29, third month, 1935, in Robert H. Dann (ed.) *The Deterrent Effect of Capital Punishment*, p. 20.

10 See note 2.

11 E. Gowers, *Life for a Life*, London, 1956, p. 8.

12 The general results of these investigations are reported in this book in the chapter on 'questionnaire and interview methods.'

13 These correlations are significant, as revealed by the chi-square test. This kind of statistical analysis when applied to materials secured by other means can be considered as a meta-level research method. It is valuable in all cases where the objective is to determine parallelism of phenomena or, if further assumptions are accepted, to define the eventual direction of their causal link. Full results of investigations on the attitudes of the Polish population towards the death penalty are presented in A. Podgórecki, *Prestiż prawa* (*The Prestige of Law*), Warsaw, 1966, pp. 78-83.

14 M. Cieślak, *op. cit.* (see note 5 above).

Chapter 9: Analysis of legal materials

1 A. Podgórecki, *Zjawiska prawne w opinii publicznej* (*Legal Phenomena in Public Opinion*), Warsaw, 1964, the chapter 'Procesy o zniesławienie (Libel suits).' The study was undertaken on the order of the Cracow Center for Press Researches.

2 The relevant article of the 1932 penal code was almost always 255, paragraph 1. Although since January 1, 1970 a new code has been in force, the 1932 stipulations were applicable at the time the analyzed suits occurred. Article 255, paragraph 1 stated: 'that whoever accuses a person or an institution of conduct or properties which can degrade them in the public opinion, or endanger the loss of confidence necessary for the relevant position, trade or activity, is subject to a term of imprisonment for up to two years and a fine.'

3 These organizational and methodical activities aimed at grasping the number of press trials to be studied are reported in such detail so as to point out that empirical investigations are often involved in technical matters which, while seemingly remote from the essential research problems, may significantly hinder access to them.

4 F. Znaniecki, *Ludzie teraźniejsi a cywilizacja przyszłości*, Lwów-Warszawa, 1934.

5 Although the research program based on court materials was finished

in 1963, these data expressed, in the main, the standpoint of the judges with respect to the cases submitted to them for decision; for a fuller analysis, it seemed worth while to address a general question to journalists asking them about their view of their role, in particular the role of a court reporter. Thus a supplementary study was made in 1965, also on the order of the Cracow Center for Press Researches, and under the scientific direction of the author. The scope of this study may seem rather limited, as only Warsaw court reporters (20 in all, and practically covering the field) were interviewed, journalists from other cities being left out for technical reasons; and no statistical comparisons were made because the sample was too small. This should not, however, obscure a significant point. The respondents were highly competent socially, politically and judicially, and they represented so much professional experience that they could certainly be considered what are called social experts. A study addressed to this kind of respondent can be seen, in some situations, as second-degree investigation, since an interview with an expert offers a synthetic experience of many individuals. It was found through this study that the respondents were clearly aware that court reporting or articles based on an analysis of one or more court cases might be an instrument of rational social influence.

6 A. Podgórecki, *Zasady socjotechniki* (*Principles of Social Engineering*), Warsaw, 1966.

## Chapter 10: The concept of a legal norm

1 M. Ossowska, *Socjologia moralności*, Warsaw, 1969, p. 252.
2 L. Petrażycki, *Wstęp do nauki prawa i moralności*, Warsaw, 1959, p. 25. Some of Petrażycki's ideas will be discussed in detail later on.
3 Essays by J. Lande collected in the volume *Studia z filozofii prawa*, Warsaw, 1959, were largely devoted to this task.
4 K. Opałek and J. Wróblewski, *Zagadnienia teorii prawa*, Warsaw, 1969, p. 38.
5 A. Łopatka, *Wstęp do teorii prawoznawstwa*, Warsaw, 1969, p. 76.
6 Z. Ziembiński, *Teoria panstwa i prawa* (part II: 'Zagadnienia teorii prawa'), Poznan, 1969, p. 29 (mimeographed).
7 B. B. Whiting, *Piaute Sorcery*, Viking Foundation Publications in Anthropology, pp. 15, 50.
8 The results reported here are related to the research on moral and legal views of the Polish society presented in ch. 5, 'Questionaire and interview methods.'
9 The above interpretation of empirical data was suggested by Maria Łoś.
10 J. Skolnick, *The Politics of Protest*, New York, 1969, pp. 335–8.

## Chapter 11: Anomie, conformism, legalism

1 R. Merton, *Social Theory and Social Structure*, New York, 1959.
2 Cf. A. Podgórecki, *Patologia życia społecznego* (*Pathology of Social Life*), Warsaw, 1969, pp. 16–31.

3 Aren't all these terms awe-inspiring?
4 P. Sztompka, 'Jednostka a normy społeczne–warianty wzajemnych reakcji,' *Studia Socjologiczne*, 1967, no. 2.
5 H. M. Johnson, *Sociology*, New York, 1960, p. 552.
6 M. B. Bass, 'Conformity, deviation . . .,' in I. A. Berg and M. B. Bass (eds), *Conformity and Deviation*, New York, 1961, p. 38.
7 S. E. Asch, 'Issues in the study of social influences on judgment,' in I. A. Berg and M. B. Bass (eds), *op. cit.*, pp. 150, 156.
8 M. Scheriff, 'Conformity-deviation,' in I. A. Berg and M. B. Bass (eds), *op. cit.*, p. 161.
9 M. Rokeach, 'Authority, authoritarianism, conformity,' in I. A. Berg and M. B. Bass (eds), *op. cit.*, p. 246.
10 T. Bilikiewicz, *Psychiatria*, Warsaw, 1969, pp. 150–1.
11 E.g. E. B. Berelson and G. Steiner, *Human Behavior*, New York, 1964; A. Podgórecki, *Zasady socjotechniki* (*The Principles of Social Engineering*), Warsaw, 1966. Chapter on 'Influencing small groups.'
12 S. Asch, 'Effects of group pressure upon the modification and distortion of judgments,' in E. E. Maccoby, Th. M. Newcomb and E. C. Hartley, *Readings in Social Psychology*, New York, 1958.
13 W. Evan and M. Zelditsch, jun., 'A laboratory experiment on bureaucratic authority,' *American Sociological Review*, 1961, vol. 26, no. 6, p. 883.

Chapter 12: Theories of the functioning of law

1 N. Timasheff, introduction in, *Law and Morality: Leon Petrażycki* by L. Petrażycki (trans. by H. W. Babb), Cambridge, Mass., 1955, pp. xxxiv–xxxv.
2 It is by no means easy to reconstruct Petrażycki's ideas on sociology in general and sociology of law in particular. He has not written a comprehensive work on these issues. The first outline of his book *Sociology* is not extant. Various material on sociology as it was seen by Petrażycki can be found in J. Lande, 'Sociologia Petrażyckiego,' *Przegląd Socjologiczny*, 1948, no. 12 and in 'Notes from Petrażycki lectures' made by his pupil, Professor H. Piętka (unpublished: in the archives of the Polish Academy of Sciences). Some elements of Petrażycki's sociology are discussed in the mimeographed reader by H. Piętka, *Teoria prawa*, part I, 'Sociologia,' Warsaw, 1947; in L. Petrażycki's *O dopełniających prądach kulturalnych; prawa rozwoju handlu*, Warsaw, 1936, and in the collective volume: *Z zagadnień teorii prawa i teorii nauki L. Petrażyckiego*, Warsaw, 1969. The best summary of Leon Petrażycki's ideas is contained in: Georges S. Langrod and Michalina Vaughan, 'The Polish psychological theory of law,' in *Polish Law Throughout the Ages*, W. J. Wagner (ed.), Stanford, 1970.
3 Emotion has, according to Petrażycki, a different meaning from the usual one. According to him 'emotion' is the basic element of psychological life. This element has a dual structure—passive and active—and is primordial to cognitive, affectionate and volitional components. H. W. Babb, the translator of the basic book of Petrażycki into English,

says: 'the Russian original says "impulses or emotions" but there is persuasive authority for the view that the author did not employ the Russian word (emotsiya) in our English sense of "emotion" (an agitated or excited state of mind).'

4 J. Lande, the most devoted pupil of L. Petrażycki, Professor of Jurisprudence, Jagiellonian University. Died in 1954.

5 J. Lande, *Studia z filozofii prawa*, Warsaw, 1956, p. 9.

6 G. Homans, *Social Behavior: Its Elementary Forms*, New York, 1961, p. 2.

7 J. Lande, *Studia z filozofii prawa*, p. 902.

8 W. B. Dröscher, *Instynkt czy doświadczenie* (*Instinct or Experience*), Warsaw, 1969, pp. 139–40.

9 N. Timasheff, *op. cit.*, p. xxxviii.

10 N. Timasheff, *op. cit.*, pp. xxviii–xxix.

11 'The Polish medieval system of law, public as well as private, is clearly distinguishable from the systems prevailing to the east and west of Poland's frontiers. It differed from the western system primarily because of the absence in Poland of a strictly feudal structure. Poland did not pass through Roman rule and did not have the prerequisites of feudalism in the form of "protection" and vassalege. . . . Moreover, the patriarchal character of Polish state feudalism made possible the early reunification of the national territory under one kind, which occurred in the fourteenth century, earlier than in Western Europe. . . . On the other hand, Poland came under the strong influence of three Western European institutions that in many ways shaped her social and cultural character. There were: first, the Roman Catholic church . . .; second, the self governing municipality . . .; and third, the concept of Christian chivalry. . . . In Polish private law, three coexistent currents, differing in origin, influenced each other and in some way merged. The first, the old Slavonic law, was customary and particularistic. The second, Roman law, was represented in the canon law. The third was the German municipal law.' W. Wasiutyński, 'Origins of the Polish law, tenth to fifteenth centuries,' in *Polish Law Throughout the Ages* (ed. W. J. Wagner), Stanford, 1970, pp. 61–2. Still it is quite puzzling why the experts in the area of comparative law (who are usually highly specialized in their type of approach) overlook, as a principle, this problem, the most important in their own field.

12 L. Petrażycki, *O dopełniajcych prądach . . .*, Warsaw, 1936, pp. 6–7.

13 *Kodeks rodzinny*, M. Grudzińska and J. Ignatowicz (eds), Warsaw, 1955, p. 543. The code of civil procedure quoted in this book has been changed, and a new one has been valid since 1 January 1965. However, the general assumptions of the former code, and the principles of contradictoriness, have been retained. The numbers of the appropriate articles in the new code are different.

14 Z. Bożyczko, *Kradzież kieszonkowa i jej sprawca*, Warsaw, 1962.

15 C. Czapów, *Młodzież a przestępstwo*, Warsaw, 1962.

16 S. Macaulay, 'Non-contractual relations in business; a preliminary study,' *American Sociological Review*, 1963, no. 28.

17 S. Szelhaus, *Młodociani recydywiści*, Warsaw, 1960, pp. 181–2.

18 J. Jasiński, 'Kształtowanie się przestępczości nieletnich w Polsce w

latach 1951–1960 w świetle statystyki sądowej,' *Archiwum kryminologii*, vol. 2, Warsaw, 1964, p. 134.

19 C. Czapów, *op. cit.*

20 J. Jasiński, *op. cit.*, p. 38.

21 V. Aubert, 'Conscientious objectors before Norwegian military courts,' in G. Schubert (ed.), *Judicial Decision Making*, New York, 1963, p. 219.

22 Leszek Kubicki, 'Udział ławników w orzekaniu,' in *Udział ławników w postępowaniu karnym. Opinie a rzeczywistość*, Warsaw, 1970, pp. 80–4.

23 J. Skupiński, 'Postępowanie przed kolegium karno-administracyjnym,' (w świetle badań empirycznych), *Studia prawnicze*, 1969, no. 23, p. 138.

24 J. Kurczewski, 'Struktura poglądów na prawo i ich powiązania wewnętrzne,' (unpublished M. A. thesis, Wydział Nauk Społecznych UW).

25 *Ibid.*

26 J. Kurczewski, 'Postawa na temat karania i zachowania sedziow zawodowych,' a communication to the International Congress of Sociology, Varna, 1970.

## Chapter 13: The concept of legal policy as a science

1 This work is related to another monograph by L. Petrażycki, concerning the policy of law: *Wstęp do nauki polityki prawa*, Warsaw, 1968.

2 L. Petrażycki, *Wstęp do teorii prawa i moralności*, Warsaw, 1930, p. 3.

3 J. Lande, *Teoria prawa*, Lublin, 1956, p. 26.

4 A. Podgórecki, *Charakterystyka nauk praktycznych*, Warsaw, 1962.

5 In this context an appeal should be repeated to call forth an institutional framework for realization of this type of reflection. As we have already said in another work, 'such institutional framework ought to take the form of a center of empirical legal investigations and a methodological center for improvement of legislation,' Cf. A. Podgórecki, *Zasady socjotechniki*, Warsaw, 1966, p. 80.

## Chapter 14: Effectiveness of the law in operation

1 T. Kotarbiński, *Praxiology*, Oxford-Warsaw, 1965.

2 The problem of ineffective work in legislative agencies, i.e. the failure on their part to issue appropriate legal enactments, has been intentionally left out. The subject of this analysis is the effectiveness of the functioning of legal precepts, not the efficiency of legislation.

3 The problem is fairly complex. Usually a given administrative apparatus realizes more than one normative act at the time, and its low performance in the carrying out of one of them may well be recompensed by its high efficiency in realizing another. Thus, if we want to appreciate the efficiency of an administrative agency, we must take into account all the normative acts realized by it, and distinguish between the effectiveness (efficiency) of a given normative act and the effectiveness of the other acts realized by the same agency.

4 W. G. Sumner, *Folkways*, 1906, and M. Deutsch and M. Collins, 'The

effect of public policy in housing projects upon interracial attitudes,'
in E. Maccoby *et al.* (eds), *Readings in Social Psychology*, New York,
1958, p. 612.
5 V. Goldschmidt, 'The Greenland criminal code and its sociological
background,' *Acta Sociologica*, vol. 1, fasc. 4, 1956, p. 248.
6 J. Hall, *Theft, Law and Society*, Indianapolis, 1952, p. 251.
7 A case study on the conversion from left-hand to right-hand traffic
which took place in Sweden in 1967 would serve as a good illustration
of some of the above mentioned ideas. Britt-Mari, Persson Blegvad,
Jette Mølle a Nielsen, *Law as a Means of Social Change: a Case Study*,
Warna, 1970, mimeographed; with a valuable bibliography.

## Chapter 15: Towards a general theory in the sociology of law

1 J. Kubin, 'The influence of fictional reference groups on youth' (paper
delivered to the Polish-Austrian symposium, Austria, 1972, unpublished material).
2 A. Cohen and J. Short, 'Research in delinquent sub-cultures,' *Journal
of Social Issues*, 1958, vol. XIV, no. 3, pp. 24–8.
3 V. Aubert, 'Conscientious objectors before Norwegian military courts,'
in, G. Schubert (ed.), *Judicial Decision Making*, New York, 1963, ch. 7.
4 The concept of the *control reference group* belongs without any doubt
to the category of notions which are generated by the analysis of
empirical studies in the area of the sociology of law. Compare ch. 6.
5 A. Malewski, *O zastosowaniach teorii zachowania*, Warsaw, 1964, p. 93.
6 *Ibid.* Elaboration of those ramifications, pp. 93–127.
7 A. Podgórecki, *Zjawiska prawne w opinii publicznej*, Warsaw, 1964,
pp. 27–98.
8 Compare ch. 5.
9 Again: the concept of 'invisible factors' belongs without a doubt to the
category of notions generated by the analysis of empirical studies in the
area of the sociology of law. Compare ch. 5.
10 The synthetic overview on several Italian studies conducted in the area
of the administration of justice is given by R. Treves, 'The administration of justice in Italy', Varese, Italy, 1971, unpublished material
(source: Research Committee of Sociology of Law, 3 Piazza Castello,
Milan). Treves quotes the work of Franco Leonardi, *Il Cittadino e la
Giustizia*.
11 R. Blom, 'National confidence in the judiciary. Tutkimussdoste report,'
University of Tampere, Finland, no. 7/1969.
12 Compare ch. 6.
13 Compare ch. 5.
14 Compare ch. 6.
15 A. Hart, 'definition', cited in H. L. Packer, *The Limits of Criminal
Sanctions*, Stanford, 1968, p. 21.
16 *Ibid.*
17 G. Calabresi, *The Costs of Accidents*, New Haven, 1970, p. 16.
18 M. Łoś, 'Law as an integrative system', unpublished paper presented
at the Conference of Sociology of Law, Nocdwijk, 1972.

19 *The Book of Lord Shang*, London, 1928, p. 285 (trans. by J. J. L. Duyvendak).
20 Compare ch. 12.
21 W. J. Chambliss and R. B. Seidman, *Law, Order and Power*, Reading, Mass., 1971, p. 504.
22 H. M. Johnson, 'The generalized symbolic media in Parsons's theory,' unpublished paper, 1972, p. 10.
23 *Ibid.*, pp. 10–11.
24 B. Kutchinsky, 'Sociological aspects of deviance and conformity,' Council of Europe, manuscript, 1971, p. 75.

# Select bibliography

AUBERT, V. (ed.), *Sociology of Law*, London, 1969.
BIERLING, E. K., *Juristische Prinzipienlehre*, 5 vols, Freiburg, 1894–1917.
CARDOZO, B. N., *The Growth of the Law*, New Haven, 1924.
CARLIN, J., *Lawyers on their Own*, New Brunswick, N.J., 1962.
CLINARD, M., *Sociology of Deviant Behavior*, 3rd ed., New York, 1968.
COHEN, J., ROBSON, A. H. and BATES, A., *Parental Authority*, New Brunswick, N.J., 1958.
CORNIL, G., *Le Droit privé, essai de sociologie juridique simplifiée*, Paris, 1924.
DAVIS, J., FOSTER, H., MAY, C. and DAVIS, E., *Society and the Law*, New York, 1962.
DUGUIT, L., *Le Droit social, le droit individuel et la transformation de l'état*, Paris, 1911.
DUGUIT, L., *Traité de droit constitutionel*, 5 vols, Paris, 1922–8.
DURKHEIM, É., *De la Division du travail social*, 6th ed., Paris, 1932.
EHRLICH, E., *Grundlegung einer Sociologie des Rechtes*, Munich, 1913. English trans., Cambridge, Mass., 1936.
EHRLICH, S., *Grupy nacisku*, Warsaw, 1962.
EVAN, W. M., *Law and Sociology, Exploratory Essays*, New York, 1962.
FLOUD, J., LEWIS, P. and STUART, R., *Proceedings of a Seminar: Problems and Prospects of Socio-Legal Research*, Nuffield College, Oxford, 1972.
FRIEDMAN, L. M. and MACAULEY, S., *Law and the Behavioral Sciences*, New York, 1969.
FULLER, L. L., *The Morality of Law*, New Haven, 1964.
GEIGER, T., *Vorstudien zu einer Sociologie des Rechtes*, Copenhagen, 1947.
GROSSMAN, JOEL and MARY, *Law and Change in Modern America*, Englewood Cliffs, N.J., 1971.
GURVITCH, G., *Sociology of Law*, New York, 1942.
HESSEN, S., 'Die Philosophie der Strafe,' *Logos*, 5, 1914.
HOEBEL, A., *The Law of Primitive Man*, Cambridge, Mass., 1954.
HOLMES, O. W., *Collected Legal Papers*, New York, 1921.

JELLINEK, G., *System der subjectiven öffentlichen Rechte*, 21st ed., Berlin, 1905.

JHERING, R., *Geist des römischen Rechts auf den verschiedenen Stufen seiner Entwicklung*, 3 vols, 2nd ed., Leipzig, 1866.

KELSEN, H., *Reine Rechtslehre*, Leipzig, 1934.

LANDE, J., *Studia z filozofii prawa*, Warsaw, 1959.

LLEWELLYN, K. N. and HOEBEL, E. A., *The Cheyenne Way: Conflict and Case Law in Primitive Jurisprudence*, Norman, Oklahoma, 1941.

MALINOWSKI, B., *Crime and Custom in Savage Society*, London, 1926.

MANNHEIM, K., *Ideology and Utopia*, (English trans.), New York, 1936.

MARX, K., *Zur Kritik der politischen Ökonomie*, Basel, 1859.

NADER, L., *Law in Culture and Society*, Chicago, 1969.

OPAŁEK, K. and WRÓBLEWSKI, I., *Współczesna teoria: sociologia prawa w stanach zjednoczonych*, Warsaw, 1962.

OSSOWSKA, M., *Social Determinants of Moral Ideas*, Philadelphia, 1972.

PERSSON-BLEGVAD, B. M. (ed.), 'Contributions to the sociology of law,' *Acta Sociologica*, 1966, no. 10.

PETRAŻYCKI, L., *Law and Morality: Leon Petrażycki* (trans. H. Babb; introduction N. Timasheff), Cambridge, Mass., 1955.

PETRAŻYCKI, L., *Vvedenie v izuczenie prava i nravstviennosti* (*Introduction to the Study of Law and Morals*) 3rd ed., St Petersburg, 1908.

PETRAŻYCKI, L., *Teoria prava i gosudarstva v svjazi c teoriej nravstviennosti* (*Theory of Law and State*), 2nd ed., St Petersburg, vol. 1, 1909, vol. 2 1910.

PIAGET, J., *The Moral Judgment of the Child*, London, 1932.

PODGÓRECKI, A., *Sociologia prawa*, Warsaw, 1962.

PODGÓRECKI, A., *Zarys sociologii prawa*, Warsaw, 1971.

POUND, R., *Law and Morals*, Chapel Hill, 1926.

PUCHTA, G. F., *Das Gewohnheitsrecht*, 2 vols, Erlangen, 1828–37.

RADBRUCH, G., *Rechtsphilosophie*, Leipzig, 1914.

RADZINOWICZ, L., and WOLFGANG, M., *Crime and Justice*, 3 vols, New York, 1971.

SAWER, G., *Law in Society*, Oxford, 1965.

SCHUBERT, G., and DANELSKI, D., *Comparative Judicial Behavior*, New York, 1969.

SCHUR, E. M., *Law and Society, a Sociological Review*, New York, 1967.

SCHWARTZ, R. D. and SKOLNICK, J. H., *Society and the Legal Order*, New York, 1970.

SELZNICK, P., 'Sociology of Law,' *International Encyclopedia of the Social Sciences*, New York, 1968.

SIMON, R. J., *Sociology of Law*, San Fransisco, 1968.

SKOLNICK, J., *Justice without Trial*, New York, 1966.

*Socialisation, The Law and Society, Journal of Social Issues* (complete issue), vol. 27, no. 2, 1971.

SOROKIN, P., *Sociology of Revolution*, Philadelphia, 1925.

SYKES, G., *The Society of Captives*, Princeton, N.J., 1958.

TARDE, G., *Les Transformations du droit*, 8th ed., Paris, 1922.

TARDE, G., *The Laws of Imitation*, English trans. New York, 1903.

TIMASHEFF, N. S., *An Introduction to the Sociology of Law*, Cambridge, Mass., 1939.

TREVES, R., (ed.), *La sociologia del dritto*, Milan, 1964.

TREVES, R., (ed.), *Nuovi sviluppi della sociologia del dritto*, Milan, 1968.

TREVES, R., and GLASTRA VAN LOON (ed.), *Norms and Action*, The Hague, 1968.

WEBER, M., *Max Weber on Law in Economy and Society*, Cambridge, Mass., 1954.

WESTERMARK, E., *Origin and Development of Moral Ideas*, 2 vols, New York, 1906.

# Index

# International Library of Sociology

Edited by
## John Rex
*University of Warwick*

Founded by
## Karl Mannheim

as The International Library of Sociology
and Social Reconstruction

*This Catalogue also contains other Social Science
series published by Routledge*

## Routledge & Kegan Paul   London and Boston

68-74 Carter Lane   London EC4V 5EL
9 Park Street   Boston   Mass 02108

# Contents

● *Books so marked are available in paperback*
*All books are in Metric Demy 8vo format (216 × 138mm approx.)*

## GENERAL SOCIOLOGY

**Belshaw, Cyril.** The Conditions of Social Performance. *An Exploratory Theory. 144 pp.*

**Brown, Robert.** Explanation in Social Science. *208 pp.*
Rules and Laws in Sociology.

**Cain, Maureen E.** Society and the Policeman's Role. *About 300 pp.*

**Gibson, Quentin.** The Logic of Social Enquiry. *240 pp.*

**Gurvitch, Georges.** Sociology of Law. *Preface by Roscoe Pound. 264 pp.*

**Homans, George C.** Sentiments and Activities: *Essays in Social Science. 336 pp.*

**Johnson, Harry M.** Sociology: *a Systematic Introduction. Foreword by Robert K. Merton. 710 pp.*

**Mannheim, Karl.** Essays on Sociology and Social Psychology. *Edited by Paul Keckskemeti. With Editorial Note by Adolph Lowe. 344 pp.*
Systematic Sociology: *An Introduction to the Study of Society. Edited by J. S. Erös and Professor W. A. C. Stewart. 220 pp.*

**Martindale, Don.** The Nature and Types of Sociological Theory. *292 pp.*

**Maus, Heinz.** A Short History of Sociology. *234 pp.*

**Mey, Harald.** Field-Theory. *A Study of its Application in the Social Sciences. 352 pp.*

**Myrdal, Gunnar.** Value in Social Theory: *A Collection of Essays on Methodology. Edited by Paul Streeten. 332 pp.*

**Ogburn, William F.,** and **Nimkoff, Meyer F.** A Handbook of Sociology. *Preface by Karl Mannheim. 656 pp. 46 figures. 35 tables.*

**Parsons, Talcott,** and **Smelser, Neil J.** Economy and Society: *A Study in the Integration of Economic and Social Theory. 362 pp.*

**Rex, John.** Key Problems of Sociological Theory. *220 pp.*

**Urry, John.** Reference Groups and the Theory of Revolution.

## FOREIGN CLASSICS OF SOCIOLOGY

**Durkheim, Emile.** Suicide. *A Study in Sociology. Edited and with an Introduction by George Simpson. 404 pp.*
Professional Ethics and Civic Morals. *Translated by Cornelia Brookfield. 288 pp.*

**Gerth, H. H.,** and **Mills, C. Wright.** From Max Weber: *Essays in Sociology. 502 pp.*

**Tönnies, Ferdinand.** Community and Association. *(Gemeinschaft und Gesellschaft.) Translated and Supplemented by Charles P. Loomis. Foreword by Pitirim A. Sorokin. 334 pp.*

## SOCIAL STRUCTURE

**Andreski, Stanislav.** Military Organization and Society. *Foreword by Professor A. R. Radcliffe-Brown. 226 pp. 1 folder.*

3

**Coontz, Sydney H.** Population Theories and the Economic Interpretation. *202 pp.*

**Coser, Lewis.** The Functions of Social Conflict. *204 pp.*

**Dickie-Clark, H. F.** Marginal Situation: *A Sociological Study of a Coloured Group. 240 pp. 11 tables.*

**Glass, D. V.** (Ed.). Social Mobility in Britain. *Contributions by J. Berent, T. Bottomore, R. C. Chambers, J. Floud, D. V. Glass, J. R. Hall, H. T. Himmelweit, R. K. Kelsall, F. M. Martin, C. A. Moser, R. Mukherjee, and W. Ziegel. 420 pp.*

**Glaser, Barney,** and **Strauss, Anselm L.** Status Passage. *A Formal Theory. 208 pp.*

**Jones, Garth N.** Planned Organizational Change: *An Exploratory Study Using an Empirical Approach. 268 pp.*

**Kelsall, R. K.** Higher Civil Servants in Britain: *From 1870 to the Present Day. 268 pp. 31 tables.*

**König, René.** The Community. *232 pp. Illustrated.*

● **Lawton, Denis.** Social Class, Language and Education. *192 pp.*

**McLeish, John.** The Theory of Social Change: *Four Views Considered. 128 pp.*

**Marsh, David C.** The Changing Social Structure of England and Wales, 1871-1961. *288 pp.*

**Mouzelis, Nicos.** Organization and Bureaucracy. *An Analysis of Modern Theories. 240 pp.*

**Mulkay, M. J.** Functionalism, Exchange and Theoretical Strategy. *272 pp.*

**Ossowski, Stanislaw.** Class Structure in the Social Consciousness. *210 pp.*

## SOCIOLOGY AND POLITICS

**Hertz, Frederick.** Nationality in History and Politics: *A Psychology and Sociology of National Sentiment and Nationalism. 432 pp.*

**Kornhauser, William.** The Politics of Mass Society. *272 pp. 20 tables.*

**Laidler, Harry W.** History of Socialism. *Social-Economic Movements: An Historical and Comparative Survey of Socialism, Communism, Co-operation, Utopianism; and other Systems of Reform and Reconstruction. 992 pp.*

**Mannheim, Karl.** Freedom, Power and Democratic Planning. *Edited by Hans Gerth and Ernest K. Bramstedt. 424 pp.*

**Mansur, Fatma.** Process of Independence. *Foreword by A. H. Hanson. 208 pp.*

**Martin, David A.** Pacificism: *an Historical and Sociological Study. 262 pp.*

**Myrdal, Gunnar.** The Political Element in the Development of Economic Theory. *Translated from the German by Paul Streeten. 282 pp.*

**Wootton, Graham.** Workers, Unions and the State. *188 pp.*

## FOREIGN AFFAIRS: THEIR SOCIAL, POLITICAL AND ECONOMIC FOUNDATIONS

**Mayer, J. P.** Political Thought in France from the Revolution to the Fifth Republic. *164 pp.*

## CRIMINOLOGY

**Ancel, Marc.** Social Defence: *A Modern Approach to Criminal Problems.* *Foreword by Leon Radzinowicz. 240 pp.*

**Cloward, Richard A.,** and **Ohlin, Lloyd E.** Delinquency and Opportunity: *A Theory of Delinquent Gangs. 248 pp.*

**Downes, David M.** The Delinquent Solution. *A Study in Subcultural Theory. 296 pp.*

**Dunlop, A. B.,** and **McCabe, S.** Young Men in Detention Centres. *192 pp.*

**Friedlander, Kate.** The Psycho-Analytical Approach to Juvenile Delinquency: *Theory, Case Studies, Treatment. 320 pp.*

**Glueck, Sheldon,** and **Eleanor.** Family Environment and Delinquency. *With the statistical assistance of Rose W. Kneznek. 340 pp.*

**Lopez-Rey, Manuel.** Crime. *An Analytical Appraisal. 288 pp.*

**Mannheim, Hermann.** Comparative Criminology: *a Text Book. Two volumes. 442 pp. and 380 pp.*

**Morris, Terence.** The Criminal Area: *A Study in Social Ecology. Foreword by Hermann Mannheim. 232 pp. 25 tables. 4 maps.*

**Taylor, Ian, Walton, Paul,** and **Young, Jock.** The New Criminology. *For a Social Theory of Deviance.*

## SOCIAL PSYCHOLOGY

**Bagley, Christopher.** The Social Psychology of the Epileptic Child. *320 pp.*

**Barbu, Zevedei.** Problems of Historical Psychology. *248 pp.*

**Blackburn, Julian.** Psychology and the Social Pattern. *184 pp.*

**Brittan, Arthur.** Meanings and Situations. *224 pp.*

**Fleming, C. M.** Adolescence: Its Social Psychology. *With an Introduction to recent findings from the fields of Anthropology, Physiology, Medicine, Psychometrics and Sociometry. 288 pp.*

The Social Psychology of Education: *An Introduction and Guide to Its Study. 136 pp.*

**Homans, George C.** The Human Group. *Foreword by Bernard DeVoto. Introduction by Robert K. Merton. 526 pp.*

Social Behaviour: *its Elementary Forms. 416 pp.*

**Klein, Josephine.** The Study of Groups. *226 pp. 31 figures. 5 tables.*

**Linton, Ralph.** The Cultural Background of Personality. *132 pp.*

**Mayo, Elton.** The Social Problems of an Industrial Civilization. *With an appendix on the Political Problem. 180 pp.*

**Ottaway, A. K. C.** Learning Through Group Experience. *176 pp.*

**Ridder, J. C. de.** The Personality of the Urban African in South Africa. *A Thematic Apperception Test Study. 196 pp. 12 plates.*

**Rose, Arnold M.** (Ed.). Human Behaviour and Social Processes: *an Interactionist Approach. Contributions by Arnold M. Rose, Ralph H. Turner, Anselm Strauss, Everett C. Hughes, E. Franklin Frazier, Howard S. Becker, et al. 696 pp.*

**Smelser, Neil J.** Theory of Collective Behaviour. *448 pp.*
**Stephenson, Geoffrey M.** The Development of Conscience. *128 pp.*
**Young, Kimball.** Handbook of Social Psychology. *658 pp. 16 figures. 10 tables.*

## SOCIOLOGY OF THE FAMILY

**Banks, J. A.** Prosperity and Parenthood: *A Study of Family Planning among The Victorian Middle Classes. 262 pp.*
**Bell, Colin R.** Middle Class Families: *Social and Geographical Mobility. 224 pp.*
**Burton, Lindy.** Vulnerable Children. *272 pp.*
**Gavron, Hannah.** The Captive Wife: *Conflicts of Household Mothers. 190 pp.*
**George, Victor,** and **Wilding, Paul.** Motherless Families. *220 pp.*
**Klein, Josephine.** Samples from English Cultures.
1. Three Preliminary Studies and Aspects of Adult Life in England. *447 pp.*
2. Child-Rearing Practices and Index. *247 pp.*
**Klein, Viola.** Britain's Married Women Workers. *180 pp.*
The Feminine Character. *History of an Ideology. 244 pp.*
**McWhinnie, Alexina M.** Adopted Children. *How They Grow Up. 304 pp.*
**Myrdal, Alva,** and **Klein, Viola.** Women's Two Roles: *Home and Work. 238 pp. 27 tables.*
**Parsons, Talcott,** and **Bales, Robert F.** Family: Socialization and Interaction Process. *In collaboration with James Olds, Morris Zelditch and Philip E. Slater. 456 pp. 50 figures and tables.*

## SOCIAL SERVICES

**Bastide, Roger.** The Sociology of Mental Disorder. *Translated from the French by Jean McNeil. 260 pp.*
**Carlebach, Julius.** Caring For Children in Trouble. *266 pp.*
**Forder, R. A.** (Ed.). Penelope Hall's Social Services of England and Wales. *352 pp.*
**George, Victor.** Foster Care. *Theory and Practice. 234 pp.*
Social Security: *Beveridge and After. 258 pp.*
● **Goetschius, George W.** Working with Community Groups. *256 pp.*
**Goetschius, George W.,** and **Tash, Joan.** Working with Unattached Youth. *416 pp.*
**Hall, M. P.,** and **Howes, I. V.** The Church in Social Work. *A Study of Moral Welfare Work undertaken by the Church of England. 320 pp.*
**Heywood, Jean S.** Children in Care: *the Development of the Service for the Deprived Child. 264 pp.*
**Hoenig, J.,** and **Hamilton, Marian W.** The De-Segration of the Mentally Ill. *284 pp.*
**Jones, Kathleen.** Mental Health and Social Policy, 1845-1959. *264 pp.*

**King, Roy D., Raynes, Norma V.,** and **Tizard, Jack.** Patterns of Residential Care. *356 pp.*

**Leigh, John.** Young People and Leisure. *256 pp.*

**Morris, Mary.** Voluntary Work and the Welfare State. *300 pp.*

**Morris, Pauline.** Put Away: *A Sociological Study of Institutions for the Mentally Retarded. 364 pp.*

**Nokes, P. L.** The Professional Task in Welfare Practice. *152 pp.*

**Timms, Noel.** Psychiatric Social Work in Great Britain (1939-1962). *280 pp.*

● Social Casework: *Principles and Practice. 256 pp.*

**Young, A. F.,** and **Ashton, E. T.** British Social Work in the Nineteenth Century. *288 pp.*

**Young, A. F.** Social Services in British Industry. *272 pp.*

## SOCIOLOGY OF EDUCATION

**Banks, Olive.** Parity and Prestige in English Secondary Education: a Study in Educational Sociology. *272 pp.*

**Bentwich, Joseph.** Education in Israel. *224 pp. 8 pp. plates.*

● **Blyth, W. A. L.** English Primary Education. *A Sociological Description.*
 1. Schools. *232 pp.*
 2. Background. *168 pp.*

**Collier, K. G.** The Social Purposes of Education: *Personal and Social Values in Education. 268 pp.*

**Dale, R. R.,** and **Griffith, S.** Down Stream: *Failure in the Grammar School. 108 pp.*

**Dore, R. P.** Education in Tokugawa Japan. *356 pp. 9 pp. plates*

**Evans, K. M.** Sociometry and Education. *158 pp.*

**Foster, P. J.** Education and Social Change in Ghana. *336 pp. 3 maps.*

**Fraser, W. R.** Education and Society in Modern France. *150 pp.*

**Grace, Gerald R.** Role Conflict and the Teacher. *About 200 pp.*

**Hans, Nicholas.** New Trends in Education in the Eighteenth Century. *278 pp. 19 tables.*

● Comparative Education: *A Study of Educational Factors and Traditions. 360 pp.*

**Hargreaves, David.** Interpersonal Relations and Education. *432 pp.*

● Social Relations in a Secondary School. *240 pp.*

**Holmes, Brian.** Problems in Education. *A Comparative Approach. 336 pp.*

**King, Ronald.** Values and Involvement in a Grammar School. *164 pp.*
 School Organization and Pupil Involvement. *A Study of Secondary Schools.*

● **Mannheim, Karl,** and **Stewart, W. A. C.** An Introduction to the Sociology of Education. *206 pp.*

**Morris, Raymond N.** The Sixth Form and College Entrance. *231 pp.*

● **Musgrove, F.** Youth and the Social Order. *176 pp.*

● **Ottaway, A. K. C.** Education and Society: An Introduction to the Sociology of Education. *With an Introduction by W. O. Lester Smith. 212 pp.*

**Peers, Robert.** Adult Education: *A Comparative Study. 398 pp.*

**Pritchard, D. G.** Education and the Handicapped: *1760 to 1960. 258 pp.*
**Richardson, Helen.** Adolescent Girls in Approved Schools. *308 pp.*
**Stratta, Erica.** The Education of Borstal Boys. *A Study of their Educational Experiences prior to, and during Borstal Training. 256 pp.*

## SOCIOLOGY OF CULTURE

**Eppel, E. M., and M.** Adolescents and Morality: *A Study of some Moral Values and Dilemmas of Working Adolescents in the Context of a changing Climate of Opinion. Foreword by W. J. H. Sprott. 268 pp. 39 tables.*
● **Fromm, Erich.** The Fear of Freedom. *286 pp.*
The Sane Society. *400 pp.*
**Mannheim, Karl.** Essays on the Sociology of Culture. *Edited by Ernst Mannheim in co-operation with Paul Kecskemeti. Editorial Note by Adolph Lowe. 280 pp.*
**Weber, Alfred.** Farewell to European History: *or The Conquest of Nihilism Translated from the German by R. F. C. Hull. 224 pp.*

## SOCIOLOGY OF RELIGION

**Argyle, Michael.** Religious Behaviour. *224 pp. 8 figures. 41 tables.*
**Nelson, G. K.** Spiritualism and Society. *313 pp.*
**Stark, Werner.** The Sociology of Religion. *A Study of Christendom.*
Volume I. *Established Religion. 248 pp.*
Volume II. *Sectarian Religion. 368 pp.*
Volume III. *The Universal Church. 464 pp.*
Volume IV. *Types of Religious Man. 352 pp.*
Volume V. *Types of Religious Culture. 464 pp.*
**Watt, W. Montgomery.** Islam and the Integration of Society. *320 pp.*

## SOCIOLOGY OF ART AND LITERATURE

**Jarvie, Ian C.** Towards a Sociology of the Cinema. *A Comparative Essay on the Structure and Functioning of a Major Entertainment Industry. 405 pp.*
**Rust, Frances S.** Dance in Society. *An Analysis of the Relationships between the Social Dance and Society in England from the Middle Ages to the Present Day. 256 pp. 8 pp. of plates.*
**Schücking, L. L.** The Sociology of Literary Taste. *112 pp.*

## SOCIOLOGY OF KNOWLEDGE

**Mannheim, Karl.** Essays on the Sociology of Knowledge. *Edited by Paul Kecskemeti. Editorial Note by Adolph Lowe. 353 pp.*
**Remmling, Gunter W.** (Ed.). Towards the Sociology of Knowledge. *Origins and Development of a Sociological Thought Style.*
**Stark, Werner.** The Sociology of Knowledge: *An Essay in Aid of a Deeper Understanding of the History of Ideas. 384 pp.*

## URBAN SOCIOLOGY

**Ashworth, William.** The Genesis of Modern British Town Planning: *A Study in Economic and Social History of the Nineteenth and Twentieth Centuries. 288 pp.*
**Cullingworth, J. B.** Housing Needs and Planning Policy: *A Restatement of the Problems of Housing Need and 'Overspill' in England and Wales. 232 pp. 44 tables. 8 maps.*
**Dickinson, Robert E.** City and Region: *A Geographical Interpretation. 608 pp. 125 figures.*
   The West European City: *A Geographical Interpretation. 600 pp. 129 maps. 29 plates.*
●  The City Region in Western Europe. *320 pp. Maps.*
**Humphreys, Alexander J.** New Dubliners: *Urbanization and the Irish Family. Foreword by George C. Homans. 304 pp.*
**Jackson, Brian.** Working Class Community: *Some General Notions raised by a Series of Studies in Northern England. 192 pp.*
**Jennings, Hilda.** Societies in the Making: *a Study of Development and Re-development within a County Borough. Foreword by D. A. Clark. 286 pp.*
● **Mann, P. H.** An Approach to Urban Sociology. *240 pp.*
**Morris, R. N.,** and **Mogey, J.** The Sociology of Housing. *Studies at Berinsfield. 232 pp. 4 pp. plates.*
**Rosser, C.,** and **Harris, C.** The Family and Social Change. *A Study of Family and Kinship in a South Wales Town. 352 pp. 8 maps.*

## RURAL SOCIOLOGY

**Chambers, R. J. H.** Settlement Schemes in Tropical Africa: *A Selective Study. 268 pp.*
**Haswell, M. R.** The Economics of Development in Village India. *120 pp.*
**Littlejohn, James.** Westrigg: *the Sociology of a Cheviot Parish. 172 pp. 5 figures.*
**Mayer, Adrian C.** Peasants in the Pacific. *A Study of Fiji Indian Rural Society. 248 pp. 20 plates.*
**Williams, W. M.** The Sociology of an English Village: *Gosforth. 272 pp. 12 figures. 13 tables.*

## SOCIOLOGY OF INDUSTRY AND DISTRIBUTION

**Anderson, Nels.** Work and Leisure. *280 pp.*
● **Blau, Peter M.**, and **Scott, W. Richard.** Formal Organizations: *a Comparative approach. Introduction and Additional Bibliography by J. H. Smith. 326 pp.*
**Eldridge, J. E. T.** Industrial Disputes. *Essays in the Sociology of Industrial Relations. 288 pp.*
**Hetzler, Stanley.** Applied Measures for Promoting Technological Growth. *352 pp.*
Technological Growth and Social Change. *Achieving Modernization. 269 pp.*
**Hollowell, Peter G.** The Lorry Driver. *272 pp.*
**Jefferys, Margot,** *with the assistance of Winifred Moss.* Mobility in the Labour Market: *Employment Changes in Battersea and Dagenham. Preface by Barbara Wootton. 186 pp. 51 tables.*
**Millerson, Geoffrey.** The Qualifying Associations: *a Study in Professionalization. 320 pp.*
**Smelser, Neil J.** Social Change in the Industrial Revolution: *An Application of Theory to the Lancashire Cotton Industry, 1770-1840. 468 pp. 12 figures. 14 tables.*
**Williams, Gertrude.** Recruitment to Skilled Trades. *240 pp.*
**Young, A. F.** Industrial Injuries Insurance: *an Examination of British Policy. 192 pp.*


### DOCUMENTARY

**Schlesinger, Rudolf** (Ed.). Changing Attitudes in Soviet Russia.
2. The Nationalities Problem and Soviet Administration. *Selected Readings on the Development of Soviet Nationalities Policies. Introduced by the editor. Translated by W. W. Gottlieb. 324 pp.*


### ANTHROPOLOGY

**Ammar, Hamed.** Growing up in an Egyptian Village: *Silwa, Province of Aswan. 336 pp.*
**Brandel-Syrier, Mia.** Reeftown Elite. *A Study of Social Mobility in a Modern African Community on the Reef. 376 pp.*
**Crook, David,** and **Isabel.** Revolution in a Chinese Village: *Ten Mile Inn. 230 pp. 8 plates. 1 map.*
**Dickie-Clark, H. F.** The Marginal Situation. *A Sociological Study of a Coloured Group. 236 pp.*
**Dube, S. C.** Indian Village. *Foreword by Morris Edward Opler. 276 pp. 4 plates.*
India's Changing Villages: *Human Factors in Community Development. 260 pp. 8 plates. 1 map.*

**Firth, Raymond.** Malay Fishermen. *Their Peasant Economy. 420 pp. 17 pp. plates.*

**Gulliver, P. H.** Social Control in an African Society: a Study of the Arusha, Agricultural Masai of Northern Tanganyika. *320 pp. 8 plates. 10 figures.*

**Ishwaran, K.** Shivapur. *A South Indian Village. 216 pp.*
Tradition and Economy in Village India: *An Interactionist Approach. Foreword by Conrad Arensburg. 176 pp.*

**Jarvie, Ian C.** The Revolution in Anthropology. *268 pp.*

**Jarvie, Ian C.,** and **Agassi, Joseph.** Hong Kong. *A Society in Transition. 396 pp. Illustrated with plates and maps.*

**Little, Kenneth L.** Mende of Sierra Leone. *308 pp. and folder.*
Negroes in Britain. *With a New Introduction and Contemporary Study by Leonard Bloom. 320 pp.*

**Lowie, Robert H.** Social Organization. *494 pp.*

**Mayer, Adrian C.** Caste and Kinship in Central India: *A Village and its Region. 328 pp. 16 plates. 15 figures. 16 tables.*

**Smith, Raymond T.** The Negro Family in British Guiana: *Family Structure and Social Status in the Villages. With a Foreword by Meyer Fortes. 314 pp. 8 plates. 1 figure. 4 maps.*


## SOCIOLOGY AND PHILOSOPHY

**Barnsley, John H.** The Social Reality of Ethics. *A Comparative Analysis of Moral Codes. 448 pp.*

**Diesing, Paul.** Patterns of Discovery in the Social Sciences. *362 pp.*

**Douglas, Jack D.** (Ed.). Understanding Everyday Life. *Toward the Reconstruction of Sociological Knowledge. Contributions by Alan F. Blum. Aaron W. Cicourel, Norman K. Denzin, Jack D. Douglas, John Heeren, Peter McHugh, Peter K. Manning, Melvin Power, Matthew Speier, Roy Turner, D. Lawrence Wieder, Thomas P. Wilson and Don H. Zimmerman. 370 pp.*

**Jarvie, Ian C.** Concepts and Society. *216 pp.*

**Roche, Maurice.** Phenomenology, Language and the Social Sciences. *About 400 pp.*

**Sahay, Arun.** Sociological Analysis.

**Sklair, Leslie.** The Sociology of Progress. *320 pp.*


# International Library of Anthropology

*General Editor* Adam Kuper

**Brown, Paula.** The Chimbu. *A Study of Change in the New Guinea Highlands.*

**Van Den Berghe, Pierre L.** Power and Privilege at an African University.

*11*

# International Library
# of Social Policy

*General Editor* Kathleen Jones

**Holman, Robert.** Trading in Children. *A Study of Private Fostering.*
**Jones, Kathleen.** History of the Mental Health Services. *428 pp.*
**Thomas, J. E.** The English Prison Officer since 1850: *A Study in Conflict.*
*258 pp.*

# Primary Socialization, Language
# and Education

*General Editor* Basil Bernstein

**Bernstein, Basil.** Class, Codes and Control. *2 volumes.*
  1. *Theoretical Studies Towards a Sociology of Language. 254 pp.*
  2. *Applied Studies Towards a Sociology of Language. About 400 pp.*
**Brandis, Walter,** and **Henderson, Dorothy.** Social Class, Language and
  Communication. *288 pp.*
**Cook-Gumperz, Jenny.** Social Control and Socialization. *A Study of Class
  Differences in the Language of Maternal Control.*
**Gahagan, D. M.,** and **G. A.** Talk Reform. *Exploration in Language for Infant
  School Children. 160 pp.*
**Robinson, W. P.,** and **Rackstraw, Susan, D. A.** A Question of Answers.
  *2 volumes. 192 pp. and 180 pp.*
**Turner, Geoffrey, J.,** and **Mohan, Bernard, A.** A Linguistic Description and
  Computer Programme for Children's Speech. *208 pp.*

# Reports of the Institute of Community Studies

**Cartwright, Ann.** Human Relations and Hospital Care. *272 pp.*
  Parents and Family Planning Services. *306 pp.*
  Patients and their Doctors. *A Study of General Practice. 304 pp.*
● **Jackson, Brian.** Streaming: *an Education System in Miniature. 168 pp.*
**Jackson, Brian,** and **Marsden, Dennis.** Education and the Working Class:
  *Some General Themes raised by a Study of 88 Working-class Children
  in a Northern Industrial City. 268 pp. 2 folders.*
**Marris, Peter.** The Experience of Higher Education. *232 pp. 27 tables.*
**Marris, Peter,** and **Rein, Martin.** Dilemmas of Social Reform. *Poverty and
  Community Action in the United States. 256 pp.*
**Marris, Peter,** and **Somerset, Anthony.** African Businessmen. *A Study of
  Entrepreneurship and Development in Kenya. 256 pp.*
**Mills, Richard.** Young Outsiders: *a Study in Alternative Communities.*

**Runciman, W. G.** Relative Deprivation and Social Justice. *A Study of Attitudes to Social Inequality in Twentieth Century England. 352 pp.*
**Townsend, Peter.** The Family Life of Old People: *An Inquiry in East London. Foreword by J. H. Sheldon. 300 pp. 3 figures. 63 tables.*
**Willmott, Peter.** Adolescent Boys in East London. *230 pp.*
    The Evolution of a Community: *a study of Dagenham after forty years. 168 pp. 2 maps.*
**Willmott, Peter,** and **Young, Michael.** Family and Class in a London Suburb. *202 pp. 47 tables.*
**Young, Michael.** Innovation and Research in Education. *192 pp.*
● **Young, Michael,** and **McGeeney, Patrick.** Learning Begins at Home. *A Study of a Junior School and its Parents. 128 pp.*
**Young, Michael,** and **Willmott, Peter.** Family and Kinship in East London. *Foreword by Richard M. Titmuss. 252 pp. 39 tables.*
    The Symmetrical Family.

# Reports of the Institute for Social Studies in Medical Care

**Cartwright, Ann, Hockey, Lisbeth,** and **Anderson, John L.** Life Before Death.
**Dunnell, Karen,** and **Cartwright, Ann.** Medicine Takers, Prescribers and Hoarders. *190 pp.*

# Medicine, Illness and Society
*General Editor* W. M. Williams

**Robinson, David.** The Process of Becoming Ill.
**Stacey, Margaret.** *et al.* Hospitals, Children and Their Families. *The Report of a Pilot Study. 202 pp.*

# Monographs in Social Theory
*General Editor* Arthur Brittan

**Bauman, Zygmunt.** Culture as Praxis.
**Dixon, Keith.** Sociological Theory. *Pretence and Possibility.*
**Smith, Anthony D.** The Concept of Social Change. *A Critique of the Functionalist Theory of Social Change.*

# Routledge Social Science Journals

**The British Journal of Sociology.** *Edited by Terence P. Morris. Vol. 1, No. 1, March 1950 and Quarterly. Roy. 8vo. Back numbers available. An international journal with articles on all aspects of sociology.*

**Economy and Society.** *Vol. 1, No. 1. February 1972 and Quarterly. Metric Roy. 8vo. A journal for all social scientists covering sociology, philosophy, anthropology, economics and history. Back numbers available.*

**Year Book of Social Policy in Britain, The.** *Edited by Kathleen Jones. 1971. Published Annually.*

Printed in Great Britain by Lewis Reprints Limited
Brown Knight & Truscott Group, London and Tonbridge    1373